2 WOMEN SLAIN: MOTIVE UNKNOWN

Because Claudia worked as a waitress, the front-page story in the *Columbus Dispatch* of December 11, 1977 touched her. She felt terrible at the thought of the dead women's bodies frozen in the icy night. She shivered in the cold as she went to work again, and as she danced, moving and bumping her body to the rock music, she glanced into the glazed eyes of the men and hoped none of them would want to kill her.

When she got home that night, she knelt beneath a sacred plaque of Jesus praying in the Garden of Gethsemane she had mounted above the door between the living room and the dining room, and she prayed for the two dead women.

She had no way of knowing at the time, she said, that these were the first of the .22-caliber murders and that their deaths would change her life.

Books by Daniel Keyes:

Novels

*FLOWERS FOR ALGERNON (filmed as *CHARLY*)
*THE TOUCH
THE FIFTH SALLY

Nonfiction

*THE MINDS OF BILLY MILLIGAN
*UNVEILING CLAUDIA

(*a Bantam Book)

Unveiling Claudia

A True Story of Serial Murder

Daniel Keyes

BANTAM BOOKS

TORONTO • NEW YORK • LONDON • SYDNEY • AUCKLAND

For Aurea, with love, as always . . .

UNVEILING CLAUDIA
A Bantam Book
Bantam hardcover edition / August 1986
Bantam paperback edition / November 1987

Library of Congress Cataloging-in-Publication Data

Keyes, Daniel.
  Unveiling Claudia.

  1. Yasko, Claudia Elaine.   2. Crime and criminals—
Ohio—Biography.   3. Mass murder—Ohio—Case studies.
I. Title
HV6248.Y37K48   1986   364.1'523'0977157   85-48043
ISBN 0-553-26502-4

Published simultaneously in the United States and Canada

Bantam Books are published by Bantam Books, Inc. Its trade-
mark, consisting of the words "Bantam Books" and the por-
trayal of a rooster, is Registered in U.S. Patent and Trademark
Office and in other countries. Marca Registrada. Bantam
Books, Inc., 666 Fifth Avenue, New York, New York 10103.

PRINTED IN THE UNITED STATES OF AMERICA
KR   0 9 8 7 6 5 4 3 2 1

Contents

Prologue

This is the true story of the beautiful, seductive, mentally ill Claudia Elaine Yasko. It is also the story of law enforcement agencies puzzled, frustrated, and caught in the turmoil of trying to solve a series of apparently random killings which for a year held the people of Central Ohio in terror.

I first learned of Claudia in mid-July 1982, when a male friend of hers phoned to ask if I would be interested in writing about the woman who, in 1978, at the age of twenty-six, had confessed to a triple homicide—three of ten killings that came to be dubbed by the Ohio press as "The .22-Caliber Murders." Though she had feared to speak out before this, he said, now she wanted to tell the world her story.

I was intrigued, and the timing was right, as I was on a leave of absence from my teaching at the university to fulfill publicity commitments for my most recent book.

The caller, who has asked me not to reveal his identity, agreed to bring her to my office the following week. In the meantime, to refresh my memory, I went to the library and read dozens of four-year-old newspaper articles on microfilm about the crime for which Claudia

Elaine Yasko and two men she implicated had been indicted by an Ohio grand jury for "aggravated murder" with death penalty specifications.

The first bold headlines brought back memories of the case:

> "LOVE-TRIANGLE THEORY ENTERS
> TRIPLE SLAYING"
> "WOMAN HELD IN TRIPLE SLAYING AFTER
> SURRENDERING TO SHERIFFS"

And later:

> "HAS SHE THE SOLUTION TO FIVE DEATHS?"

But the newspaper photographs did not prepare me for the very tall, beautiful young woman who walked through the door of my office at noon on the following Monday, July 19, 1982.

She sat in the chair beside my desk, crossed her long legs, and clasped her hands. Her red nails were perfectly manicured, and she wore rings on all her fingers.

"I appreciate your willingness to meet me," she said in a soft, liquid voice. "Some of my friends tell me my life would make an interesting book. Would you consider writing my story?"

"That depends," I said. "I'd have to question you in depth, and you'd have to reveal yourself. It might be embarrassing. It could be painful."

She touched her throat. "I'm not ashamed of the things I've done or the way I live. Let me ask you, Mr. Keyes—"

"Call me Daniel," I said.

She smiled. "Daniel . . . that means *Judge of God*." Then she frowned. "I forgot what I was going to ask you." She tried to remember. "That's one of my problems," she said. "You must never interrupt me or I'll lose my train of thought."

I should have heeded the warning twinge her words gave me and realized that trying to interview a subject with a short attention span could turn into agony for both of us. But something about her fascinated me—an

odd combination of seductiveness and vulnerability—
and told me there was a story here.

She brightened again. "Oh, I remember. I wanted
you to explain how we'd be working together, if you decide to do the book. I don't drive, and I couldn't ask my
friend to bring me out here too often."

"That wouldn't be necessary. After my publicity
tour ends, I'd go to Columbus once a week and we could
talk for two or three hours each time—or whatever you
could handle."

Her shoulders slumped in relief. "Oh, that's great. I
thought I'd have to pay someone to drive me out here,
and I don't earn much money at my job." She worked
part-time as a cocktail waitress at the Sessions bar of the
Columbus Sheraton Hotel, she said, and her income was
mostly tips.

"But I'm agreeing only to begin gathering material
to see if there's a story," I reminded her.

"You'll want to do it," she said. "I know."

"Why do you want the book written?" I asked.

She sighed and stared past me. "What happened to
me in 1978 still haunts me. If I see it in a book, between
covers—the way you did for Billy in *The Minds of Billy
Milligan*—then maybe I can exorcise the memories of
the victims."

"I can't promise that will happen."

"It will. You'll see," she said with confidence.

When she left, the scent of her perfume lingered in
my office. I sat there and wondered what I was letting
myself in for.

The people I talked to about Claudia were divided in
their opinions about her. Prosecutors and law enforcement officers actually involved in the case were certain
that she had participated in the triple homicide or, at
least, had been at the scene of the murders.

Yet most of the media had been sympathetic toward
her, including *Playboy*, which in its December 1978 story
"A Close Call for Claudia" had insisted that details of
the crime she had revealed in her nine-hour Sheriff's Department interrogation had been spoon-fed to her by the
detective in charge of the case. Because 1978 was an elec-

tion year, many TV and press reporters charged that pressures on the deputies and prosecutors to solve a triple homicide had led them to excesses. Claudia, it was generally acknowledged, had been used and victimized.

The idea of telling the true story of this beautiful, mysterious woman appealed to me. If she thought putting the truth into a book would help her dispel the memories haunting her, that was fine too.

It just didn't turn out that way. The truth kept changing.

On a cold November 26, 1982, four months after our meeting, I drove to Columbus to interview Claudia for the first time.

The friend who had phoned and introduced her to me had also warned me that the neighborhood she lived in was one of the highest crime areas in the city. He felt sorry she had to live in such a terrible location and admitted that whenever he visited her he carried a gun.

Turning into the narrow street behind her house, I parked opposite her back door as she had instructed. Though it was afternoon, the streets were deserted, and I was already getting edgy. There is something very embarrassing about being frightened in the middle of the afternoon. I looked up and down the alley carefully before I unlocked the car, stepped out, and walked very quickly to the back door of Claudia's apartment.

She had been watching for me through her window. As she opened the door to let me in, something clattered to the floor.

I jumped.

"Oh, damn!" she said. "I forgot." She bent and picked up a long butcher's knife.

"What's that for?" I shouted, backing away with a vision of her plunging it into me.

She looked at me in surprise.

"I keep it wedged above the hinge so if someone pries my lock while I'm asleep it'll fall and wake me. This place has been broken into three times. I'm really scared here alone, and it gives me something handy to protect myself."

It took a few seconds for me to regain my composure. Finally I went inside and she relocked the door, shoving the knife back into its place.

"Make yourself comfortable," she said. "I have to go to the bathroom."

Her apartment was a one-room efficiency, the kitchenette separated from the sleeping-living room by two cabinets covered with bottles of hair products, makeup, vitamins, and cans of food. The place smelled of scented talc and perfume. Propped up on the dresser, a studio-type greeting card with the illustration of a large ugly-looking toad proclaimed the motto:

> Swallow a live toad before breakfast
> and nothing worse will happen to you
> the rest of the day.

Thank God she had a sense of humor.

I moved aside a pile of old newspapers and bills on the couch to make room to sit and placed my tape recorder on the arm of her rocking chair.

Claudia frowned when she came back and saw it. "What's that for?"

"I always work with a tape recorder," I said. "I have to be able to go back over our conversations to make sure I get things right."

"I understand," she said, sitting down and rocking hard, "but I don't like it."

I grabbed the recorder before it fell off and moved it to the couch beside me. "After a while you'll forget it's there."

"I doubt it," she said as she tensed her muscles and then relaxed. "But fire away."

"First, I'd like to get some background. Tell me about your childhood. What was it like when you were growing up?"

She shook her head. "I don't remember. My childhood was miserable—the worst part of my life."

I was about to ask why, but when I saw the tears in her eyes I kept silent.

Instead, as she talked freely about her arrest, indictment, and imprisonment, I realized she was steering the interview.

When I got back home and listened to the tape, I discovered that during the three hours we had spent together, Claudia had told me nothing more than I had already found out from the newspapers.

I should have broken it off at that point. But I didn't. I was already caught up in the excitement of searching for the untold story of what had really happened in Ohio in 1978, and learning what part Claudia had played in those brutal killings.

I

---

*Claudia and
the
.22-Caliber
Murders*

Part One

Victims and Suspects

One

1

Central Ohio had been in the grip of one of the coldest winters on record, recovering from what Columbus newspapers had called the "Killer Blizzard of '78." Governor James Rhodes, in declaring a state of emergency, had referred to the storm as "a killer looking for victims."

On the night of Monday, February 13, Franklin County Sheriff's Deputy George Nance drove west on icy Interstate 70 responding to a call for a routine house check just outside Columbus city limits. The manager of Mickey's Eldorado Club, he'd been told, had telephoned because his boss, Mickey McCann, and Christine Herdman, the go-go girl who lived with him, hadn't come in to work that night, and no one at his home was answering the phone.

It was almost ten o'clock when Deputy Nance made his way slowly to Ongaro Drive. The street was quiet, lights from luxury ranch houses reflecting onto snow-covered trees and lawns. As Nance pulled to the curb in front of the McCann house, he saw a green Ford station wagon parked on the right side of the driveway.

He got out of the cruiser and plodded through deep

11

drifts to the small porch, illuminated by light from inside the house. He rang the bell, tried the doorknob, and when no one answered he moved to peer through the front window.

A woman lay on the floor in the passageway.

Nance rushed back to the cruiser, radioed the sheriff's dispatcher, and described what he'd seen. He was going inside to find out if she was dead or alive, he said, and he needed backup and a detective.

Circling the house, Nance looked for footprints, but fresh snow covered everything. When he saw that the door alongside the garage had been pried open, he entered cautiously, his service revolver drawn, and passed through a summer porch decorated with rattan furniture, African masks, and spears. The place was hot; he noticed that the thermostat had been turned all the way up.

The woman, in her seventies, clad in a short bathrobe over a white print nightgown, lay in the passageway between the summer porch and the living room. She had been shot once in the shoulder and three times in the right side of her head. Her hair and face were covered with blood, and .22-caliber shell casings lay strewn on the blood-spattered floor. From the sickening odor, Nance guessed she had been dead a day or two.

He moved quickly, checking all the rooms. Mattresses had been tossed aside, sheets pulled off, drawers emptied onto the beds.

As Nance opened the door leading from the kitchen to the garage, frigid air hit his face. He switched on the light and was shocked to see the body of a young dark-haired woman lying on her back. Her boots stood beside her, surrounded by the scattered contents of her emptied purse. Her rust-colored slacks, zipper torn to the crotch, had been pulled down to her knees, revealing white, blue-beaded, theatrical panties. She had been shot once in the right shoulder, twice in the forehead, and once in the right cheek.

The blood on her face had frozen.

Nance was relieved to hear the sound of cars pulling up. The medics got there first; then the local township police, who had picked up his radio call.

*   *   *

When Deputy Nance's first call for backup came over the radio at about ten-thirty, Franklin County Sheriff's Detectives Howard Champ and Tony Rich responded.

Sergeant Champ, in his mid-forties and prematurely white-haired, was a natty dresser who usually wore three-piece suits and sported gold and diamond rings. For the past three years he had been supervisor of the Sheriff's Organized Crime and Narcotics Bureau. Champ was lean, cool, and tough.

Detective Tony Rich, with his dark blond wavy hair, brush mustache, and blue eyes, gave the impression of someone always deep in concentration. Heavyset and six-foot-one, he looked like a middle-aged football player.

During the forty-five-minute drive from the substation to Ongaro Drive, the two compared notes on Mickey McCann. Mickey's Eldorado Club (a so-called "club" for owners of Cadillac Eldorados) was located in the sleazy west-side section of Columbus known as the Bottoms. Rich knew it was going to be closed down for six months because one of McCann's go-go girls had violated a Columbus ordinance against nude dancing in a club that sold liquor. Rich had been to the club once to meet an informant who introduced him to the owner—the only time he had ever met Mickey.

Howard Champ had heard street talk that McCann ran a high-stakes poker game in the back room and that he was involved in narcotics and prostitution. But the only indictment had been five years ago, when McCann was convicted of income-tax evasion.

When they arrived at McCann's house, Champ discovered he was the first senior sheriff's detective on the scene, and he took charge of the investigation. He knew he had a big case on his hands—the biggest of his career. He listened to Deputy Nance's report as they went through the rooms, told Rich to start photographing the house inside and out, and had one of the other officers place inverted drinking glasses over the .22-caliber bullet casings so that no one would accidentally disturb them before the Crime Scene Search Unit arrived.

After he saw the two bodies (later identified as those of McCann's mother and Christine Herdman), Champ tried to call headquarters to get Sheriff Harry Berkemer to put out a warrant and a bulletin to pick up Mickey

McCann, but the phone was dead. The wires at the northwest corner of the house had been cut.

"I don't want to put this stuff out on the radio," Champ said to Nance. "See if any of the neighbors will let us use their phone."

The people across the street allowed the detectives to set up a communications post in their home, and Champ trudged through the deep snow to make the call to arrest Mickey. He thanked the people in the house for their hospitality and was about to dial when Tony Rich came to the doorway.

"Howard, better forget the warrant on Mickey and get back over there. His body's in the garage between the driver's side and the wall. Those trash bags must've blocked Nance's view."

Champ notified Sheriff Berkemer about the triple homicide and went back to the McCann house. Squeezing in between the closed garage door and the rear of the Cadillac, Champ shone his flashlight along the driver's side.

Mickey's corpse was on its back. The knee sock on the right leg had been pulled down to the ankle, and the trousers had been pulled down over the hips. McCann had been shot once in the right knee. Champ's flashlight showed that McCann's blue silk shirt had been pulled out of his trousers, as if someone had been looking for a money belt. The light illuminated McCann's face, revealing his toupee tilted forward, askew, almost down to his eyes. He had been shot five more times in the head: twice in his forehead, twice in the back of his head, and once in his mouth.

The Crime Scene Search Unit arrived, diagrammed the house, photographed the scene, and collected physical evidence: sixteen .22-caliber casings and two live .22-caliber cartridges on the floor, along with four hazelnuts. The wooden handle of the young woman's purse found in the garage had been shattered by a bullet. The red Cadillac Eldorado with a white top, parked near the far wall of the garage, had a flat right-front tire and a dent in the passenger-side door where it had been struck by a stray bullet.

In the finished basement, panels had been removed from the ceiling, stereo speakers had been torn apart, and wood paneling had been pried loose from the walls.

There was a bullet hole in the living room picture window.

Champ and Rich stayed with the Search Unit through the night. At noon of the next day they returned to the Sheriff's Department, exhausted and frustrated. The biggest, most brutal murder case in Franklin County's history was going to dominate their lives until it was solved. Before they could get a few hours of sleep they would have to face the press.

Reporters pressed into the small office at the Franklin County Jail shouting questions. Someone asked Champ's opinion of the theory that, because of the head shootings, the murders might be the work of a professional hit man.

"What I can tell you, gentlemen," he said, "is that this wasn't your ordinary burglary. This was planned. I believe the shootings grew out of an armed robbery. Mickey McCann was known to carry large amounts of money with him. The mother was apparently killed first. Then the killers waited for McCann to return home. He and his girlfriend Christine Herdman were ambushed in the garage between four and five-thirty Sunday morning, February twelfth."

A "source close to the investigation" told reporters it had been rumored that McCann owed $50,000 to Las Vegas gamblers. Another "unnamed source" suggested that the Cincinnati-Dayton organized crime family had been involved in a power play to take over Mickey's Eldorado Club.

The *Columbus Citizen-Journal* of February 17, 1978, highlighted another theory:

LOVE-TRIANGLE THEORY ENTERS
TRIPLE SLAYING

Sheriff's deputies have added a new direction to their investigation into the Far West Side triple slaying—a love triangle. . . .

The nature of the slayings and the series of events indicates a viciousness usually associated with crimes of passion, detectives feel. . . .

Actually, the sheriff's detectives were considering *two* possible love triangles. Although the young go-go dancer victim, Christine Louise Herdman, had been living with McCann for several months, her estranged husband, James Herdman, was notified of her death, questioned, and then released. He was not considered a suspect.

The second love triangle included McCann's twenty-six-year-old assistant manager, Mary Frances Slatzer. Champ speculated that because of her jealousy over Mickey's recent relationship with Christine Herdman, Mary might have had something to do with the murders.

Champ brought Mary Slatzer in for questioning again and again. Despite her insistence under intense interrogation that she had nothing to do with the killings, she remained his prime suspect until he checked out her alibi that she had been with her father—Auxiliary Deputy Bob Slatzer.

In the weeks that followed the triple homicide, sheriff's detectives interrogated hundreds of contacts and informants: every associate, relative, friend, and past acquaintance of Mickey McCann, as well as every known patron of Mickey's Eldorado Club. Mary Slatzer provided Champ with a notebook Mickey had kept of people who owed him money or who held a grudge against him, and Champ assigned Tony Rich and Steve Martin, as well as other deputies, to follow up all names—but they led to nothing. The search was broadened to include groups who might have the background to commit such professional killings: bikers, ex–police officers, the military.

When the case against Mary Slatzer fell apart, Champ was left with no significant suspects.

Until Claudia Elaine Yasko came into the picture.

2

During the early hours of March 12, 1978, exactly one month after the triple homicide, Officers William Brinkman and George Smith of the Columbus Police Department were working as off-duty uniformed guards at an all-night Western Pancake House on the north side of Columbus.

Brinkman noticed a very tall, beautiful woman with long dark hair enter with a man and another couple. The group took a booth not far from the officers, ordered their food, and as they began talking both officers heard the name "Mickey McCann."

After a while, the tall woman rose and approached them.

Brinkman felt that her green eyes looked troubled.

"Do you want to know something about the McCann murders?" she asked him.

Brinkman smiled. "What do you know about them?"

"A lot," she said.

"C'mon, sit down," Smith said. "What's your name?"

"Claudia Yasko," she said, sitting beside Smith. "And I've got a problem. I've got to get away from my boyfriend."

"You mean the guy who came in with you?"

"Oh, no. He's just a friend. I'm talking about Bobby Novatney, the man whose apartment I share. He wants to kill me. Could you help me move out?"

"I don't think so," Smith said. "Not unless a crime has been committed."

"You were saying something about the McCann murders?" Brinkman said.

She nodded, childlike. "I know a lot about them."

Answering the officers' questions rapidly and intensely, she told them she was divorced and was using her maiden name. She said she was currently a waitress at the Image Gallery, a restaurant on High Street. "Mickey McCann came there a lot," she said. "Before that, when I worked at the Latin Quarters, he saw me dance and offered to pay me double if I'd dance for him. But I wouldn't, because everyone knows Mickey turned his waitresses and go-go dancers into hookers."

Brinkman tried to recall what he had read about the murder scene. "All right, Claudia," he said, "can you remember anything unusual in the McCann house?"

"You mean, like about the pictures?"

"Yeah," Smith said, "what can you tell us about them?"

"They were taken down from the walls."

"Now why was that done?" Brinkman asked.

She looked at him slyly. "Well, you ought to be able to figure that out."

"I could," Brinkman said, "but I'd rather you told me."

"To look for money and drugs," she said, "because a lot of people knew Mickey hid stuff behind the pictures."

Brinkman didn't remember anything in the news about pictures being taken down, and he was trying to decide whether to call the Franklin County Sheriff's Department now—at four in the morning—or wait until later and talk to the detective in charge of the investigation. He made a note of Claudia Yasko's address.

"I guess the best thing for you to do," Smith said, "is move out of your apartment, and don't give your boyfriend the new address."

"Well, if anything happens to me, I want you to remember his name is Robert Raymond Novatney, and his buddy's name is Deno Constantin Politis."

Claudia walked unsteadily back to her friends, whispered to them for a few moments, and when they got up to leave and paid for their breakfasts, she turned and waved good-bye to the two officers.

Though the McCann triple homicide had happened in Franklin County, outside the Columbus Police Department's jurisdiction, Brinkman had been following the case. He knew that every major murder news story brought out two kinds of people: mentally disturbed individuals anxious to participate vicariously in the perverse thrill of murder by getting their names in the headlines, and others who might become copycat killers.

At first, Brinkman sensed that Claudia Yasko might be one of the mentally ill, and probably had nothing to do with the murders. But as he watched her walk away he felt uncertain. He had to be careful not to let her beauty influence his judgment. He glanced at her tall figure moving out the doorway, and then back at Smith.

"I think," he said, "I'd better call the Sheriff's Department in the morning."

3

Detective Howard Champ and his brother, Detective Don
Champ, pulled up in front of 1126 South Wilson Avenue,
parked, and knocked on the front door. After a short
wait, they heard someone coming down a flight of stairs
and then saw a man peer at them suspiciously through
the door window. He had a young face with black hair, a
dark mustache and neatly trimmed goatee.

"We're from the Sheriff's Department," Howard
Champ said, "and we'd like to talk to someone in the
house."

"We're not dressed," the man said. "Let us get
something on."

"That's okay," Don Champ said. "We'll wait."

The previous morning Howard had spoken to Officer Brinkman about the incident at the Western Pancake
House. Since the Image Gallery where Brinkman had
said Claudia worked was just a couple of blocks away
from the Sheriff's Department, Champ had decided that
night to drop in and pay her a visit.

The Image Gallery was a dinner theater, decorated
like a nineteenth-century brothel, with textured red velvet wall covering and crystal chandeliers. Waitresses
wore black slacks and sequined jackets. The action was
onstage, where two naked women were dancing.

When Champ had identified himself and asked to
speak to Miss Yasko, the blond manager said Claudia
was busy working and didn't have to talk to him at the
club if he didn't have a warrant. He decided then to pay
Claudia Yasko a visit at her home the following day. He
called his brother, Don, also a deputy detective, and said
he'd like him along while he questioned her in the morning.

Now, as they waited to be let in, Howard wondered if
this was going to be another wasted day.

The bearded young man in the finally came back and
unlocked the door. He was six feet tall, thin, and had a
cold, hard expression.

"What's your name?" Don Champ asked as they went inside.

"Robert Raymond Novatney. What's this all about?"

"I know there's a young woman named Claudia Yasko living here," Howard Champ said. "We'd like to ask her a few questions."

Novatney gestured towards the steps, indicating the apartment was on the second floor. They followed him up, entered the living room, and saw that the place was shabby but clean. The baseboards were lined with books: philosophy, psychology, and science fiction.

"Who's the reader here?" Don Champ said.

Novatney glared at him. "I am."

A tall woman shuffled out of the bedroom in a white nightgown, apparently still half-asleep.

"Why'd you wake me, Bobby?" she mumbled. "What's the matter?"

"She took her medication this morning before she went to sleep," Novatney explained. "She works until three and doesn't get to bed till four or five, and if she doesn't get about twelve hours, she's a zombie."

Her eyes were closed now, and she rocked groggily back and forth.

"Hey, Laudie," he said, "hang on there, babe."

"Are you Claudia Yasko?" Howard asked.

She nodded, eyes still closed.

"We're detectives from the Sheriff's Department and we'd like to talk to you, Claudia. We need your help."

She parted her lids laboriously until they were half open, like cat's eyes. "Me? Help you? How?"

"First, what kind of drugs are you on?" Howard asked.

"Haldol and Cogentin. Prescription medication from my doctor. I don't take street drugs of any kind."

"I'm glad to hear that," Don Champ said. "What do you take those medications for?"

Claudia, who had been focusing on Howard, turned abruptly towards Don and, losing her balance, stumbled against him. "Oops! Sorry . . . I'm not really awake yet. What was your question?"

"I asked what you took the drugs for."

"I have problems with my cognition, sometimes,"

she said. "Haldol's a real strong psychotropic drug. Do you know what that is?"

Don Champ said he did.

"Well, my psychiatrist has been treating me for schizophrenia, common latent type. Do you know what that means?"

"Tell us," Howard said.

"It's the kind where I come and go, though most of the time I'm tuned in to reality. It's related to the other kind of schizophrenia, but it's not. . . . You're looking confused."

"That's all right, Claudia—or is it Laudie?"

She smiled and nodded towards Novatney. "That's what Bobby calls me."

"Well, then, Claudia. We'd like to talk with you and Bobby separately. Is that all right? My brother, Don, will talk to Bobby in the kitchen, and you and I can talk in the living room."

She shrugged and led the way, her tall, slender body moving sensuously. Even in a dazed condition she exuded sexuality.

"Claudia, did you have breakfast at the Western Pancake House on the north side of Columbus the other day?"

"You mean the one in the Patio Center on Morse Road?"

"Yes."

She thought a moment and then looked confused. "What's the question?"

"Were you there?"

"Yes, for breakfast."

"And did you talk to two Columbus police officers?"

"I . . . I don't remember." She yawned long and hard.

"Officers Brinkman and Smith say you approached them and told them you knew details about the murder of Mickey McCann."

She suddenly came wide awake and looked fearfully towards the kitchen. "I can't talk about that here."

"Why?"

"Bobby would kill me. I'd be a dead woman."

"Would you be willing to talk to us at headquarters?"

"You'd have to tell Bobby you're taking me in for

questioning on some other charge—bad checks or something. But get me out of here."

"All right," Champ said. "I'll take care of it."

Since there was no telephone in the house, Howard went to the kitchen and told his brother to use the car radio to check out the two of them.

"Standard procedure," he told Novatney, who was starting to look very agitated. "By the way, do you have any coffee? Laudie is asleep on her feet. Caffeine might help."

Novatney went to the cupboard and pulled out a jar. He dumped three heaping teaspoons of instant coffee into a cup, filled it with warm water from the tap, stirred, and started towards the living room.

"Wait in the kitchen until my brother gets back," Howard said. "I'll give her the coffee. There are a few more questions I want to ask her."

In the living room, Howard discovered Claudia had dozed off sitting up on the couch.

"This might perk you up," he said, lifting her head and putting the cup to her lips. "Bobby made it good and strong."

She opened her eyes, looked at him dumbly, and sipped. Suddenly, she choked and spat it out. "Jesus! I can't drink that shit!"

Howard heard Novatney pacing in the kitchen, obviously worried about what Claudia might be saying.

"Whose apartment is this? Yours or Bobby's?"

"We share it," she said. "I'm paying the rent and most of the bills right now because he isn't working. But I'd say it belonged to both of us."

"Are there any weapons in the house?"

She looked at him silently for a long time, making up her mind, then nodded. "Bobby's got one in the bedroom, one in the dining room, and another one in his car. He bought me a derringer for my birthday, to protect myself with. But what good is a gun if I'm incapable of pulling the trigger?"

"Do you have any objection to our searching the house?"

"Don't you need a search warrant or something?"

"Yes, but you could give us permission. You don't have to, of course . . ."

"It's okay with me. That's why you asked me whose apartment it is, right?"

Champ nodded.

"But Bobby has to give his permission too, doesn't he?"

"Let's ask him," he said, leading her by the arm towards the kitchen, where Novatney was still pacing. "Hey, Bobby, will you and Claudia voluntarily allow my brother and myself to search this apartment? Now, I don't have a search warrant, and you can refuse. But I'm asking for your cooperation."

Novatney's eyes moved from Champ to Claudia and back to Champ again. He leaned on the sink, trying to appear casual. "What are you looking for?"

"Only weapons," Champ said.

Novatney swallowed. "Well, if it's only weapons, okay."

Just then Don Champ returned and called his brother aside. "Novatney has a record. Small stuff. I can't find any active warrants on her."

"Nothing?"

"I checked with our department and the Columbus Police. Nothing."

"All right," Howard said, "they've given me oral permission to search the apartment. Let's see what's here."

They found a .38, a .45, a .22 rifle, and Claudia's derringer. When they found some marijuana in the bedroom, Novatney became upset, but Howard Champ reminded him that they were looking only for weapons.

"We'll take these guns in just to check them out," Don said. "Someone'll let you know when you can claim them."

When Howard got Claudia alone in the living room again, he asked if she really knew anything about the McCann homicides.

"I won't talk where Bobby can hear me. I'll just tell him you're taking me down to headquarters on an open warrant."

He could see she was getting quite upset now, though from time to time she let out an enormous yawn.

"Can we leave right away?" she asked.

"Why don't you get dressed?" Howard said. "We've

notified our supervisors. They'll be here in a little while, and then we can go."

She went into the bedroom and changed into a black dress. "Bobby," she called out, "they've got a warrant on me for bad checks. I've got to go downtown with them."

Howard was relieved when Captain Herdmann (no relation to the victim Christine Herdman) and Lieutenant Davey finally arrived. Of all the people the department had checked out, Claudia Yasko was the first to admit direct knowledge of the triple homicide, and he wanted his supervisor to be present when he brought her in for questioning.

"Can I go along?" Novatney asked, obviously upset at the thought of leaving Claudia alone to talk to the police. "I'd like to ride down in the car with her."

"That won't be possible," Don Champ said. "We'll have to follow regular procedures."

"I'm calling my lawyer."

"You go right ahead and do that," Howard said.

Claudia put on her brown cloth coat and left with the deputies, clutching her collar tightly in the brisk March wind. As they got into the unmarked police car, Don at the wheel and Howard in the back with Claudia, Novatney ran across the street to use his brother's phone.

The moment the deputies' car pulled away from the curb, with Herdmann and Davey following, Claudia put her head back and sighed deeply. "Ohmygod, I thought we'd never get out of there. I don't ever want to go back to that apartment. Can you help me move out?"

She was talking very fast now—the sleepiness had worn off and she was in a hysterical mood—babbling about Novatney. He was a heroin addict, she said, and to support his habit he occasionally dealt dope. "But I pay all the bills, and he doesn't contribute a nickel. Everything he gets goes into his veins."

Champ didn't want to question her about the McCann killings until they got to headquarters. He hadn't yet advised her of her rights, and though he knew he had stumbled on to something very important, he wanted to be careful.

"I don't see why you stay with him," he said. "In addition to being a beautiful woman, I can see you're very intelligent."

The sultry warmth of her laugh surprised him.
"Bobby wouldn't agree with you about the intelligent
part," she said. "He calls me a flake because I have a
mental problem. And he and his friend Deno Politis talk
about me right in front of me, as if I'm too stupid to understand."

"They do that a lot?"

"Oh, yes. And Bobby makes me do things I don't
want to do. I could tell you things you'd never believe."

Champ smiled. "I'm sure I'll believe what you tell
me."

She rambled on for the fifteen minutes it took to get
downtown. He listened, but carefully steered her away
from any mention of the homicides.

Don Champ pulled the car around Front Street to the
Sheriff's Department entrance, and Howard led her inside. Herdmann and Davey parked behind them and followed.

Claudia hung back, staring at Howard as if he'd be-
trayed her. "This is the Franklin County Jail! I don't
want to go to jail!" she screamed. "Why are you bringing
me here? Why am I being arrested?"

"You're not under arrest, Claudia. You're here because you volunteered to give us some information. The
Sheriff's Department is right upstairs. That's where
we'll have our little interview."

4

As Howard helped Claudia off with her coat, he noticed
what appeared to be a dried bloodstain on the collar. He
would say nothing about it. Not yet. First he had to use
all his skill developed over the years as a polygraph spe-
cialist to gain her confidence, test her memory, and get
the truth out of her.

Howard decided Captain Herdmann's office would
be more private than the Detective Bureau, and the captain brought out a large reel-to-reel tape recorder and set
it on his desk. Don Champ and Lieutenant Davey excused
themselves.

When Claudia was seated, Howard turned on the tape recorder and pointed the microphone in her direction. "Claudia," he began, "first of all I want you to completely understand who you are talking to. My name is Sergeant Howard Champ. This is Captain Ron Herdmann. He's in charge of the Investigative Division of the Franklin County Sheriff's Department. I work for him. At the present time I'm primarily concerned with a triple homicide that occurred on the west side of Columbus on, or about, February 12, 1978. Now you are sitting in the Franklin County Sheriff's Department. Is that correct?"

"Yes."

"Did you come down here voluntarily to talk to us about this matter?"

"Did I?" she asked.

"Did anybody force you to come down here?"

"No."

"Do you feel you have information we should know in reference to the McCann homicides?"

"Yes."

"Do you mind if I call you Laudie?"

"That's fine."

"Laudie, due to the fact that we're talking about a very serious crime, I'm obligated by law to advise you of your rights. Can you read and write?"

She took the card he handed her, and as he indicated, read it aloud. When she got to the words: *"I have read the statement of my rights shown above. I understand what my rights are,"* she said, "I really don't understand anything. I'm so mixed up and confused."

"Let me have the card," Champ said.

He went over the rights card with her line by line, and each time he asked if she understood, she said she did. But when he came to the words: *"I understand what my rights are,"* she said, "Not completely."

"What questions do you have about them?" he asked, restraining his impatience.

"I'm worried about them finding out that I snitched. I want to be protected. I want to make certain that anything I say won't come back on me."

Champ asked, "Are you referring to Robert Novatney or Deno Politis?"

"Right," she said. "I would want Deno and Bobby to think you found it out from another angle."

"Laudie, you're talking about a different aspect of the investigation, as opposed to understanding your rights. Once we find out everything you want to tell us, then we can tell you how we can keep your involvement to a minimum—if that's possible. I don't know until I know everything you want to tell me."

"Okay."

It took nearly an hour, as they went over it again. Finally, Champ paused and spoke slowly. "These are your constitutional rights. Do you understand them now?"

"Yes," she said.

Champ asked her to acknowledge that fact by writing in the time—2:35 P.M.—and the date. "Today is March fourteenth," he said.

"I can't even write," she said. "My medicine makes me so screwed up. Three . . . fourteen . . . what year is this?"

"Nineteen seventy-eight," he said.

"May I have some water?"

"Certainly. In fact, would you like a cup of coffee?"

"Please. That medicine has some harmful side effects. You get dehydrated."

After asking a few questions about her background, Champ pointed out that his primary purpose was to find out what she knew about the McCann homicides. "Do you have any information like that?"

She said she did.

"Did you know Mickey McCann?"

"Not personally."

"Did you know Mickey McCann's mother?"

"Yes."

"How would you happen to know her?"

"By being invited to dinner in her home."

"Oh, you've been in her home?" Champ said, surprise showing in his voice. "On how many occasions?"

"In the past three years, I've been there every six months. Now how many times would that be in three years? I can't even count."

"And who gave you these invitations?"

"Mamma," she said, referring to McCann's mother.

At that point, Lieutenant Davey entered the office and sat beside Captain Herdmann. Champ asked Claudia to describe the house, which she did accurately. She said the outside was beige, with bushes and shrubbery. One floor—no upstairs. Describing the kitchen, she said there were lots of cabinets, because Mamma was a good cook.

"Wow! I just realized something about the table!" she said. "There used to be an antique table of real heavy oak wood, and there was—I don't know for certain—but I guess if you removed the leaf out of the big table there was narcotics stuffed up inside. That table was removed from the home right like a few weeks before the—you say *triple homicide* because you don't know about the *fourth* body, right?"

"No, I don't know anything about a fourth body," Champ said, his voice tightening, "right now."

"Okay, so you call it the *triple homicide*," she continued. "That table was removed. The pictures on all the walls were removed."

"Tell me," Champ asked, "when was the last time you were in the house?"

"Right before Valentine's Day. That's February fourteenth, right? I was there a couple of days before. . . . Sunday was the twelfth. I'll never forget February twelfth."

"Why?"

"Are you kidding? That's when those four people were murdered."

"What murders are you talking about?"

She stared at him, confused. "Are we talking about the same thing?"

"Well, that's what I'm trying to determine. Why does February twelfth stick out in your mind?"

"That date . . . was the day that Mamma and Mickey and Chrissie and this other chick died."

"All right, let me ask you this. Who did you go out to the McCann house with? . . . Who was with you?"

"Novatney in the Oldsmobile. He drove."

"And who else?"

"There wasn't anybody else in our car, but Politis followed in . . . his girlfriend's car. See, [name deleted] just got out of the state hospital not too long ago. Anything you tell her to do, she'll just do it. And she won't even question you . . . she's like me. They use people like [us] to do things for them. And we don't realize what we're doing. And then something like this happens."

"Did [she] ever go into the house?"

"I don't think so. I never saw her enter. I don't think she's been there."

Champ bit off his words crisply. "Did you go into the house? Now, we're talking about the night that Mickey and Mamma and Chrissie were killed. Did you go into the house?"

"Yes."

"Okay, what was the first thing you observed when you went in . . . ?"

"Well, we went in through the back, so I saw the kitchen first."

". . . When you first went into the house, were Mickey and Chrissie there yet?"

"I don't remember . . ."

"You did see Mamma, though?"

"Oh, yeah. She was crying . . . terribly upset. I tried to talk to her but I couldn't understand a word she said . . ."

"What did Deno say to her?"

"Wow! He told her to shut up in a real sarcastic tone of voice, and made it clear he didn't want to hear any more crying."

"Where did this happen?"

"In the kitchen."

"In the kitchen?"

"That's where she was when I first went in the house through the back door. She was in the kitchen leaning up against the cabinet above the sink, kinda holding her head and complaining that she had a severe headache."

"Were you there when she was shot, Laudie? I know you didn't want to see her shot, but were you there?"

"Yes," she whispered.

"Who actually shot her . . . who actually pulled the trigger?"

"Deno."

Champ shifted around in his chair. "So you're telling me—and there's no question in your mind, that you actually saw Mrs. McCann—who you refer to as Mamma—you're actually telling me that you saw her shot and killed, is that correct?"

"I hate to admit it."

"*Did* you see it?"

"You'll protect me. Nothing's going to happen to me, right?"

"We will give you as much protection as is necessary to keep you away from these types of people."

"I won't ever be in a courtroom type of situation where I will have to speak right in front of their faces?"

"I cannot make you any guarantees like that, Laudie. But you would be fully protected from this point on. . . . and if you do not think I have the authority to give you that kind of assurance, I'm certain that he [the lieutenant] does . . ."

Lieutenant Davey leaned forward. "I just came in on the tail end of your questioning . . . I'm curious about a '*fourth body.*'"

Claudia explained eagerly. "See, the original plan was that Mamma's body, Mickey's body, and Chrissie's body and this other chick, this hooker, all the bodies were supposed to be removed from the house . . . and they were all supposed to be disposed of somewhere, but they only managed to get one of them out of there."

"Let's take it step by step . . ." Champ said, growing impatient at the way her answers were jumping around. "Were you close enough to see Mrs. McCann killed?"

"Yes, a few feet away."

"And where did this occur? What portion of the house?"

"In the kitchen."

Champ knew very well the mother had been shot and killed in the passageway in front of the fireplace. "Exactly in the kitchen?"

"Well, she dropped down, but see they were supposed to remove all the bodies from the house, and they were dragging them around and rearranging them and things. Pictures were removed from the walls. And, first of all, the phone was disconnected—cut. . . ."

"Was Mickey home yet? . . ."

". . . He had not gotten home yet."

"All right, what was Deno Politis and Robert Novatney doing while you were waiting on Mickey to get home?"

"They were talking about the money . . . about that fifty grand and the heroin and/or cocaine."

"Did they expect to find fifty thousand dollars on Mickey?"

She nodded. "They knew he had it."

"How did they know?"

"There was another Mickey who's biracial. He knew for certain . . ."

"How many people were involved?"

"Chrissie had two people shooting at her at once. One went down her throat. And here on the side of her head. It was yuck."

"Did you see her shot?"

"I was seeing it and looking away and then more would happen and I was looking away. And I knew my mind was not functioning . . . I can't remember . . . 'cause the whole thing is so screwed up inside my mind . . ."

"All right, what was Mickey doing while they shot Chrissie? Where was he?"

"I think he was outside on the driveway or the street . . ."

Champ had seen McCann's body inside the garage between the Cadillac and the wall. "Are you certain you're not confused?"

"I am definitely *very* confused. Trying to figure out. I don't even know where I was during this whole thing. And trying to remember where Bobby and Deno and the other Mickey, the Biracial Mickey, and these other people were . . ."

Champ was annoyed. Some of the things she was saying could only have been known by someone who'd been at the scene of the crime. Other things were impossible—as if she were mixing fact and fantasy. He asked her about Christine Herdman's body after her death.

"You mean her boots were removed?" Claudia said.

"Did you see her boots were removed?"

"Her boots were removed because of heroin or cocaine, but . . . I don't know if she was carrying dope in her boots and they wanted the dope so they removed her boots . . ."

"All right," sighed Champ. "Let's back up. Who shot Chrissie?"

"I'm not certain. It wasn't Deno, and it wasn't Bobby either. And it wasn't the Biracial Mickey. It was another man whose name I don't know. I don't even know if I'd recognize his face if I saw him."

"Where was Chrissie killed, Laudie? You were there. You know where she was killed."

"I keep thinking about the bedroom."

"She wasn't killed in the bedroom," Champ said.

"But there was a conversation that took place in the bedroom before she was shot."

"Do you know how many times she was shot?"

"Chrissie? Many times," she said. "Down the throat. Her open mouth. Lots of bullets hit her head. But her heart—I can still remember her chest—you could actually see her chest going up and down and her heart was pumping more blood, and there was a pool of blood like this . . . 'cause more blood kept spurting out of her head out her mouth."

Champ's voice turned harsh. "I'm going to tell you something. *I don't believe you.*"

She gasped. "Why not?"

"I just don't believe . . . I know some things about this. I was one of the first officers on the scene, and I don't believe what you're telling me."

Claudia rasped hoarsely, "If I'm telling you something that's not true, I'm not intentionally lying or anything."

Considering her for a moment, Champ asked if she would show him the position of Chrissie's body on the floor.

Claudia lay down, stretched out, legs and arms spread—and she had it just right. But she was unable to say what other things had been taken from Chrissie's body, and she couldn't recall in what room her body had lain. Finally, pressured, she said Chrissie had ended up in the living room.

"I'm guessing," she said.

"If you were there, you wouldn't have to guess. Have you reached a point . . . that you're fearful to tell me anything?"

"Yes," she whispered, "and I'm starting to lie."

"I don't want you to lie."

"I *am* lying. I was totally honest with you up to a point, and then I just started lying."

"Okay. Now do you want to start telling me the truth?"

"No."

"Why don't you want to start telling me the truth?"

She said with earnest intensity, "Well, there's some things that only the people that were present there know. Okay? . . . And by the process of elimination Novatney and Politis are going to figure out it was me."

Champ reminded her that he had promised to protect her, and advised her against going back to live with Novatney. The department, he said, would arrange for protection, but she would have to start being honest with him.

Claudia then described seeing hazelnuts on the floor, Chrissie's red address book, the clothes the victims were wearing, and the way they had been disarranged. All correct. But when Champ asked her the locations of the bodies she got the locations wrong. Champ made her describe the death scene again, and asked where she had been when Chrissie was killed.

"I'm trying to picture myself someplace, and I can't . . . it's a blank really . . . I was out of touch with reality . . ."

Champ's voice took on the tone of a stern but understanding father. "Laudie, can you walk out of here today—and you're just a young, a very attractive young lady—can you walk out of here today and live with this the rest of your life?"

She was on the verge of crying. "If anyone gets convicted because of something I said, I feel like I'm committing suicide."

Champ reviewed the murders over and over, each time pressing until she remembered a detail. Finally, eight hours into the interview, when he asked her again who had held the gun that killed Christine, Claudia said, "I'll be totally honest with you, but I'll have to act it out."

"You do anything you want as long as you tell me the truth and nothing but the truth."

"Tell you the truth and nothing but the truth. The

gun was in my hand, my left hand—I'm left-handed—and
I didn't have the strength at that point—my finger—my
finger was not strong enough to pull the trigger back.
Bobby reached around me or something and put his
hand over my hand and"—she made the sound of a gun
being fired—"and that was the truth."

Champ had her describe the death of Mickey Mc-
Cann. "Who did the shooting?"

"Bobby."

"And who?"

"I helped hold the gun," she said, "just like with
Chrissie. My finger was on the trigger but I wouldn't
pull it back, so Bobby put his finger over mine and
pulled the trigger back."

As the interrogation neared its ninth hour, Champ
finally said, "Okay, I think you're getting tired, Laudie,
and we're going to discontinue the interview at this time.
Have you told me the complete and honest truth to everything now?"

She laughed nervously. ". . . It's really hard for me to
give you honest answers."

"I can understand that."

"I've lied about each and every one of the bodies in
the beginning."

"That's because you were close to the bodies, isn't
it? . . ."

"I took the life out of those bodies, don't you understand?"

"I understand."

It was ten-thirty at night, and the interrogation was
coming to an end. Champ arranged for his new prime
suspect to be taken to the Ramada Inn North with a female deputy to stay in the room and a male deputy to
guard the outside.

"Have I mistreated you in any way?" Champ asked.

"No. No. No. Not at all," she said. "You've been very
nice—very gentle—very kind."

5

The next morning, Captain Herdmann called the Franklin County Prosecutor's office and asked for someone to come over and consult with them. Assistant Prosecutor James O'Grady dropped by, read through the sheriff's file, and listened to the confession tapes carefully, going over sections again and again.

"Do you have Novatney and Politis?" O'Grady asked Champ.

"Not yet. I've sent deputies to look for them, but we haven't found them yet."

"There's enough here to bring before a grand jury," O'Grady said. "You have probable cause to arrest the woman. But I'm telling you this, I won't indict her until the two men are also in custody."

Claudia was brought from the Ramada Inn back to the Sheriff's Department at three o'clock in the afternoon, and Champ and O'Grady questioned her again. They were troubled by the inconsistencies in her confession. She had described the house and the victims' wounds accurately, but her statement about the locations of the bodies didn't match the facts. She'd remembered correctly the position of a riding mower in the garage, but she'd referred to Mickey's red Cadillac as "a small foreign car." And although Mickey's body had been found in the garage, she said he'd been shot outside the house, in the snow. She suddenly recalled that there had been a blue bowl of unfinished cereal in the kitchen sink. Because no one remembered seeing that, Champ sent a deputy down to the McCann house to check.

A few minutes later he was handed a message that attorney Lew Dye was on his way over to talk to Claudia. When Champ showed her the message, she shook her head. "He's Bobby's lawyer. I don't want to see him. I won't talk to him."

"All right," Champ said. "You don't have to if you don't want to."

Champ knew Lew Dye as a criminal defense attorney

with a large clientele of drug dealers, prostitutes, and pimps—a practice Dye himself had referred to as "poor people's law." His car, a gold-and-black Rolls-Royce with "LEW DYE" license plates, was a familiar sight to German Village's legal community, a section of Columbus close to the jail.

Howard Champ didn't like him or trust him.

6

Lew Dye crossed the patio from the courthouse to the jail with long strides, headed for the sheriff's office. He was five-foot-ten, solidly built, with blond hair combed forward in a wave to cover his receding hairline. His pale blue eyes were closely set and his gaze was a constant frown.

Bobby Novatney had called him shortly after Claudia was taken in for questioning. "Something phony's going on," Bobby had said. "There's no way of knowing what she might be saying to Champ, and Claudia's the kind of woman who can be talked into saying or doing anything."

Bobby was right. The few times Dye had met Claudia, he'd gotten the same impression—that she was highly suggestible.

"See if she's been arrested and charged with something," Bobby had said, "and post bond if you can."

Dye said he would do his best. He had represented members of the Novatney family for many years and felt he knew them well. Bobby's father, whose forebears had emigrated from Bohemia before the turn of the century, had brought his wife, Mary, to live in the tough, depressed Bottoms area of Columbus. After she'd borne him Bobby, Chris, Andy, and little Marlene, he'd left her, and Mary Novatney had raised her children alone and proudly. Ever since his father had gone, Bobby—a self-taught bright young man who felt there was nothing he could learn from school—had been constantly in trouble with the Columbus police for fighting, drinking, and petty theft.

Lew Dye made a dozen phone calls trying to locate Claudia, but the sheriff's deputies, including Howard Champ, denied having Claudia in custody and denied knowing her whereabouts. Calls to the prosecutor's office, the attorney general, and the jail all produced the same result. Dye felt everyone was stonewalling him.

He didn't let that stop him. Before he became a defense attorney, he'd been a prosecutor and before that he'd studied psychology. He always made it a practice to know the people he had to deal with: who they liked, what they had for breakfast, where they drank, and who they slept with. Everything about everybody. And armed with this information, he had become an expert at plea bargaining.

This morning he learned from one of his informants that Claudia had been kept overnight at the Ramada Inn North and had just been returned to the sheriff's office.

Though Champ told him Claudia didn't want to talk to him, Dye knew she was like a child and would change her mind once she saw him.

Entering the Detective Bureau office, he saw her sitting at one of the desks. When he'd seen her in the past, accompanying Novatney to court hearings, Dye had noted her cool distant gaze, the face that made him think of cover girls on glamour magazines. Vulnerable now, cheeks puffy, face pale, eyes red-rimmed, her tall body trembling, she still had that aura of sexuality.

She jumped up and ran towards him. "Help me, Lew," she sobbed. "I'm not feeling well. My head's not right."

Dye asked to speak to her privately, and they let him use Captain Herdmann's office.

"Why didn't you want to see me?" he asked when they were alone.

"I'm all confused," she mumbled. "I don't know what's going on."

Dye believed that, but he also suspected Claudia was in a state of panic now, accepting anything anyone said to her. In her naiveté she would believe the sheriff's deputies were trying to help her. Seeing someone she knew, she had done a turnabout and would cling to him for security.

"Do you want me to represent you?"

"Yes. Yes. I know you. I trust you."

"I understand from some of the deputies that you've done some talking."

"I told them about Bobby threatening to kill me, and—"

"Hey, don't go into details here. These offices aren't supposed to be bugged, but I've heard of attorney-client conversations being taped."

"What should I do?"

"Keep your mouth shut from now on. Don't talk to anyone but me. Bobby called me yesterday, after they picked you up. He's out of his head with worry."

When Dye returned her to the outer office, Champ told him of her signed confession and of the warrants now being issued for her arrest, as well as those for Robert Novatney and Deno Politis on charges of burglary, robbery, and aggravated murder.

"You're making a mistake," Dye said. "This woman never killed anyone."

Champ shrugged. "O'Grady says we have enough for a grand jury."

Dye knew the veteran chief prosecutor O'Grady well, having faced him in the courtroom many times. He shrugged and nodded at Champ. "You're leaving yourself open to a lawsuit, Howard."

"That may be, but we have probable cause." Champ turned to her and said, "Claudia Yasko, I'm sorry but you're under arrest."

Her eyes opened wide, and she shrieked, "Arrest? What are you talking about? When you brought me here, you said I wasn't under arrest!"

"You weren't then, Claudia. But you are now."

She was crying and trembling, holding on to Lew Dye's arm for support. "Why am I arrested? What for?"

"For killing three people," Champ said.

She screamed at him as he put handcuffs on her wrists. "I didn't kill anybody! I swear to God, I'm not a murderer."

The phone rang and Champ answered it, listening for a moment and nodding as he hung up. "That was the deputy I sent out to the McCann house," he said. "You were absolutely right, Claudia. There's a blue bowl with some cereal just where you said it was, in the kitchen sink."

Dye followed as a woman deputy led Claudia out of the office, down through the rear stairway, along the narrow corridor with its surveillance TV cameras, through the gated stairwell, past the jail. The deputy took Claudia out through the Front Street exit and put her into a police van. Dye got into the van, held Claudia's hand, and tried to comfort her as they drove south of Columbus to the Women's Correctional Institute.

"I'll have you out of there in two weeks," he said. "I'm going to get your record expunged, and it'll be just like this never happened."

Suddenly she smiled. "I never thought I'd get a big part like this." She rested her head against the side of the van. "I always hoped for a starring role. I've acted before—small parts in a couple of exotic films—but playing the lead in a murder drama could make me a star."

Dye stared at her. "You think you're making a movie?"

She slapped at his hand playfully. "Oh, come on, Lew. You saw those cameras in the jail hallway and the TV cameras outside. I just hope I've got a good contract with a lot of money, because acting is hard work."

Twenty minutes later, the police van pulled up to the women's prison, a one-story building surrounded by barbed wire. The matron led her inside, and the barred door at the far end of the corridor opened to admit her.

"Hang in there, Claudia," Dye said, waving goodbye. "I'll be in court first thing in the morning filing a motion to suppress your confession. I'll see you tomorrow."

As the prison door clanged shut behind her, Claudia asked the matron what day it was.

"Wednesday."

"I mean what day and month. I know it's 1978."

"March fifteenth," the matron said, uncuffing her.

Claudia smiled. "I had a feeling about that. Things happen to me around the Ides of March."

After being photographed and fingerprinted, Claudia was given the prison uniform of navy blue slacks, sneakers, and a white shirt with the black-inked letters over her pocket: C. YASKO. Noticing more TV cameras on the walls, she smiled and did her best to give an Academy Award performance.

The matron took away her rings and the clips from her hair, leaving it to hang loosely down to her hips. Claudia was put into the first of six tiny holding cells, with a steel bunk, a sink, and a toilet. Her cell, across from the control center, enabled her to see the bank of TV monitors and the cameras pointed at her. She laughed and waved.

If only her mother could see her now. . . .

Two

1

Martha Yasko learned what had happened to her daughter when Bobby Novatney called five minutes before the eleven-o'clock news and told her Claudia had been arrested and would probably be on TV.

Martha thought he was joking, but what a strange joke. She was surprised at his call because, during a phone conversation two weeks earlier, Claudia had confided to her that she wanted to leave Bobby. Martha had assumed she'd done it. Though Martha found Bobby Novatney a bright, well-read young man, she'd never liked him. She knew he had often been in trouble with the law. It worried her when she learned that he was involved in drugs.

When the TV news came on, Martha and her fifteen-year-old daughter, Nancy, watched, stunned, as a hand-cuffed Claudia, in jeans and denim jacket, smiled and waved to the cameras.

When the newscaster said Claudia had been arrested for the triple homicide, and that two possible accomplices were soon to be apprehended, Martha screamed.

"What are they saying? Have they gone mad?"

Nancy was crying. "Claudia . . . that's impossible. She could never hurt anyone."

Martha staggered out of the chair, wailing, walking in circles. "We've got to do something. What can we do? Who can we call? We need a lawyer. Who can we get? Call somebody, tell them it's all a terrible mistake."

Nancy was afraid her mother might have a heart attack.

"I know!" she sobbed. "I'll call Pop. He'll tell us what to do." She ran to the phone, tears blurring her eyes as she dialed the number of the Columbus Police Department. Pop would know. Pop would help.

Detective Sergeant Bill "Pop" Steckman was not her own father, but the father of one of her school friends. Ever since Nancy's mother and father had been divorced—almost nine years ago—she had spent so much time at the Steckman home that she considered them her second family.

Now, learning that her sister had been arrested for murder, Nancy naturally turned to Bill Steckman for help. The telephone operator at the Central Police Station connected her with the Detective Bureau Homicide Squad, and when Steckman answered with his deep, soothing voice, she told him what she and her mother had heard on the news.

"Can you help Claudia, Pop? She couldn't have done what they say. She's had mental problems, but she couldn't even hurt an insect. What should we do? Where should we—?"

"Get hold of yourself, Nancy. You've got to keep control. I'll do what I can. Let me talk to your mother."

Martha took the phone, still sobbing, and Steckman spoke softly, his voice reassuring even though he said there was not much he could do. "I can't intrude on Sheriff Berkemer's investigation. Franklin County is out of my jurisdiction."

"Oh, God . . ."

"But now, just wait. I'll talk to some of the detectives I know up at the Sheriff's office. I'll make sure they know she has a history of mental illness—"

"Oh, bless you, Bill."

"There's something you can do, Martha. When you

visit Claudia at the women's jail, you might ask her some key questions about this whole business."

"Yes . . . yes, of course. Just a minute and I'll get a pencil."

Steckman slowly dictated a list of questions designed to clarify and explain Claudia's knowledge of details of the crime.

2

As Lew Dye sat beside Claudia in Municipal Court for a preliminary hearing the following day, he noticed her dazed and confused expression when she glanced around the crowded courtroom from time to time with an embarrassed smile. It was obvious she couldn't follow the proceedings.

He sensed his new client was going to give him problems.

She had an incredible ability to confuse people. He discovered that to understand what she was driving at he had to listen to her—stand back—and then carefully analyze what she was saying. When he was with her he had to take more notes than usual because he had to go over them again and again to make sense of her stories.

Dye entered her plea of Not Guilty and also filed a motion to suppress her 158-page confession to Howard Champ on the grounds that it had been obtained under duress, and that, as someone mentally ill, she had not been competent to waive her constitutional rights. A court investigator confirmed to Judge Richard Ferrell that Claudia's history of mental illness dated back to the age of fourteen, that she was now under medication and was currently classified by the Ohio Department of Mental Health as one hundred percent disabled.

The attorney general's office countered Dye's argument with Champ's claim that Claudia had appeared completely rational when she described details about the McCann homicides that had never been released to the press, details that could be known only by someone who had been at the murder scene. She had, he insisted,

willingly, knowingly, freely signed a confession to having
participated in the brutal triple homicide.

Prosecution attorneys informed Judge Ferrell that
they intended to turn the evidence over to a grand jury
the following Tuesday.

Judge Ferrell took Dye's suppression motion under
advisement and set Claudia's bond at $150,000 for each
victim—a total of $450,000.

As Claudia was led from the courtroom, she again
laughed gaily and waved her manacled hands. Her good
spirits confused reporters and TV commentators, and
they later bombarded the sheriff's detectives with questions.

Despite the fact that Howard Champ had gone to her
home, taken her in for interrogation, and kept her overnight under guard at a motel, Champ told the press that
at nine o'clock the previous night Claudia had walked
into the Sheriff's Department and surrendered to the detectives on her own.

3

When Detective Tony Rich learned that Claudia Yasko
had implicated Deno Constantin Politis as an accomplice
in the McCann murders and that Sheriff Berkemer now
wanted him picked up, he was upset. He had questioned
Politis at length about the killings just two weeks ago.

Politis was a well-known tough character on the
west side of town, and Rich knew he had frequented
Mickey's Eldorado Club, and even had a few arguments
with McCann in the past. He had figured the thirty-one-
year-old tough guy a good suspect, and had arrested him
on an aggravated robbery with a gun. Now Rich was frustrated because Politis had been arrested twice and released twice in the past two weeks.

He pulled the file and reviewed what had happened.

On February 24, not quite two weeks after the Mc-
Cann murders, Officer G. Goldsberry had arrested Deno
Politis at 3:20 A.M. in Kroger's supermarket at 515 West
Broad Street. The store clerk, Douglas Stormant, had ob-

served Politis's nervousness at the checkout counter.
When Politis, after paying for a jar of garlic powder, had
reached down for his change, a lamb chop slid out of the
open sleeve of his denim jacket onto the counter. Flustered, Politis then pulled a second lamb chop from the
other sleeve and offered to pay for them. Because it was
Kroger's policy to prosecute every case of shoplifting,
Stormant called the Sheriff's Department.

Goldsberry reported that by the time he arrived on
the scene Politis had been taken up to one of the second-
floor security offices. While Politis shifted around in his
chair, Goldsberry noticed that on the floor behind the
suspect's foot there was a small gun. As he stood, Politis
gently nudged the gun under the desk.

Since there was no way Goldsberry could prove the
gun belonged to Politis, he arrested him for theft of
the lamb chops. After Politis was handcuffed and in the
cruiser, Goldsberry went back into the store and confis-
cated the gun—a blue .25-caliber semiautomatic Beretta
loaded with a chrome clip containing nine bullets.

Politis was able to convince the judge that he was a
responsible citizen with his own home-siding business,
truck, and tools. Since the charge was only "a misdemeanor of the first degree," he was ordered to appear in
court on March 6 and released on his own recognizance.

On February 28, four days later, Politis came to the
Franklin County Detective Bureau to report that his .25-
caliber Beretta had been stolen. Once he admitted own-
ing the Beretta, that was enough for Rich who changed
the lamb-chop theft charge from a misdemeanor to "aggravated robbery while carrying a concealed weapon."
He arrested Politis on the spot.

It wasn't only the lamb-chop theft that had made
Rich question Politis about the triple homicide. Politis
had shot a man to death in 1969 in a west-side Columbus
bar and had been tried for second-degree murder. The
jury's verdict had been "self-defense" and he was acquit-
ted.

During Rich's questioning of Politis about his having carried a gun when he stole the lamb chops, Rich had
brought up the triple homicide, as he did with everyone
he questioned. Politis admitted to having known Mickey
McCann for many years, admitted to having quarreled

with him, and admitted to having dated the go-go girl Christine Herdman three times.

Rich had spotted Politis as a suspect then, two weeks before Claudia Yasko confessed and implicated him. Now Rich could barely hide his frustration. One week ago, on March 8, a Municipal Court judge had thrown out the "armed robbery" charges because no civilian prosecution witness had actually been present to testify that Politis had the gun with him while he stole the two lamb chops.

Sheriff Berkemer's order was to find Deno Politis and bring him in, but to be careful, because he was most likely armed and dangerous.

Three

1

When Martha Yasko visited the Women's Correctional Institute a week after Claudia's arrest, she noted that the outside looked like an ordinary building—except for the barbed-wire fences.

Inside, visiting conditions were poor. On the left wall of the corridor, four metal stalls with narrow ledges and phones stood like open telephone booths. At her eye level the rectangular slash of a six-inch peephole would enable her to see part of her daughter's face when Claudia was allowed to enter the booth and was locked in on the other side. Both would have to stand to make eye contact, and they would have to communicate by phone.

A short while after Martha arrived, Donna Zag, the red-haired matron, brought a smiling Claudia to the visitors' area, let her enter the cubicle, and locked the bars shut behind her.

"Why are you upset, Mamma? There's nothing to worry about. This is the greatest opportunity I've ever had. You never believed I'd make it as a real actress, and now you see I've got a starring role."

"What are you talking about?"

"Don't you understand this is all a movie? We're

47

making a film about a brutal triple murder." She pointed to the TV monitor on the wall behind her. "Look at the cameras all around us."

That was the way it had always been with Claudia. As a child, she would take a few details of reality and embroider them with fantasies. She had always dreamed of being an actress. For years, Martha had worried about Claudia's habit of retreating into her never-never land, but now she was grateful for her ability to transform the reality of prison into a world of make-believe.

"We called Pop Steckman," Martha said, "and he's going to check into some things for us. He's taking a personal interest in your case. Pop suggested a few questions. Let's concentrate on them for a minute."

Claudia nodded eagerly.

Martha took a slip of paper from her purse and read aloud: "Before you were picked up for questioning, did anyone from the Sheriff's Department ever ask you to get information for them off the street?"

Claudia shook her head. "Never."

"Were you at the scene of the murders—at Ongaro Drive?"

"No, Mamma, I was never there."

"Then where did you get the details? How did you know what was in the house? How did you know how the murders happened?"

Claudia put her fingers to her lips and closed her eyes as if trying to recall. "I heard about it from Deno. I heard him tell Bobby that when he was picked up on a robbery charge two weeks after the murders, Detective Tony Rich questioned him about the McCann case, and that's how he found out a lot about the scene and the way it happened. That's how I knew."

Martha felt a great sense of relief. That explained it. Just as it had always been with Claudia, someone had given her a few details and she'd elaborated it into her own complete story, with herself at the center of things.

"Was Bobby involved in the murders?"

"No!" Claudia said. "Bobby had nothing to do with it."

"Is there any way you can prove you weren't there that Sunday morning? Don't you usually go somewhere for breakfast after work?"

Claudia hit her palm against the side of her head. "Yes! Yes! Now that you mention it, I remember. I think I went out with Lenny White, and someone—a girl was with us—yes, it was Ginger who works at the Image Gallery with me."

"Who's Lenny White?"

"Oh, he's a very nice man. I've known him for months. He owns his own eighteen-wheeler and does long-distance hauling—mostly pigs. The girls at the Image Gallery call him 'Pigman.' Lenny comes to the Image Gallery when he's in town and takes me out to breakfast, and sometimes he drives me home. We went out to breakfast after work."

"Wonderful—two witnesses to your alibi. Everything is going to be all right, Claudia."

"That's what I said, Mamma. The film will be a great success. I'll be famous."

When Martha Yasko left the Women's Correctional Institute, she called Bill Steckman at the Detective Bureau and relayed Claudia's answers to his questions.

"I can't interfere, Martha," he said after they talked for a while, "but I'll do what I can."

Steckman later called Sheriff's Detective Steve Martin. One of his own men knew Martin well and spoke highly of him. He felt Martin would understand he was not nosing into his territory.

"Look, Steve, about the McCann case," he said. "I don't mean to butt in, and I'm not asking for any information. I just think you guys ought to know you have a very unstable person on your hands."

2

On March 17 the *Columbus Citizen-Journal* ran the story.

SHERIFFS HUNT SECOND SUSPECT IN WEST SIDE TRIPLE SLAYING

Sheriff's detectives were searching Thursday for a second suspect in the Feb. 12 slaying of three far West Side persons.

Claudia Yasko . . . was arrested late Wednesday and charged with three counts of aggravated murder . . .

Sheriff's Sgt. Howard Champ said Miss Yasko contacted detectives about 1 P.M. Tuesday and supplied details of the slayings known only by someone who was there while they were committed . . .

When she said she was afraid she would be killed if she returned home, detectives placed her in protective custody . . .

Champ gave no information about the possible relationship between Miss Yasko, the suspected accomplice and the murder victims.

Miss Yasko has been under mental care since she was 14 years old but appeared "completely rational" when she talked with detectives, Champ said.

Three days later, the order was given to arrest Politis at the trailer court where he lived with his girlfriend. At 4:10 A.M. five deputies, including Officer Goldsberry, Tony Rich, and Howard Champ, knocked and announced themselves. When Politis's girlfriend, Elsie May Benson, answered the door, they showed her the warrant for Politis's arrest.

She pointed to the room where he lay sleeping, and all five deputies, guns drawn, entered the room, awakened Politis, and told him he was under arrest for the murders of Christine Herdman, Mrs. Dorothy McCann, and Mickey McCann.

Politis, startled and angry, shouted that he had nothing to do with killing anyone. It was all a goddamned mistake, and they were arresting the wrong person.

"Don't let them search my house!" he shouted to Elsie May as they handcuffed him and led him out to the Sheriff's cruiser. "I don't want them in my house!"

They drove Politis to the county jail, booked and slated him at 4:30 A.M., and in less than an hour he was behind bars for the third time in four weeks.

When Mary Novatney opened her front door and saw her son Bobby's agitated face, she knew something terrible had happened. He said that after reading the article in the *Citizen-Journal* about the Sheriff hunting for a second suspect, and the part about Claudia being afraid she'd be killed if she returned home, he had the feeling he was being set up, and he was afraid to go back to the apartment.

Now in the house where he had grown up, he was raging like a wild man, shouting that there was no way of knowing in what kind of mess crazy Claudia had implicated him. He had come to stay in his old room until he could figure out what to do, he said.

When he had gone up to his room, the small, wiry, white-haired Mrs. Novatney went to the kitchen to get her son something to eat. She realized that her oldest son was once again terrified that he was being framed for a crime he hadn't committed.

It upset her that the fear of being framed and his hatred of the police went back such a long way. She remembered clearly the day Bobby and his youngest brother, Andy, had been arrested after they were caught inside Hoover Dam with explosives. Street talk was that the explosives belonged to one of the bar owners connected to organized crime. But Bobby and Andy had told her what really happened.

One morning in the last week of July the previous summer, Bobby had decided he wanted to go fishing at Hoover Dam. He, his friend Frank, and Andy took some fishing gear and a few six-packs and drove out to the dam.

The fishing was slow, and Andy, exploring, discovered that one of the doors leading down inside the wall of the dam was unlocked. He yelled to Bobby that he was going inside, and Bobby grabbed a couple of beers and went with him. Frank stayed outside and kept fishing.

Andy said they hadn't gone more than a few yards when suddenly the area was filled with Marine and Park Police, guns drawn. Bobby and Andy, hands raised, started up the stairs, when Frank, who'd brought along some leftover firecrackers from the Fourth of July, lit one and sent it exploding down the passageway. Then he took off in Andy's car.

When Bobby and Andy came up, they found themselves surrounded by armed officers, with a police helicopter hovering overhead.

They were arrested and booked for criminal tres-
pass and for possessing explosives within the dam. Lew
Dye defended them. The charges were dropped to a misdemeanor, and the brothers were fined and released. But
the Hoover Dam experience made Bobby more bitter
than ever at law enforcement officers.

"That's what the police can do," he had told his
mother. "They can take something like a little fishing ex-
pedition and build it up so they can throw a guy into
prison."

Now he was back home, hiding in his old room because he feared the police were going to frame him for
murder.

Late Monday night, March 20, Mary Novatney heard
banging on the front door. She put on her robe, went
down to peer through the window, and was startled to
see Sheriff's cruisers in front of the house, blocking off
the street on both sides.

Bobby, who had come down behind her, said, "I'm
getting out of here. I'm going out the back door."

"Bobby," his mother said, "stay put."

The silver-haired plainclothes officer on the porch
called out, "I'm Sergeant Champ. We know your son is
inside, and we'd like to talk to him."

"Do you have a warrant?" she asked.

"No, but I'd like to see him."

"Just a minute," she said. "I'll ask him."

She rushed to the telephone, found Lew Dye's home
number, and told him what was happening.

"Tell Bobby to stay cool," Dye said. "Under no circumstances is he to go out, and don't let those officers in
the front door. Put Bobby in your bedroom, and tell him
to stay there until he hears from me."

At four in the morning, Lew Dye called back and
asked if the deputies were still outside. Bobby checked.
The porch and street were deserted.

"All right now, Bobby, get some sleep, if you can,
and come to my place first thing in the morning. We'll go
down to the sheriff's office together."

Next morning, as he left, Bobby kissed his mother
good-bye. "You may not see me again," he said, "because they're gonna kill me."

"Don't say that," she insisted.

"They want me for murder. You know what they can do."

"Don't think like that, Bobby," she said, crying as he slipped out the back door. "Don't talk that way."

That evening on the TV news she learned that Lew Dye had gone with Bobby when he turned himself in at the Sheriff's Department.

She screamed as she heard the reporter say that at four-thirty on March 21, indictments had been handed down by the Franklin County grand jury: Claudia Elaine Yasko, Robert Ray Novatney, and Deno Constantin Politis—all now in custody—were each indicted for multiple counts of felony murder and murder with prior calculation and design.

All with death-penalty specifications.

3

Lew Dye found Claudia's arraignment a harrowing experience. It lasted just about forty-five minutes, but he felt a deep anger at having to stand there with a terrified client in open court to hear the entire indictment read. After each of the three separate aggravated-murder counts with death-penalty specifications the State asked that she be electrocuted until dead.

Dye looked at Claudia out of the corner of his eye and saw her still smiling—as if embarrassed at causing so much trouble—but also pale and trembling. She might still believe she was filming a scene in a movie, but the Prosecutor's words frightened her.

Dye had decided that if they really went for the death penalty he would do whatever was necessary to save her. He would fight the case in the news media. He knew that was considered unethical, but he didn't consider it wrong to save someone completely innocent from being electrocuted. When he heard the specifications being read, he knew that was what he'd have to do.

Being a good Republican, he had first tried to use whatever political clout he could muster. Not that he was friends with George C. Smith. He had never been friends with prosecutors. Some of them had been his friends be-

fore they took that position, but he felt one had to draw
the line. Being close to a prosecutor could give a defense
attorney a jaundiced view, he thought. And at the last
moment in court, when you had to put in your final dig, a
prosecutor might ask you—as a favor—to ease up. And
he couldn't do that and defend his clients.

Dye watched Assistant Prosecutor James O'Grady in
the courtroom. Jim had been around, he knew. First-
generation Irish from New York—Green Irish, not Or-
ange Irish—and active in the Shamrock Club. Once he'd
gone into Jim's office and found him listening to Wagner.
It was important, he told himself, to understand the men
you had to fight in court.

Dye felt that O'Grady's boss, Prosecutor George C.
Smith, was the strongest politician in Columbus. You
served George Smith well and you became a judge or got
some other plum, because George knew how to get his
people appointed to higher offices. Shortly before the arraignment, Dye had called for an appointment to talk to
him and O'Grady. He'd come to that meeting with the
idea of saying: "Gentlemen, drop this. You know she's
not guilty. The whole thing is a bad mistake and it's going to hurt George's chance to be elected."

Dye was hoping Smith would buy the idea and drop
the case. He did not want to destroy George Smith. Up to
now Dye had been friends with the top Republicans in
Columbus, and he knew a young Republican attorney
like himself could get hurt by rocking the political boat.

But to save Claudia he would take that chance.

When he had gotten to the Prosecutor's office he was
told by Jim O'Grady and an administrative assistant that
George couldn't see him. He knew damned well George
was out of town, politicking.

Dye told them politely, softly, "Well, gentlemen, national media are interested in this case. If you don't see
the light, all hell's going to break loose and it's going to
destroy George's political chances, his political career."

O'Grady said they had to do what they thought was
best, call the shots as they saw them. With solid evidence
that couldn't be ignored and with the tapes, they had no
choice but to go forward with the case.

"But you know the background," Dye had argued.
"You know her condition. You know Champ had her

locked up in a motel room and was spoon-feeding her."
Dye tried to lay the situation out for them, but they
weren't interested. "There'll be articles in national
publications," he said, knowing he was pressing too
hard.

Although he sensed something odd was going on, he
hadn't become aware until later of George Smith's total
involvement in the case. He learned that George himself
had met with Champ to coach and advise him. Franklin
County's triple homicide, it seemed, had become a siz-
zling political issue.

Hustler, whose publisher Larry Flynt had been a Columbus resident, had actually been the first magazine
interested in doing something with the story. Though
Dye wouldn't commit himself right away, he knew he
could use *Hustler*'s interest as leverage. He'd told a local
TV reporter that a national magazine wanted to high-
light the case. He wouldn't tell her which one, because
nothing was final, and he had no intention of following it
up if the Prosecutor would drop the case. But when the
reporter pressed him for information, he told her only
that it was one of the "girlie" type magazines.

A few days later, he'd gotten a call from *Playboy* Senior Editor Bill Helmer asking about Claudia and mentioning the possibility of help from the Playboy
Foundation. Helmer told him that once Hugh Hefner decided to go with a case, it was carte blanche. It seemed
that the Columbus reporter, in calling around to check
the story, hoping to find out what magazine Dye was
dealing with, had aroused *Playboy*'s interest.

Now, as Dye left the courthouse and watched them
take Claudia away in the cruiser, he made his decision.
He would do anything, go anywhere, fight anyone, to save
her life—even if it meant accepting help from magazines
like *Hustler* and *Playboy*.

4

Tony Rich was feeling that old frustration again.

On Friday, March 31, Judge William Gillie released
Deno Politis on recognizance bond under orders to re-

port to court officials by phone each day until his murder trial.

Deno's attorney had arranged for him to take a polygraph examination, and Deno had passed all the questions except one. The polygraph indicated he'd lied when he said he hadn't been in Mickey McCann's house at the time of the deaths. But the technician explained that the aberration could have been caused by some childhood problems Politis had with *home* or *house*.

Deno said he would never again take a lie-detector test, knowing it could be wrong.

The following Thursday, April 6, at 10:40 A.M., the Prosecutor was able to get a "true bill of indictment" from a Franklin County grand jury against Politis for having had a gun in his possession during the lamb-chop robbery. Rich got another warrant for Deno's arrest.

Shortly before 1 A.M. on Saturday, April 8, the body of seventy-seven-year-old Jenkin T. Jones was discovered by his daughter and her husband, at his isolated home on Route 37, not far from Newark, Ohio. Jones had apparently been lying on his couch reading a magazine, when he was shot through the glass panel of his front door. The .22-caliber bullet had entered his back. The killer or killers had then broken in through the front storm door and shot him five more times—four to the head—and then dragged his body to the first-floor bedroom; .22-caliber shells were scattered on the floor.

Two dogs had also been shot in the basement and two more in an outside pen. One dog was found alive under the shed.

Licking County detectives estimated that the killer or killers had taken their time searching the house. The cluttered rooms and the fix-it shop behind the home had been ransacked.

Jones, a gregarious man according to neighbors, had been a self-employed general contractor, a mechanical genius who made tools and parts for customers all over Ohio. He was known to keep large amounts of cash on hand to buy motors at sales.

Licking County Sheriff Max Marston sent the .22-caliber shells to the Bureau of Criminal Identification and Investigation (BCI) in London, Ohio, for routine check. Though the murder pattern, especially the large number of shots to the victim's head, was similar to that of the McCann homicides, no one connected the two crimes.

The murder of Jenkin T. Jones in Newark, Ohio, received very little publicity in Columbus.

Tony Rich rearrested Deno on the lamb-chop "aggravated robbery" charge on April 11, but the judge released him the same day on his own recognizance.

Someone said they ought to put in a revolving door at the county jail, just for Deno.

The following Friday, having also passed a lie-detector test administered by the Columbus Police Department, Bobby Novatney was released on $75,000 recognizance bond and went to live with his mother while awaiting his murder trial.

Mary Novatney was saddened by the change she saw in her son. Though in the past he'd had a quick sense of humor and a ready wit, now that seemed gone. No jokes. Few smiles. He talked of his ordeal in prison with a sense of horror and told his brothers he had died many times in his nightmares. During his three and a half weeks in the Franklin County Jail he had believed the detectives were going to frame him, build a case against him, and send him to the electric chair.

Although he and Deno had been released on bond, the charges against them and their trials for murder were still pending. Of the three, that left only Claudia in prison to await her trial. Bobby told his family he was torn between forgiving Claudia because of her mental illness and wishing she would die in the electric chair and rot in hell.

Four

1

After thirty days in protective isolation, during which time she showed no sign of being dangerous, Claudia was permitted into the prison recreation room an hour each day. Most of the other women inmates, having seen her on television, resented her notoriety.

On April 24, Claudia entered the recreation room as a group of women was watching a soap opera. She sat alone at a table, wondering when the film director would come and tell her what scene they were going to shoot that day.

When the guards were out of earshot, a young blonde woman approached her.

"You goddamn bitch! You're gonna spend the rest of your life in Marysville or Lima. That's where you belong for killing my friend."

Claudia cringed. "I don't know what you're talking about. I didn't kill anybody."

"Don't lie, bitch!" shouted an enormously fat dark-haired prisoner. "You killed Chrissie, and you'll get it."

The loud talking attracted one of the guards, who warned them they would all lose visitation rights and commissary privileges. That settled things down for a while, but suddenly the guards were called away from the dayroom by reports of a fire in a wastebasket.

As the blonde approached her again, cursing, Claudia tried to explain. "I'm here only because we're making this movie about a triple homicide. Burt Reynolds is in it, and Sally Fields. I don't think I should have to actually stay in a cell—they could put me up in a hotel, and let me come in every morning for the scenes—but it's my first big part and I can't complain too much."

"Yeah? Look around you, bitch!" the blonde said. "This joint is real. I'm real. And I'm gonna kick your ass."

"But the TV cameras. Why would they have cameras on all the time if we weren't making a movie?"

"Because they always have TV monitors in max security, you crazy asshole. You're here because you're a murderer."

Claudia stared and sobbed, "You're the one who's crazy. You don't know what you're talking about."

The blonde looked around to make sure the guards hadn't come back and punched Claudia in the right eye. Claudia fell to the floor, and others joined in kicking and cursing her. The fat woman jumped on top of her, and Claudia passed out.

A nurse and a guard carried her back to her cell. When Claudia regained consciousness, she discovered her body was bruised, her left ankle sprained and very swollen. Why, she wondered, would the movie producers allow the extras to hurt her? Something was terribly wrong, she realized, and she would have to find out what was going on.

Claudia had to hop or crawl from place to place. For her court appearances she was carried outside and given crutches, but—since they were potential weapons—she was denied their use inside the prison.

2

The following Monday, May 1, the *Citizen-Journal* headlined another murder:

"MINISTER'S SLAYING HAS WIFE, FRIENDS
BAFFLED."

The previous day, Sheriff Dan Berry of Fairfield County, just east of Franklin County, had been called to investigate the murder of Reverend Gerald Fields, the thirty-five-year-old minister of the nearby Berean Baptist Church.

Fields had carried a gun one night a week while making his rounds as a temporary substitute security guard at the Wigwam, a private club on a 100-acre wooded retreat owned by Wolfe Industries, which also owned the *Columbus Dispatch*, WBNS-TV and radio, and the Ohio National Bank.

According to Sheriff Berry, Fields had apparently been shot numerous times while patrolling the compound.

A dump truck parked at the maintenance barn had its left window shot out, and there were bloodstains on the side of the truck, as if the victim had fallen against it. Berry speculated that Fields then staggered three hundred yards back to the bunkhouse, where the killer or killers finished him off. Eighteen spent .22-caliber cartridges were found on the ground. Nine of the bullets had hit Fields in the legs, chest, and head. The time of death was fixed within an hour of twelve-thirty in the morning, after Fields had keyed into his time clock during his hourly rounds.

Fields had then been dragged behind the bunkhouse to hide his body. The dead man's pockets had been turned inside out. His wallet and his .38 Colt revolver, identifiable by its broken handle, were missing. Sixteen deputies with bloodhounds searched the grounds all day Sunday, and late in the day they found Fields's billfold, credit cards, and driver's license.

According to news stories, Fields had taken the job just before Christmas as a favor to the manager of the Wigwam, who was also a member of his church. Since the weekend night security guard had quit, Reverend Fields had agreed to fill in—from nine o'clock Saturday morning, to five o'clock Sunday morning—until the company found a replacement. His primary duty had been fire protection. There had been no major security problems.

When his wife, Virginia, awoke and discovered that her husband was not yet home, she said she knew something was wrong. She told the *Citizen-Journal* reporter that she set out to find him. "I didn't know if he'd be there [at the Wigwam] or lying along the road somewhere, but I knew he was in trouble."

Fields, a graduate of the Appalachian Bible Institute, had started his small Berean Church in 1973 in a room at the local elementary school, and by 1975 he and his congregation had built the wooden church and the parsonage where he lived—all with their own hands. Until his murder, he had lived there with his wife and three children.

The following day, Sheriff Berry said that six of the bullets recovered from Fields's body would be sent to the BCI to be compared with those from the murders committed in adjoining Franklin and Licking counties, in which large numbers of .22-caliber bullets had been fired into the heads of the victims.

If ballistics showed the gun to be the one used in the other killings, Berry told reporters, he would seek help from law enforcement agencies in the other two counties.

But it had been two and a half months since the triple homicide, and if the same .22-caliber gun turned out to have been used in five serial murders, the Franklin County Prosecutor would have a hard time bringing to trial a prime suspect who had been locked up in the women's prison during the last two of the five killings.

3

Lew Dye felt sure of himself as he entered Judge Paul W. Martin's courtroom on May 4, 1978, for the suppression hearing to bar the Prosecutor's use of Claudia's 158-page confession as evidence in her murder trial.

Once again, Claudia behaved oddly for someone facing the death penalty. At times she seemed dazed and

confused. At other times she listened intently as if trying
to comprehend what was being said about her. Frequently she would turn and wave to reporters.

Dye planned to call as his first witness Claudia's
psychiatrist, Dr. Byron Stinson, Associate Professor of
Psychiatry at Ohio State University's Medical School,
who would testify as to Claudia's history of mental illness. Then he would call Bobby Novatney, who would describe her recent behavior.

The prosecution would call only one witness to argue that Claudia had given the confession openly, freely,
and in an apparent sound mental state—Detective Sergeant Howard Champ.

Dye smiled at O'Grady, confident that Judge Martin
would never allow that cockeyed confession to be used as
evidence against a mentally ill defendant.

After being sworn in, Dr. Stinson, the tall, slightly
overweight psychiatrist in his early sixties, referred to
his notes as he testified. Claudia, he said, had been hospitalized under his care at Upham Hall three times: October 1974, after her return from Hawaii; October 1976;
and September 1977, for periods of two or three months.
His diagnosis was *"schizophrenia, common latent type."*

"What does that mean?" Dye asked.

"It's a condition described by Hoch in 1949," Stinson said, "characterized by pan-anxiety—really panic
attacks—pan-hysteria, and pan-sexuality. It's a curious
kind of diagnostic—the new diagnostic nomenclature
will be out this year and will be called borderline schi-
zophasia [sic]. It's related to schizophrenia, but . . . the
patient is at times tuned to reality. . . . I have seen her
over a number of years . . . and the diagnosis has always
been the same. Claudia's type comes in areas of judgment, in dealings with her surroundings, usually in a
sexual way. She gets into curious kinds of sexual situations."

He looked at Claudia as she smiled up at him. "For
instance, the first occasion we saw her was after she had
been divorced . . . and then she gets in a state of panic,
feels like . . . the world is falling around her and so on—
and she comes in the hospital and is pretty well divorced
from the surrounding world, lost, kind of in a fantasy,
and it requires a while to crank her down."

Lew Dye asked him how that diagnosis related to her contact with reality and to her surroundings.

"Claudia seems to prefer to live in the eye of a storm," Stinson said. "She is always seeking out curious kinds of relationships with marginal people in terms of her social contacts. Bisexuals, homosexuals, prostitutes, go-go dancers. She gets involved in these situations and begins to imagine she is part of the syndicate, the Mafia, which is going to involve her in white slavery. All kinds of curious fantasies become closely interwoven with reality until there is a point where somebody lets her have it . . . rejects her . . . and then she has one of these panic attacks and seeks, really, the protection of the hospital."

Stinson described the symptoms of her panic attacks: "sleeplessness, pacing, poor appetite, crying spells and spells of hysterical shouting . . . very demanding, threatening to sue, worrying about others coming to harm her . . . in all, just very unpleasant to be around."

The doctor recalled that when Claudia had first been admitted to Upham Hall in 1974, she had given him a long involved story of having been kidnapped in Hawaii by the Mafia and forced into white slavery, from which she'd escaped.

In 1977, she had been hospitalized after calling the police, saying she had seen a woman being stabbed in an alley behind her home. But no body was found; there was no corroboration.

Stinson pointed out that after the "stabbing incident" Claudia's voice had become progressively more hoarse, until on the day of admission to the hospital her voice had disappeared completely. "This hoarseness and this phobia," Stinson said, "are part of this pan-hysteria . . ."

Dye reviewed the details of the McCann homicides, and the subsequent interrogation of Claudia by Detective Howard Champ, during which she had made her confession. Dye asked Stinson if that was similar to statements she had made for other crimes.

"Claudia is like a chameleon," Stinson explained, "like the little cocker spaniel . . . an extreme need to please which certainly could be brought out by questioning. I think Claudia would give you anything you wanted if you had her in a cohesive situation. She might well do it in a noncohesive situation. Her behavior takes on her surroundings . . . She meets other people's demands."

Dye asked, "If Claudia were given some information . . . about a murder case . . . from the interviewer, would it be possible, not just possible but *very probable*, that Claudia would reiterate all this and put herself in as one of the principals?"

Stinson nodded. "Claudia is very capable of involving herself, almost like a spider weaving a web, constructing parts of reality and fantasy until . . . to a degree that I can never tell—and I really paid much attention in treating her—where the fabrication ended and the truth began."

During cross-examination, Assistant Prosecutor James O'Grady reviewed Stinson's comment that "Claudia was a person living in the eye of a storm, in the curious scene in Columbus."

"Well," Stinson said, "the *curious* I don't recall [saying]. She certainly has always picked a kind of demon world, the fringe of social propriety, I suppose you call it."

"The people she made reference to," O'Grady asked, "her friends and associates . . . did she tell you about two go-go girls that had in fact been murdered?"

"No."

"Had you yourself ever read about that in the newspaper, the unsolved murder of two go-go girls—one from here and one from Dayton?"

Stinson said he had not.

After a few questions about the treatment of Claudia's disorder, O'Grady asked if Dr. Stinson had read Claudia's statement, or if he had heard the taped confession. When Stinson said he had not, O'Grady pressed the point. "So I take it you could not even attempt to give any opinion on what actually was said in that statement, that is . . . the tone of voice . . . without having heard it."

"None at all."

"Okay, I take it you also could not venture an opinion as to whether or not Claudia, when she was first talking to the deputies, was able to understand what her rights were and things like that?"

"Certainly not from the specifics, no."

"Thank you, doctor," O'Grady said. "That will be all."

On redirect examination, Lew Dye summarized the earlier testimony, and asked, "Doctor . . . would you make a judgment based on your professional expertise, involvement with Claudia, and experience in these matters, did she in fact commit these murders in your opinion as a psychiatrist?"

"I'm not too aware of the facts of the case," Stinson said, "but I'm very familiar with Claudia. I just can't believe—I do not believe—that Claudia is capable of committing murder or has committed murder."

Howard Champ, when called to the witness stand, described how he had learned about Claudia from the officers who had spoken to her in the restaurant. Dye had him describe the events that resulted in her being taken to the Sheriff's Department and then reviewed the confession.

Trying to clarify Claudia's shifting moods, Dye asked, "Do you recall indicating to me that she did not want to see me . . . then when I got over to headquarters she came in screaming to see me? Do you recall that? You were quite surprised at her reaction."

Champ's reaction was hostile. "I do recall that after talking to you about it, she was going into some type of hysterical act."

"Do you recall that you commented to me that the way she was acting was related to drugs, and so on, and was faking, she was not really that bad off?"

"It was my opinion," Champ insisted, "that after her initial meeting with you, she did go into an act—yes."

Dye pressed Champ on Claudia's having taken medication during the interrogation, the circumstances surrounding the search of the apartment, and her comments during the confession. "Did you find that what she told you was actually the way your investigation indicated things took place?"

"We were amazed at the amount of information she had concerning the crime scene itself . . . the position of the bodies, the type of wounds they received and the areas where these wounds were in proportion [sic] to the body."

Dye pointed out that both Deno Politis and Robert

Novatney had passed lie-detector tests, convincing the Franklin County Prosecutor that they had nothing to do with the murders. He reminded Champ that two weeks after the murders, Politis had been arrested for theft at the Kroger supermarket, and that in questioning him Detective Tony Rich might have revealed information that Politis then passed along to Claudia.

Champ said he had been sitting nearby while Rich was interrogating Politis, and that less than fifteen percent of the conversation pertained to the McCann homicides.

Dye hammered away at Howard Champ about the points in the confession during which Claudia had admitted lying to confuse her interrogator, and the times she had said she wished to remain silent.

Judge Martin interrupted that line of questioning. "Mr. Dye, I think this is one of the things I'm going to be called upon to decide when the transcript is reviewed. I'm not interested in his opinion."

When Champ was excused, Dye's associate, William Fleck, rose and said, "I have one more witness. We are calling Robert Novatney, Your Honor."

After Novatney was sworn in and gave the court his address, he was asked if he knew Claudia Yasko. When he said he did and was asked to identify her in the courtroom, he looked directly at her and pointed in her direction. In answer to Fleck's questions, he described having met Claudia approximately a year earlier, and said they had been living together.

When asked if Claudia had ever admitted to knowledge of a crime before the present situation, Novatney said that three or four months ago, Claudia claimed to have seen a young girl murdered outside their home, and had called the detectives.

In response to Fleck's questions about Claudia's fear of being killed, Novatney said, ". . . [She was afraid of] various people that I don't know about . . . [There was] some incident that happened in California or Hawaii. She stated that she was in fear of her life."

"Can you supply us with any particular conversation she may have stated . . . ?" Fleck said.

Novatney shrugged. "Quote, there are people out there that want to kill me, unquote."

Fleck got Novatney to confirm the fact that Deno Politis had come to the house after having been arrested on a petty theft charge and had described, in Claudia's presence, details he had learned of the murders.

During cross-examination, Prosecutor O'Grady asked Novatney if Claudia had ever mentioned other criminal activity. When Novatney looked at him blankly, O'Grady added, "Did she also have knowledge of any other criminal activity such as explosives up at Hoover Dam?"

"Object!" Fleck shouted. "That is getting—it's irrelevant."

"Overruled," said the judge.

Novatney nodded. "She stated that she had that knowledge."

"Uh-huh. You say she stated she had some knowledge of some explosives at Hoover Dam? What did she say happened up there?"

Novatney bristled. "Well, I don't know. You know more about that than—"

"You don't know what she stated?"

"Yeah."

"How do you know she stated something?"

"Well, I was at my attorney's office going over the transcript of the confession she made."

O'Grady looked triumphantly at Fleck and then at Dye. "And who was your attorney, for the record?"

"Lew Dye."

O'Grady got Novatney to admit that Claudia hadn't actually named him or his younger brother as having been involved in the Hoover Dam incident, and then asked, "Why did you automatically assume it's yourself and younger brother, if no one is named?"

Novatney glared at Claudia. "She accused me of murder. Why not?"

After a few more minutes of cross-examination, weakening Novatney's credibility as a witness, O'Grady dismissed him. Judge Martin told the attorneys he was taking the matter under advisement.

At approximately the same time Claudia's hearing was being conducted in the Hall of Justice, sheriffs from three counties were being informed by the Bureau of

Criminal Identification and Investigation that the .22-caliber automatic pistol that had killed McCann, his mother, and Christine Herdman in Franklin County was the same weapon that had killed Jenkin T. Jones in Licking County and Reverend Gerald Fields in Fairfield County.

No one mentioned the obvious—that Jones and Fields had been murdered while Claudia was still in prison.

4

When Claudia returned from the court hearing and Donna Zag let her into her cell, Claudia lay on her cot and wept.

"C'mon, perk up, kid," the matron said. "Nothing could be that bad. I want you to read my palm again. I told my two oldest daughters what you said last time about me becoming a grandmother. The part that's got them worried is when you said one of them would have a terrible hard time in childbirth."

Claudia stared at her, still dazed. "What are you talking about?"

"My palm, honey. I'd like you to read my future again."

Claudia shook her head and moaned. "I don't want to look into the future anymore."

"What do you mean? You're a great fortune-teller, Claudia. Why not?"

"Because I heard my psychiatrist talk about me in court. He says I construct fantasies—like a spider weaving a web. And now I know—" Her hand gestured to include the whole prison. "This isn't a movie set." She touched her bandaged foot. "And this wasn't a filming accident during a scene." She glanced up with tears in her eyes. "He said at times I'm tuned in to reality. Well, it's sure reality time now."

"Anything I can do for you, Claudia?"

"Jesus has deserted me. You might as well just leave me alone too."

When Zag left, Claudia sat silently on her cot for a

while, eyes closed, trying to understand what it all meant. If she wasn't starring in a movie, then she was under indictment for a real murder. She had heard them read the death-penalty specifications. The prosecutors had asked that she get the electric chair.

Claudia heard a scraping noise and saw two workmen putting up a ladder outside her cell to change a long fluorescent bulb. They were talking about finishing this job and going to dinner. As they spoke, she realized that since they were between her cell and the control room, the officers' view of her through the monitor would be obstructed.

She could take her own life now, and no one would see or stop her. The porcelain toilet. There was water in the bottom.

She dropped to her knees, the pain making her left ankle too unbearable to walk on. She crawled to the toilet bowl and looked down. Put her hand into the water—it was cold and clean. She had to do it now, before anyone came. She murmured, "Sweet Jesus, forgive me, but I know you will take me to a better place." And with one deep breath she pressed her face into the bowl, and let her breath bubble out for a moment—and inhaled.

Against her will, feeling the water up in her nostrils, her face came up. She forced it down again and again, but suddenly she was gagging . . . and choking . . . and vomiting . . . and the noise of her choking brought unwanted help.

Guards took her to the infirmary. When they found out she was going to be all right they put her back into her cell under strict supervision.

She wept. She wanted to die in a manner of her own choosing, not in the electric chair. Oh, dear God, not in the electric chair. She didn't want them to shave off her long black hair, and strap her down, and send the high voltage through her body.

All her life she had been against capital punishment; now she knew she had been right.

Five

1

On Saturday, May 6, 1978, nearly two months after Claudia had been arrested and imprisoned, the *Columbus Citizen-Journal* gave the five brutal killings their label:

"THE .22-CALIBER SLAYINGS."

They ran two front-page stories.

The first quoted Franklin County Sheriff Harry Berkemer as saying, "Apparently there is somebody kill-crazy running around. I'm afraid we're going to have some more murders." Berkemer admitted that sheriff's detectives from the three adjacent counties where these murders had been committed (Franklin, Fairfield, and Licking counties) had failed to turn up any clues from informants. "Things are very quiet," he said. "There is no street talk . . ."

The second story explored Claudia's involvement:

HAS SHE THE SOLUTION TO FIVE DEATHS?

The answer to five or more brutal slayings may be locked in the tormented and confused mind of Claudia Elaine Yasko.

Although it appears that she was wrong in telling sheriff's deputies two men [Novatney and Politis] were involved in the shootings of Robert "Mickey" McCann, his mother and his girlfriend, deputies believe she must have been present when the killings occurred.

"It's weird, the things she knows about the McCann murders," says Berkemer. "She tells you something and you think she's lying, but you go back to the pictures taken at the scene and you find out you were wrong and she's right. . . ."

"She is a mystery," Sheriff Berkemer admits.

Some officials told reporters that they still intended to hold her and try her for aggravated murder. Other officials pointed out that—since her detailed knowledge of the murder scene had been publicized, and since the murderers were still at large—to release her on bond now would be the equivalent of giving her the death penalty.

On Friday, May 12, Lew Dye filed a motion requesting that Claudia be freed on bond. Since her co-defendants, Novatney and Politis, had been released on recognizance bonds, he argued, it was not fair that she alone remain in prison. Judge Paul W. Martin put off ruling on this motion until he was ready to rule on Dye's earlier motion to suppress her confession.

Dye also requested that Claudia be permitted to take a lie-detector test, with the stipulation that the results be used in court regardless of the outcome. Since Politis and Novatney had submitted to polygraphs, he argued, due process demanded that Claudia be given the same opportunity.

Prosecutor O'Grady objected and to Dye's astonishment Judge Martin turned down the request.

Afterwards, a disappointed Lew Dye met with reporters and released a "Statement of Alibi" he intended to file with the court.

"Claudia was in somebody's company from the time she went to work until she got home next morning," he read from his prepared text. "She worked at the Image

Gallery that evening, February eleventh, until two thirty
A.M., and then afterwards went with two friends, one
male and one female, to a Western Pancake House for
breakfast. After breakfast, she remained in their company until she got home, where she lived with Robert
Novatney."

The following Friday, May 19, Judge Martin overruled Dye's motion to suppress Claudia's confession and
refused to release her on bond. She had been informed of
her rights, the judge decided, and had "knowingly, intel-
ligently, and voluntarily" waived them.

Once again Lew Dye was surprised. He'd been certain the court would throw out the confession of a mental patient interrogated while under medication. Now he
had mixed feelings about the "release on bond." Per-
haps Claudia *was* better off in prison until her trial.
Though her knowledge was interwoven with lies and fantasy, he felt she knew a great deal more than she was telling him.

In addition to the things she might have learned
from Politis, she most probably knew street people who
had passed along details of the crimes. But if word ever
got back to those who had talked or those behind the killings, that she *did* have information—that she did know
the murderer or murderers—she would be in real danger.

Dye no longer hesitated to use the press to fight
Claudia's case. He had been feeding stories to reporters
and TV newscasters. His next tactic was to accept the
help offered by *Playboy* magazine. The Playboy Foundation Defense Team was providing manpower, resources,
and funds for cases, anywhere in the country, in which
the defendant was not receiving justice. Dye could see
that this case—a beautiful, vulnerable, mentally ill
woman being unjustly held in prison and threatened
with the death penalty—was just the kind of case they'd
go for. There'd be a story in it for them as well.

Dye told *Playboy*'s Bill Helmer that the defense
needed more information, more people to do legwork,
and more witnesses interviewed. Claudia's confession,
he pointed out, was gruesome and hair-raising but also
plausible enough. Unless he could counter it point by
point, the case was lost.

Dye pointed out that, as often happened in cases like this, the prosecution was dropping hints that the risk of Claudia's conviction and a possible death sentence could be avoided if Dye offered to have Claudia committed to a civil mental hospital. It was obvious to most people connected with the case, he said, that the Franklin County Prosecutor was hoping to appear successful in a sensational, highly publicized case without even having to go to trial.

Helmer asked Dye to provide him with a summary of the events for the Playboy Foundation, and Dye spent most of that weekend in his office dictating his notes. But when the newspapers came out on Monday, May 22, he had another multiple murder to add to his report. A couple whose home was just inside the city limits of Columbus had been shot to death with a .22.

The case came under the jurisdiction of the Columbus Police Department. Although city homicide detectives were reluctant to associate the Columbus killings with the earlier .22-caliber slayings until ballistics results were in, the *Columbus Dispatch* made the connection:

DOUBLE MURDER SIMILAR TO
.22-CALIBER KILLINGS

A couple whose bullet-riddled bodies were found Sunday afternoon in their secluded Morse Road house, may be the latest victims in a series of murders linked by a .22-caliber automatic weapon.

Over the weekend, on the north side of Columbus, forty-seven-year-old Jerry L. Martin, who had recently been promoted to general manager and vice president of the Perma Stone Company, and his wife, Martha, had been found shot to death. When a nephew had come to the home for a cookout on Sunday to celebrate Martha's fifty-first birthday and found no activity, he entered the house and discovered the bodies.

Jerry Martin, six feet, five inches and 225 pounds, had apparently been shot through a window while he lay on the couch watching television. Two .22-caliber shell casings lay on the ground outside the house, near the window. Then he was shot again at close range several times in the head.

Martha, dressed in a black suit, was found dead in the hallway, shot numerous times in the head. As in two of the earlier cases, the telephone wires outside the house had been cut. Bedrooms had been ransacked. The motive appeared to be robbery.

Neighbors told a *Dispatch* reporter that Mrs. Martha "Marty" Martin had been a loan officer at the City National Bank, where she had worked for thirteen years. Jerry Martin hadn't much money and "was just a man who went to work every day." The Martins had been married for eight years (it was the second marriage for each) and they had moved into the house on Morse Road three years ago. The couple often entertained friends at their home. Though they had not been currently active in any organizations, Jerry had been one of the original volunteers for the Whitehall Fire Department.

By Friday, May 26, the Bureau of Criminal Identification and Investigation confirmed that the Martins had been murdered by the same gun as Jones, Fields, and the three victims at the McCann house—seven deaths now linked by one weapon. To the dismay of several city detectives, "a source close to the investigation" revealed the details of the murder weapon to the *Columbus Citizen-Journal* which ran the front-page story with the headline:

"SAME GUN LINKED TO SLAYINGS."

The weapon, according to the story, was a semi-automatic .22-caliber Stoeger Luger manufactured in West Germany. The Stoeger Luger, known as a "junk gun" that frequently misfired and jammed, had been one of the pistols most widely sold through mail-order houses until 1968, when a federal law was passed prohibiting selling handguns through the mail, except to gun dealers.

2

The first Columbus Police Department detective on the scene of the Martin murders was Sergeant Bill Steckman of Homicide—the same "Pop" Steckman who had once considered adopting Claudia's sister, Nancy—and he was put in charge of the city's investigation of the .22-caliber killings.

The six-foot-tall, blond-haired, blue-eyed detective had just started wearing a hearing aid and was still a bit self-conscious about it. He spoke in a soft, throaty voice that echoed from deep inside his chest. The Homicide Bureau was his life, and the way "Steck" conducted that life was praised by prosecutors and defense attorneys alike.

Most of Steckman's work days became eighteen hours long now, and it was common knowledge that he practically lived in the Detective Bureau.

Every new suspect had to be checked, double-checked, and cleared. Steckman had to supervise the interrogation of more than two hundred people who might have been directly or indirectly involved in the murders.

The .22-caliber killings, Steckman soon learned, were becoming more important than anything else in his life. All he had to do was be patient, and it would come: the clue, the lead, the break. And when it did, he would be ready, because he knew his job. Homicide investigation was his world: he dreamed it, he lived it, he loved it.

Born and raised just outside Columbus, he had been a policeman for fourteen years—eight as a homicide detective. While an officer, he had taken three years of paralegal training at Capitol Law School. It was as if all the training of his life had prepared him for this incredible case.

Even before the Martins were murdered, he'd followed the investigations connected with the .22's. From the time Nancy Yasko had first phoned to ask if he could help Claudia, he'd been in constant touch with county detectives who had sought his advice on the McCann

homicides. At that time he had even asked for and been
sent a copy of Claudia's confession.

It amazed him that some sheriff's detectives still
thought that Novatney, Politis, and Claudia had something to do with the murders. As soon as he was put in
charge of the .22's, he interviewed Claudia and Martha.
He went through Champ's interrogation carefully and
checked out Claudia's descriptions of the murder scene.

He was satisfied that on the night of the homicides a
great number of people, including street people, had
been taken to the McCann home while the murder scene
was being processed—for a valid reason, to be sure: To
identify the bodies. Those people had gone back to bars
and parties, and told other street people everything they
saw. And Claudia had picked up the information, bit by
bit by bit.

He knew by now that if someone gave Claudia the tip
of a finger, she quickly took the whole hand. He accepted
that. His answer to those who asked: "How did Claudia
know what she knew?" was that street people, as well as
police officers who had been at that scene and talked too
much, were the source of her information.

After the Martin murders, Steckman, on behalf of
the Columbus Police Department, made an agreement
with the other law enforcement heads from the two cities
and three counties involved in the investigation that
whoever actually broke the case would get everything
from the others—all the arrests and all the evidence connected to the crimes.

It was logical, he felt, because theoretically each
agency already knew what everybody else knew. It was
too important—too many people had died—for depart-
mental rivalry to be allowed to play a part in the arrest
and conviction. Jealousy, everyone knew, made detectives play a different kind of game while the investigation was in progress. But, he insisted, when and if the
case broke, then it was time for everybody to come together.

He made the agreement informally, through private
conversations, and he took full responsibility for it. It
had to be that way, he felt, because the problems of
catching serial killers were difficult enough, but when
detectives and their superiors—hoping to be credited

with breaking big cases—guarded their own information, the killers gained an advantage.

He was well aware of other serial murder cases making the news across the country—"Son of Sam" and "The Hillside Strangler"—and the special problems of the kind of crime that covered different jurisdictions.

Unlike mass murderers, who killed a number of victims at one time and place, most serial murderers moved from city to city, stalking their victims across city, county, or state lines, over weeks, months, and even years. Because different law enforcement agencies were involved—county sheriff's deputies, city police, and the FBI, each concerned primarily with their own cases—detectives often didn't notice the patterns. Conflicting investigative methods, interdepartmental jealousies, and prosecutors overreacting to the political pressures of a fearful and outraged public, often gave serial killers the advantage. Among the most difficult criminals to apprehend, most often, when they were arrested, it was by accident.

But many of them—like "Jack the Ripper," who killed six women in London in 1888, and the "Zodiac Killer," who murdered anywhere from six to thirty-seven people in California, Nevada, and Oregon between 1966 and 1974—were never caught.

So, despite the well-known rivalries between the Columbus police and city and county detectives in Newark and Licking and Franklin counties, Steckman, by taking it on himself to make a winner-take-all deal, encouraged the five law enforcement agencies to work together.

Some of his own colleagues on the Columbus Police Department disagreed with him and began criticizing his methods and his approach. Others resented the way he seemed to pay no attention to investigations done by any but his own men, the way he trusted no one's information but his own, insisting on personally checking every lead that came along.

In addition to organizing all the material his own department had gathered independently during the months of the seven murders, Steckman now faced the task of trying to coordinate five law enforcement agencies—sheriffs and their deputies in three counties and police chiefs and their officers in two cities.

From now on, he would devote every waking moment to what everyone called "the .22's" until the killer or killers were caught, arrested, prosecuted, and behind bars.

Steckman moved all the files and evidence connected with the serial murders into one small room and posted crime-scene photographs and maps of the three adjacent counties on the walls.

Everyone who knew about it called it "Steck's War Room."

Six

1

Two weeks before her June 12 trial date, Claudia was in the prison shower when matron Donna Zag stuck her head in and said, "You've got visitors. Your attorney says they're from *Playboy*."

Claudia rinsed off the soap, stepped out of the shower, and wrapped her long hair in a towel. "Hey, maybe they want me for the centerfold," she said, laughing. "It's too late for May or June. Maybe I'll be Miss July."

She put on her prison uniform and, with Donna Zag helping her, she limped around the control center, past the dormitory, into the visitors' area. Beyond the telephone-booth-like cells was the "Attorney's Room."

As she entered, Claudia saw Lew Dye and two other men on the other side of the wired-glass window. She picked up one of the phones.

"Claudia, these people are here to help you," Dye said. "I don't know if you remember when I told you I was going to ask the Playboy Foundation in Chicago for assistance. Well, Bill Helmer is a senior editor at the magazine." He gestured towards the short, bald man with a mustache, wearing a western-style shirt, Levi's, and boots, sitting with his chair tilted back.

"And this is Russ Million. He's one of *Playboy*'s private investigators all the way from Austin, Texas." Dye nodded in the direction of the six-foot, slender, thirtyish man with a handlebar mustache and sandy hair down to his collar line. Russ Million wore a striped shirt, conservative tie, and a blazer.

It struck her as odd that the man from Texas was dressed like a businessman while the little editor from Chicago wore western clothes.

Bill Helmer asked why she had limped in, and Claudia described her beating. She hadn't received much medical attention for her ankle, she said. "They just gave me an Ace bandage. I know my foot's getting worse because my toenails fell out."

As they talked, Russ Million became impressed with Claudia. He had interviewed many imprisoned women, but there was something special about her—an unusual combination of sexuality and spirituality.

Helmer told her the Playboy Foundation had decided to help and would pay all future expenses to assist Dye in preparing for the upcoming trial. What they wanted from Claudia in return was permission to do a story later on. She agreed.

"I have to go back to Chicago tomorrow," Helmer said, "but Russ will stay in Columbus to work with Lew. You're going to have plenty of support before you go to trial, and it won't cost you a penny."

After they left and Donna Zag took her back to her cell, Claudia cried again. She wept every day now that her fantasy of acting in a movie had been shattered. Her face became so puffy at times that Donna would get some ice from the commissary to help bring down the swelling.

Before she went to sleep that night Claudia had a vision that Jesus came to her cell and said she no longer needed to worry because the Lord was working in mysterious ways.

2

When the three men left the women's prison, Lew Dye invited them to stay at his home outside Columbus. They accepted his hospitality, and he drove them to his 112-acre estate in his gold-and-black Rolls-Royce. In addition to being a defense attorney, he told them, he was also an avid fly-fisherman, a rugby enthusiast, and a farmer in the tradition of his Seventh-Day Adventist forebears. After dinner that evening, they sat out back sipping Scotch and discussing the .22-caliber killings.

Dye had a theory and wanted their help and backing to check it out.

Because of the execution-style head shootings, Dye said he felt that organized crime was behind it all. He'd heard from some of his clients that a new cocaine supplier was trying to muscle in on the Columbus area. Since McCann probably had dealt in narcotics, Dye theorized, he might have tried to switch to the new supplier. Dye speculated that the other victims had been involved in the cocaine traffic in minor ways—such as picking up packages dropped from private planes—and that the brutal executions were the Dayton/Cincinnati syndicate's way of setting an example.

The next day, Bill Helmer went back to Chicago, but not before he learned that BCI had released new information. The .22-caliber Stoeger Luger used in the seven murders, it now turned out, had also been used six months earlier—on December 10, 1977, in Newark, Ohio—to gun down Joyce Vermillion and Karen Dodrill, in the parking lot of Forker's Café.

The Newark Police Department, reconstructing events of that December night, learned that Karen Dodrill had decided to go to Forker's Café to cash her paycheck. When Joyce Vermillion, the bar waitress, said her husband couldn't pick her up as usual, Dodrill volunteered to return at closing time and drive her home.

As they left the café, both women were shot at least nine times—most of the bullets in the head. Spent .22-

caliber cartridges had been found near the bodies. The case had not been solved.

The *Columbus Dispatch* quoted a source "close to the investigation" who theorized that since all nine of the related murders had occurred on a Saturday or Sunday, the .22-caliber killings might be part of some ceremony for initiation into a gang.

The New York Times on June 3, 1978, reported that the nine .22-caliber murder cases covered five different jurisdictions, with each law enforcement agency pursuing its own investigation.

"Although they say they are coordinating their efforts," the article pointed out, "there are signs of strain that may have led to a less than complete sharing of information." The *Times* revealed that Newark, Ohio, police officers were blaming Franklin County Prosecutor George C. Smith for having disclosed the make of the gun, and feared that if the killer or killers struck again, they might use a different weapon.

Unable to reach George C. Smith for comment because he was in Cincinnati campaigning for the Republican nomination for Ohio attorney general, the *Times* reporter wrote:

> He [Smith] is preparing to try Claudia Yasko, a waitress, for the McCann murders, because Miss Yasko volunteered a confession to the Franklin County Sheriff's Department in mid-March. But Franklin County detectives barely concealed their scorn for Mr. Smith's contention that Miss Yasko is one of the killers.
>
> "You get people who want to confess all the time when there is something sensational going on," a Columbus detective said with a shrug, "and they are not usually the people you want."

Furious at the *Times* article and at the statement that Franklin County detectives were blaming him for what some people were calling "The Yasko Fiasco," Smith protested. "The Sheriff's detectives were the ones who pressured *us*," he said. "*They* were the ones who went up to the prosecutor's office and sat outside O'Grady's door."

3

With the revelation that the Newark killings of the two
women had been done with the same gun as the other
.22's, Russ Million decided that Dye's cocaine-
conspiracy theory seemed farfetched.

Million asked *Playboy* for more help, and editor Bill
Helmer arranged for a second private detective, Lake
Headley from Las Vegas, to assist in the investigation.
Headley drove to Columbus from the *Playboy* offices in
Chicago and placed himself at Million's disposal. He was
a tall, slender man in his mid-forties, with a long, thin
face, dark hair rising straight from a deep widow's peak,
and an aquiline nose.

With an introduction from Claudia's mother and sister, Headley and Million were able to meet Sergeant Bill
Steckman, who accepted their offer of help and gave
them leads to track down. Steckman told them that several of the women at the Image Gallery suspected Lenny
White, the big truck driver with the limp, whose cargo
had earned him the street name of "Pigman."

Headley and Million snooped around Pigman's home.
Through the window of what looked like a den or office,
they saw copies of the .22-caliber articles taped to the
wall. They also learned that the go-go girls found Pigman
very odd. "He comes into a tit-bar," the girls told Headley, "but when we strip, he turns his back to the stage."

Headley and Million interviewed Pigman one night
at the Image Gallery and discovered him to be cool and
composed as he told how he enjoyed taking young
women, like Claudia, out to breakfast after their work
was done. When Lew Dye reminded them that Pigman
was Claudia's alibi, the *Playboy* detectives realized they
were in the position of trying to discredit the defense's
most reliable witness—another dead end.

Million and Headley tried several times to reach Prosecutor George Smith, but their calls were never returned.
After Assistant Prosecutor O'Grady agreed to meet them,
when they arrived at his office, his secretary told them
curtly, "He had to go out for something *important*."

It seemed to the *Playboy* investigators that everyone they tried to talk to either avoided them or sent them off on wild-goose chases. They were particularly annoyed that whenever they went out to interview people, Lew Dye would insist on being present. He would never let them out of his sight.

Half a year had passed since the first of nine killings, and it soon became apparent to the out-of-town investigators that the citizens of Central Ohio were living in deep fear. Some families bought guns. Many bought more secure locks. Everyone kept doors locked day and night. What horrified most people was that the victims weren't being killed in bars or out on the dark streets or in high crime areas. Innocent citizens were being brutally murdered in what should have been the safety of their own homes. And the terror of the murder method, shooting men and women many times directly in the face, sickened and outraged everyone. The public demanded action from their politicians and the police.

On June 2, the day before Claudia's twenty-seventh birthday and ten days before her scheduled trial, Lew Dye arranged for the Ohio Public Defender's Commission to give her a lie-detector test. It was administered in a private room at the prison and took two hours. The questions she was asked included:

"Were you actually there when Mickey McCann was shot?"

"Did you see Mickey McCann at the time he was shot?"

"Have you ever actually been inside of the McCann home?"

"Do you suspect anyone in particular of killing Mickey McCann?"

Her answer to each question was, *"No."*

In his evaluation, the polygraphist wrote:

Based upon an analysis of the charts of this examination, it is the opinion of the undersigned polygraphist that Ms. Yasko appeared to be truthful when she denied any guilty knowledge of or involvement in the murder of Mickey McCann.

Seven

1

On June 8, four days before Claudia's scheduled trial, Franklin County Prosecutor George C. Smith caught everyone off guard when he dropped all charges and asked the judge to release her from custody. The court entry of *Nolle Prosequi* read in part:

> At the time of her indictment there was more than a substantial basis for considering Miss Yasko not only a prime suspect but a participant in these homicides, particularly in view of her 158-page statement of March 14, 1978. The ongoing investigation, however, and the present climate of the community is such that the State is of the opinion that it would be fair to neither party to proceed with a trial on June 12, 1978.

It was signed: *George C. Smith and J. O'Grady, Prosecuting Attorneys.*

Franklin County detectives were upset at the prosecutor for dropping the charges and so was the press. The following morning the *Citizen-Journal* carried the front-page story:

MURDER CHARGES AGAINST YASKO ARE DROPPED

Claudia Elaine Yasko, the 27-year-old former waitress police believe may hold a key to at least three of the nine slayings committed by the so-called .22-caliber killers, was a free woman Thursday night after nearly three months in jail. . . .

O'Grady said a trial "at this time" would be "unfair either to the state or to Miss Yasko herself. . . ."

"The public is getting so incensed that they're going to say, 'Yeah, we got one of them: let's convict her,' or they're going to think that since someone else is obviously still out there killing, she's innocent."

The afternoon *Dispatch* was more critical:

MURDER SUSPECT IS RELEASED

The Franklin County prosecutor's office, faced with a put up or shut up deadline Monday in a murder case with statewide political implications, decided Thursday to shut up. . . .

While Prosecutor George Smith was in Washington hosting a conference on prosecuting career criminals, his top assistant James O'Grady decided there was not enough evidence to prosecute Claudia Elaine Yasko. . . .

Smith has been out of his office much of the past months campaigning for state attorney general, leaving O'Grady to deal with the Yasko trial preparations. . . .

The Sunday *Dispatch* needled the prosecutors in its "Analysis of the News":

DROPPING OF CHARGES IN McCANN
MURDERS LEAVES PUZZLE

Why were indictments sought by the Franklin County prosecutor's office against Claudia Yasko, Robert Novatney and Deno Politis . . . ?

Smith told *The Dispatch* that O'Grady is handling the .22-caliber murder case and should be consulted for information about it. O'Grady has been relatively quiet except for a squeak when he asked that the charges against the three defendants be dropped. . . .

Some deputies are still puzzled about the dismissal of charges against Miss Yasko. . . .

Lew Dye celebrated. He had warned O'Grady and Smith, and they hadn't listened. Now they had become the laughingstock of the Columbus legal community, and Smith's chances of becoming Ohio Attorney General were fading fast.

Immediately after Claudia's release on June 8, Russ Million and Lake Headley arranged for a *Playboy* photographer to meet them at the Women's Correctional Institute and went with Lew Dye to get Claudia out. During the ten-minute drive from the courthouse, they assured Dye that since the .22-caliber killings were continuing, *Playboy* was still on the case. Million felt that the pattern of weekend murders was about due to be repeated, and they wanted to be close by to get the story.

They also agreed it was most urgent to get Claudia out of prison, into the car quickly, and to Dr. Byron Stinson at Upham Hall on the Ohio State University campus. First, because of her mental condition, Million said, but more important, because if the killers believed she knew something about them, there could be someone outside the women's prison waiting for her.

Lew Dye brought Claudia out of the jail as the *Playboy* photographer took pictures. But when they started towards Dye's Rolls-Royce, they were intercepted by a TV team. Those accompanying her let her give a brief interview, and then headed for the Ohio State University Medical Center, assuring her she would be safe at Upham Hall.

Dr. Stinson described Claudia upon her fourth admission to Upham Hall: ". . . Black waist length hair, bangs. Lots of makeup. Large gold earrings, lots of jewelry, mini-dress and lots of thigh showing. Heels (and she is a tall woman). Keeps complaining, 'I can't remember.'

Lots of empty laughter, crying spells. Empty distant cheerful preoccupation. Some flushes of warmth. Seductivity always in high gear."

His diagnosis: *"Schizophrenia, latent type."*

When Lew Dye came to visit Claudia, he explained—as he had over and over again during the past three months—why he hadn't arranged her release from prison sooner. He had done it to save her life because she was safer behind bars. And it was important that everyone on the street spread the word that she was mentally ill and couldn't remember anything about the murders.

"You're in danger," he said. "So the thing is to stay here in the hospital and to keep your mouth shut."

2

The following day, the Franklin County Prosecutor also officially dropped the charges against Deno Politis, and a hearing was scheduled for the following Monday to do the same for Robert Novatney. Prosecutor O'Grady made a point of informing the press that if new evidence turned up, charges would be refiled against the three suspects.

Novatney gave an interview to a *Columbus Dispatch* reporter, expressing his anger at having been indicted in the first place. "George Smith, the man that's in office now, I believe he planned to get elected on this . . ." he was reported as saying. "I felt I was a pawn. I don't understand why they can get away with it . . . just pick up somebody off the street and arrest them for three counts of murder."

He still didn't know why Claudia had implicated him in the McCann murders, he said, and he hadn't spoken to her since. "They knew she had mental problems, and she is so easily led. I think her confession mostly was manufactured. The information she didn't make up, I think they gave her." He told the reporter that though he and Claudia had been living together for more than a year when she was arrested, "we never really had much of a relationship. I felt sorry for her and thought I could help her."

He admitted to having been previously arrested about ten times for misdemeanors like public intoxication, but never anything as serious as murder. Now people would always think that since he had been charged with murder he must be guilty. "No matter where I go, my name is going to be on this. Outrage is the first word that comes to mind. They ruined my whole life; I have no future here right now."

Bobby, high on his anger, made plans for lawsuits against Claudia, against the detectives, against the prosecutor, against the state of Ohio. Then his anger subsided and he told his mother and brothers that Claudia was mentally ill and he no longer held a grudge against her.

On June 11, 1978, three days after Claudia's release, the *Columbus Dispatch* hinted that charges against the three suspects had been dropped for political reasons:

> ... This is also a bad time politically for the office of Franklin County Prosecutor George Smith to lose a murder trial attracting national attention.
>
> Smith is running as the Republican nominee for Ohio attorney general, and the nine ".22-caliber murders," as they have been dubbed, are drawing as much publicity as the Son of Sam shootings in New York City and the Hillside Strangler slayings in Los Angeles ...

When Claudia—the last of the trio indicted for the McCann murders—was set free, and there were no longer any prime suspects for the .22-caliber murders, many people in Central Ohio bought guard dogs and kept their guns loaded and ready behind double-locked doors, living in greater fear than they had ever known.

Eight

1

After a stay of four days at Upham Hall, Claudia was discharged at four o'clock on the afternoon of June 12, 1978, the date she was to have been tried for murder.

As Pigman helped her into his loaded eighteen-wheeler parked on the lot outside Upham Hall, the pigs were squealing in the heat and Ohio State University students were watching and laughing. Claudia waved and laughed along with them.

Pigman drove Claudia to her mother's house on Columbus's east side, but winding Easthaven Drive was too narrow to maneuver the trailer, so he left it at the curb and they walked the rest of the way. Martha seemed pleased to see him and insisted he spend the night.

He slept on the couch. The next morning, when he looked out the front window, he discovered a sheriff's cruiser parked across the street.

"Looks like we're being watched," Pigman said.

"That's outrageous," Martha said. "I'm going out there to see what he wants."

When she approached the cruiser and demanded to know why the deputy was watching her house, he told her, "Mrs. Yasko, I'm just doing my job. What I'd really like to do is to come inside and talk to the truck driver."

"You're not coming into my house unless you've got a warrant."

"Sorry you feel that way, ma'am. I'll just wait here a while, until he leaves."

But by late afternoon the deputy was gone, and Pigman said he had to be rolling before all those pigs died of the heat. "I'm really coming back for you, Claudia. I promise you that."

When Pigman returned a week later, he convinced Claudia she needed to get away from Columbus for a while. It would be good for her, he said, to go on the road with him. Claudia thought it was a great idea.

They traveled together, delivering pigs in Indiana, Illinois, Wisconsin, and Minnesota. She helped him with the loading, unloading, and checking of the livestock. Though they slept in the cab of the truck, he never made a pass at her, and she was pleased that he respected her need for privacy, that it was enough for him to be with her, to help her forget her ordeal.

Pigman decided they'd celebrate the Fourth of July with a good dinner and the night in a motel. He picked up the afternoon newspaper from the machine in the lobby and showed Claudia the news story: The previous day, July 3, 1978, the U.S. Supreme Court, in the case of Sandra Lockett against the state of Ohio, had overturned Ohio's death-penalty law.

"What does that mean?" she asked.

"Well, your indictment carried death-penalty specifications, but now, if and when the real .22-caliber killer or killers get caught, the most they can get is life in prison."

"I'm glad," Claudia said, "because I'm against the death penalty for anyone."

Pigman looked at her and smiled. "I've thanked God a dozen times that I was with you that morning. But I've never ceased to wonder how you were able to tell all those things about the murder scene."

She laughed. "I'm psychic . . . you know that."

"I don't believe in that horse pucky."

"Well, there's no other explanation."

"And one other thing. I never mentioned this to the

police, but I'll never forget that you predicted Mickey McCann's death *before it happened*."

"Doesn't that prove I can predict the future?"

He shook his head. "What it proves, honey, is that you haven't told me everything."

"You don't trust me, Lenny," she said, pouting. "You're accusing me of—"

He stared into his rearview mirror. "Goddamn!"

"Don't blaspheme, Lenny. You know how I feel about—"

"Honey, I hate to tell you this, but I've noticed that goddamned blue Chevy on and off for the past two days."

"What do you mean?"

"What I mean, baby, is we're being followed. I'd sure like to know if it's the law or a murderer."

For the rest of the trip home, Claudia sat huddled back in the passenger seat, cringing in fear.

When they got back to her mother's house, Claudia asked Nancy to call Pop Steckman to see if he knew what was going on. Steckman said Claudia and Pigman were being tailed and watched by Franklin County sheriff's deputies to see where they went and with whom they associated.

"Howard Champ won't rest until he has me back in jail!"

Steckman said it wasn't Champ, because he was no longer a detective. Champ had been transferred to an administrative job and was now deputy director of the Franklin County Jail.

When Claudia hung up, she felt her body grow cold and she began to shake. She looked up at Pigman and whispered, "I don't want to die."

Claudia, now obsessed with the idea that the killers knew her mother's address, begged him to help her move out. Pigman found her an apartment in German Village. It would be her secret place, she said, where she could hide out until the .22-caliber murders were solved.

2

At the beginning of November 1978, eleven months after the first .22-caliber murders in Newark, Ohio, the December issue of *Playboy* was released and Claudia became a local celebrity. A photograph, showing Lew Dye helping her through the barred doorway of the county jail, was featured prominently on the page. Claudia hated the article. Terrified by the renewed notoriety, she felt certain that now the killer would recognize her on the street. She rarely went out, except for the one or two days a month Pigman came to the apartment.

The "Playboy Casebook" feature by Bill Helmer summarized the story of the McCann murders and criticized the prosecutor and the Sheriff's Department:

A CLOSE CALL FOR CLAUDIA

An Ohio case raises the question: how many innocent people have gone to prison because they lacked the money and the means to defend themselves?

The article pointed out that the Franklin County Prosecutor, George Smith, "who happened to be running for a higher state office, seemed especially anxious to try a suspect and declare a victory . . .

"Claudia's blow-by-blow confession was largely fiction based on widely reported facts," said the *Playboy* story. "A jury might have been expected to believe it in the absence of any rebuttal, but not an experienced police officer or a prosecutor. Almost every question was answered wrong, inconclusively, or with a groggy question. Her few right answers were virtually spoon-fed, or arrived at by a process of elimination. . . ."

Prosecutor George C. Smith responded to the *Playboy* article, in the November 3 *Columbus Dispatch:*

PLAYBOY ARTICLE A "HATCHET JOB"
SMITH CONTENDS

". . . The most incredible aspect of this whole thing is that *Playboy* magazine did not even discuss the case with myself nor anyone else in this office. Nor did they discuss this case with the deputy sheriff in charge of the investigation.

"The whole thrust of the article is so distorted . . ." Smith said, "I believe it is so obviously timed to have an impact on this election that that fact will also be obvious to the people in our community."

Smith said he does not know who is behind the "hatchet job" but hopes "this will become known."

James O'Grady, the assistant prosecutor who handled the case, called the article "a piece of crap" that "doesn't come close to attempting to tell the truth. . . ."

More than six months had passed since the killing of Mr. and Mrs. Martin in Columbus—the last two of the nine murders—and most people in Central Ohio were beginning to feel the nightmare was over. Many speculated that like "Zodiac" and "Jack the Ripper" the .22-caliber killer or killers had probably just quit, or left the area, or died.

But after the *Playboy* article, Sergeant Steckman, unwilling to take chances with Claudia's safety, alerted police on duty in German Village to keep watch on her apartment. A lot of people were saying that whoever had done the murders would now surely come after her and that she would not be safe until the killer or killers were caught.

Part Two

Detectives and Killers

Nine

1

At about ten-forty-five on the night of December 4, 1978, shortly after the *Playboy* article was published, the driver of a new blue Omni parked his car on Euclaire between Livingston and College avenues on the east side of Columbus. He turned out the lights, pulled a ski mask down over his face, and reached into a small leather satchel for his silencer-tipped gun. Stepping out of the car, he buttoned his hooded parka, moved quickly into the alley between the garages, and waited.

Joseph Annick, a fifty-six-year-old assistant adjutant of the American Legion, pulled his tan car up to his garage at about midnight, turned in at an awkward angle, and had to pull back and enter a second time. He sat in the car for about ten minutes, revving the engine to charge his battery.

A native of Cleveland, who had spent most of his boyhood and adult life in Columbus, Annick had served with the Army in World War Two. Known as a quiet and private bachelor, he was currently the American Legion post's activities director in charge of arranging details for Ohio state conventions, social activities, and special legion projects.

When Annick turned off the ignition and got out of the car, the masked man moved into the garage around to the driver's side and fired a full clip of nine shots. Five of them hit Annick. When the clip was empty, the man lowered the garage door, took a flashlight out of his satchel, and searched the dead man. He then removed a billfold from his victim's back pocket, revealing close to three hundred dollars, credit cards, and a driver's license. He shoved the wallet into his pocket and pulled Annick's trousers down to check for a money belt. Finding nothing else, he picked the car keys up from where they had fallen and searched the trunk. There was only a dark blue-green blanket and a spare tire.

The killer opened the garage door, let himself out, and closed it behind him. Then he walked to his own car and drove away.

Annick's sister, knowing he had been visiting a friend on the north side of Columbus, had expected him to return at about eleven-thirty. When he hadn't returned by a quarter past midnight, she went down to the garage across the street from their apartment building to see if the car was there. She screamed when she found his body sprawled on the ground.

Columbus detectives checked the area and learned that Annick had last been seen alive at a neighborhood grocery store, where he'd stopped to buy some snacks between eleven and midnight. His missing wallet suggested robbery as the motive.

Although Annick had been shot five times in the chest and stomach by a .22, police told reporters there was no reason to believe this killing was related to the .22-caliber murders.

2

Five days later, on Saturday evening December 9, 1978, a couple in their thirties went Christmas shopping for toys at the Woolco Department Store in Columbus's Great Southern Shopping Center. When the man with black-rimmed glasses and a goatee presented a Visa card for payment, cashier Cheryl Young checked and saw it was on the hot list of stolen credit cards. She alerted her supervisor, Janet Barton, who called the Visa credit center to double-check.

"I've had lots of problems with that card," the man said impatiently, offering to pay cash. "I don't know if I'll keep it."

"Just hold on," Barton said. "I've got to clear this."

The woman with him left the checkout line to walk back into the store, and a few seconds later, the man hesitated, as if not sure what was expected of him. Then he left the line and followed her, leaving the credit card behind. When the cashier noticed the couple leaving by another exit, she alerted managerial trainee Jeff Slovak, who pursued them out into the parking lot and confronted the man as he was about to get into his Chrysler station wagon.

The timid, quiet-looking man at first refused to go back to the store but changed his mind when a Columbus police officer on special duty joined them. The woman got into their station wagon and drove away.

In the Woolco office, at the policeman's request, the man turned over a Social Security card, a Sohio credit card, and a Blue Cross membership card—all in the name of Joseph Annick, the murdered legionnaire. He also turned over another Social Security card bearing the name Edward Grumman. A short while later, Gary James Lewingdon was arrested and taken to the Columbus Central Police Station to be questioned for trying to use a stolen credit card.

In the third-floor Detective Bureau of the Columbus Police Department, at eight o'clock on the evening of December 9, balding but boyish-looking Homicide Detective Jerry McMenemy took charge of Gary James Lewingdon shortly after his arrest. He advised the prisoner of his rights. Lewingdon signed the form, waiving his right to remain silent and his right to have an attorney present.

On a hunch, McMenemy decided not to reveal he was a homicide detective. Instead of taking Lewingdon to the Homicide Bureau, he led him into the Check and Credit Section and—pretending to be interested only in the fraudulent use of a credit card—said nothing about the Annick murder. McMenemy, who had a small recorder in his jacket pocket, taped the interview.

Answering McMenemy's questions about his background, Lewingdon said he was employed as a technician at Rockwell International in Columbus and had lived for the last eight months on East Main Street in Kirkersville, Ohio. He had previously lived in Newark, Ohio. At both addresses he lived with his wife, Delaine, to whom he'd been married for about a year. Before his marriage, Lewingdon said, he had lived with his mother until the age of thirty-seven.

A records check showed he had previously been arrested by Columbus police on petty larceny, possession of criminal tools, carrying a concealed weapon, and indecent exposure. There were no convictions.

To questions about his use of Annick's credit cards, Lewingdon admitted making purchases with them at K-mart, Rink, and Ontario, before being caught by the clerk at Woolco after he had purchased forty-five dollars' worth of toys for his wife's children. Asked how the cards had come into his possession, he insisted he'd found them the previous day, when he'd been forced to stop on the highway to change a flat tire and had noticed them on the grass by the roadside.

"What was the weather like?" McMenemy asked.

"Dry and windy," Lewingdon said.

"Not true, Gary. You don't mind if I call you Gary, do you? I happen to know for a fact that it was raining constantly."

McMenemy reached for Lewingdon's wallet, lying on the desk in front of them. "Do you have any other pieces of paper with Annick's name on them? Do you mind if I look?"

Lewingdon shrugged. "Yeah, go ahead."

Going through the wallet, McMenemy saw nothing of Annick's, but he was surprised to see a receipt from the Cartridge Case Store in Newark, Ohio, for a .22-caliber semiautomatic Sturm Ruger and some ammunition. The receipt was made out in the name of Delaine Lee Grumman.

"What's this, Gary?"

Lewingdon looked at the receipt, then up at the detective, and slumped back into his chair, shrugging and turning his palms up in a gesture of hopelessness. "She bought it for my birthday present."

McMenemy phoned his partner, Detective Charles "Sam" Womeldorf, and told him what he'd discovered. While waiting for Sam to arrive, McMenemy asked Lewingdon why he had gone out and bought the toys with the dead man's credit card.

"I figured this would be a good opportunity to get the gifts for Christmas."

"Three kids, huh?"

"Yeah, nice kids. I plan to adopt them."

After his partner, Womeldorf, arrived, McMenemy, following another hunch, decided to see if he could provoke Lewingdon. He pointed out that Joseph Annick had been found dead in his garage with his trousers pulled down, and he wondered if there was anything sexual going on between the two of them.

Lewingdon's face flushed with anger, the first time the placid, bespectacled man had revealed emotion. "Hell, I'm not a homo. It wasn't anything like that at all."

"Then tell me what happened."

Lewingdon confessed to the murder of Joseph Annick.

He'd been watching the area, he said, and knew Annick arrived at his garage regularly between eleven and eleven-thirty at night. After parking his own car nearby, he had waited on the corner. The street light illuminated the alley, and Lewingdon said he had considered shooting the light out but decided not to.

McMenemy could hardly believe his luck—the hunch working, his breaking the Annick murder case so easily.

"Wouldn't that have been risky, the noise of the shot?" McMenemy asked.

"No, I had this silencer on my gun—made it myself—and it wouldn't have made much more noise than a cap gun going off."

When Gary finished describing the killing of Annick, McMenemy exchanged glances with Womeldorf and decided to play another long shot. "You know, Gary, it's awful strange. Here you are using a .22. Are you involved with the .22-caliber murders?"

Gary tipped his chair back, looked up at the ceiling, and slowly ran his tongue around his lips as if they were dry. All he said was, "You're intelligent."

"What do you mean?" McMenemy said, teasing. "C'mon, it's obvious you're trying to copy them, using a .22."

Gary smiled. "You're close."

"Hey, what are you saying, Gary? C'mon, are you involved in them?"

"I don't want to start a circus at this time."

"Look, Gary," Womeldorf said, "the .22 we're looking for is a Stoeger Luger. Were you involved in that?"

"The gun I have isn't the one you've got the poster on."

McMenemy felt the hairs on his neck bristle. Lewingdon's .22 Sturm Ruger was very similar to the .22 Stoeger Luger, and he would have to be pretty familiar with the gun that police in three counties were looking for to know the difference between them.

"Where will we find the Ruger you shot Annick with?" McMenemy asked.

There was a long pause, as if Lewingdon was making up his mind. Then he shrugged. "At my home, in a leather satchel in the hall closet. You'll find Annick's wallet there, with his driver's license. What's left of the money—about fifty bucks—will be on a shelf in my bedroom closet."

"What did you do with the rest of the money?" Womeldorf asked.

Gary sighed. "Paid bills. Fifty-nine dollars for a gas bill . . . and other bills."

"Okay," Womeldorf asked, "any other guns?"

"When you go to the house, you'll find three .22 handguns, a Glenfield rifle, a 410 shotgun, and a 30-30 rifle." He smiled as if embarrassed. "You won't have to tear the house up. There's a workshop area down the basement, and just off to your left there's a box. When you position yourself right at the workshop area, just look down from your left. In that box you'll find two .38's . . ."

At 9 P.M., McMenemy went into the adjacent Homicide squad room and called his supervisor, Sergeant Bill Steckman, at his home.

"Look, Steck, we've got a guy named Gary Lewingdon here who's admitted killing Annick, and I've got a receipt for a .22-caliber automatic Sturm Ruger. I figure on getting a search warrant in Licking County to go through his house, and I'm going to need help."

"Hang on," Steckman said. "I'm coming in. Give me half an hour."

McMenemy went back into the interview room.

"I want to ask you one more time, Gary," McMenemy said, still jokingly, because he didn't believe Lewingdon was involved in anything but the Annick murder, "were you involved in the .22-caliber killings?"

Gary smiled shyly and ran his tongue around his lips again. "Just go get the guns. When you get the guns, you'll be back to talk to me."

Steckman arrived at the Detective Bureau at about nine-thirty, and McMenemy told him what they had. Not only had Gary Lewingdon confessed to the Annick murder, but he wouldn't deny being involved in the .22-caliber killings.

"All right," Steckman said, "call Bob Cupp and Clarence Sorrell, and tell them to get down here." Then he phoned the Licking County Sheriff's Department and asked Lieutenant Paul Short for help.

By one o'clock on the morning of December 10, Gary Lewingdon was belt-shackled to be transported to the Franklin County Jail. He looked at McMenemy and Womeldorf, circled the dial of his watch with his finger, and smiled.

"I'll have approximately an hour and a half to sleep, because it's going to take you twenty minutes to get to Kirkersville, forty-five minutes to do a search warrant, and twenty minutes to come back. And then you will talk to me."

After Lewingdon had been taken away, Detective Steve Martin of the Franklin County Sheriff's Department joined Steckman, and together with several other city detectives, they headed east to Kirkersville. Lieutenant Paul Short, Chief of Detectives of the Licking County Sheriff's Department, met them on Main Street in front of Gary Lewingdon's white frame house.

Behind the house, the land sloped sharply downward. The yard was filled with junk. There were no lights on inside and no sign of Lewingdon's Chrysler station wagon. Steckman walked onto the porch and knocked on the front door but got no response. He sent Detectives Womeldorf and Eisel to go with Lieutenant Short to get a search warrant from a judge in nearby Newark. Then he and the others settled down to wait for their return.

As Steckman waited for his officers and Lieutenant Short to return with the search warrant, he reviewed the list of guns Gary Lewingdon had said they would find in the house. He was especially interested in the .22-caliber Sturm Ruger Lewingdon's wife had bought for his birthday, the gun he had used to kill Annick. It was odd, he thought, that the receipt should have been made out to Delaine Lee Grumman. The name had been familiar, and Steckman had found it in his records.

It now turned out to be one of the many curious turns this case had taken, an informant not followed up, an important connection overlooked, critical information all but forgotten—until now.

He wondered what Lieutenant Paul Short's reaction would be when he learned about the receipt, and realized that he had actually interviewed Gary Lewingdon's wife under the name of Dee Grumman last July 18, but hadn't followed up the lead.

Steckman remembered that when Short first brought the incident to his attention last summer, he didn't seem to take her seriously. Short had said her allegations were probably nothing more than a domestic quarrel between families—a spite charge to cause trouble. She had told Short, as she had told the Kirkersville Chief of Police a month before she went to Short, that she believed her brother-in-law, Thaddeus Charles Lewingdon, was probably the .22-caliber killer.

When Steckman had asked to talk to her, Short said that was impossible because she didn't trust the Columbus Police Department, and she would only talk to Licking County detectives. Steckman asked for a follow-up, but he made a memorandum of the fact that he never heard anything further.

And here they were waiting for a warrant to search her home for possible murder weapons. Not that he blamed Paul Short. It was a mistake anyone might have made. Hindsight was just too easy.

3

It was six o'clock Sunday morning before Short, Eisel, and Womeldorf got the search warrant from a judge in Newark and headed back to Kirkersville. Short drove, and listened attentively as Womeldorf described the receipt for the .22 Sturm Ruger his partner had found in Gary Lewingdon's wallet. The moment Short heard that it had been made out to Gary Lewingdon's wife in the name of Delaine Lee Grumman, he remembered her all too clearly.

It had been last July 18 that Dee Grumman had walked into the Licking County Sheriff's Department and demanded to speak to the Chief of Detectives. She was fidgety and restless, her wild brunette hair in ringlets above angry dark eyes. Her lips pressed tightly accentuated the bump on her nose that looked as if it had once been broken.

Short had invited her into his office, asked her to be seated, and turned on the tape recorder. She sat on the edge of the chair and kept pulling her white cardigan sweater tightly around her, emphasizing her full breasts.

Although the Kirkersville Chief of Police who had sent her here had already filled him in on Mrs. Grumman's story about her brother-in-law being the .22-caliber killer, Short listened to her story attentively. Charles, she said, didn't make as much money as her own husband did, and yet he'd been buying things he couldn't afford—like a new truck and a microwave oven for his wife.

Charles had once asked her husband to tell his wife that the two of them were working weekend evenings polishing floors, so he could justify the late hours and the extra money he brought home. But that, she insisted, was a lie.

She admitted to Short that she didn't get along with her brother-in-law, that he had threatened her and her children. She'd had a garage sale several weeks earlier, and one of his boys had stolen a hundred dollars from her dresser drawer. Another one of his children had started a fire in her house.

She had warned Charles that she would go to the police, and he had threatened her, saying that if she did, she, her three children, and his own brother wouldn't live very long.

When she reiterated the charge that she believed Charles was the .22-caliber killer, Short asked if she had any proof: the gun, knowledge of the victims, any information like that.

She squirmed and finally blurted out that she once had worked for Mickey McCann as a go-go dancer, but that she had quit because he made her dance nude.

She talked of Mickey's Eldorado Club as a place for gambling, narcotics, and prostitution. Also, she said, Mickey got some money from two men and set her up to be raped by them in the alley behind the club. And McCann had pressured her, she charged, to have sex with a Columbus Police Department detective from the vice squad in return for a cover-up of McCann's gambling operations and liquor violations. The officer, she recalled, was about forty, average height and build, and his name was Leadsworth.

Short, who before his present job had worked for several years as an auxiliary deputy for the Franklin County Sheriff, had been interested in her accusation that someone in the Columbus Police Department was on the take. Would she be willing to go with him to the Central Police Station and look through photographs in police yearbooks to see if she could pick out Leadsworth? She agreed and he drove her to Columbus.

Though she had described the vice squad officer with whom she'd been forced to have sex as a forty-year-old man, she picked out the picture of a young officer who had never even worked in the Columbus P.D. Detective Bureau and had never been on the vice squad. That was a dead end.

After they got back to Kirkersville, Short said he would check out her brother-in-law, and he would get back to her.

Later that same day, Franklin County Detectives Steve Martin and Tony Rich, who had been in Licking County interviewing a possible .22-caliber suspect, had dropped by, and Short had let them listen to the Dee Grumman tape. Both Rich and Martin said they wanted to talk to her.

Short told them the woman wouldn't have anything to do with the Franklin County Sheriff's Department or the Columbus Police Department because she didn't trust them. He had checked out her story, found that her brother-in-law Thaddeus Charles had an excellent work record, and decided not to question him.

Now, Short knew he would have to live down the knowledge that with officers from all over the state hunting for the .22-caliber killers, he'd had a direct lead five months ago that might have broken the case, but he hadn't made the connection.

The irony was that this morning, he was going to help Bill Steckman search Dee Grumman's house for evidence and the murder weapons.

At six-forty-five Short pulled up in front of the Lewingdon house and handed Steckman the warrant. Steckman knocked on the door again, announced he was from the Columbus Police Department with a search warrant, and requested permission to enter. Getting no response, he broke the glass window in the front door, reached in, and unlocked it from the inside.

"All right, each of you knows what you're looking for," he told his men. "We'll use the living room as the center of operations. When you find something, bring it here."

In the hall closet, as Gary Lewingdon had said, they found the 30-30 carbine, a .22-caliber rifle with a home-made silencer, and a briefcase filled with various types of ammunition.

In the basement they found dozens of .22-caliber slugs and a homemade wooden target—hand-drawn circles with a bull's-eye that someone had used for practice—braced against the wall built into the hillside.

Of the two .38-caliber revolvers they found, one with a broken handle fitted the description of the weapon

taken from the body of Reverend Gerald Fields in Fairfield County—the first direct connection between Gary
Lewingdon and the .22-caliber murders.

But they hadn't found the key evidence, neither Annick's wallet nor the Sturm Ruger, where Gary had said
they would be. Steckman guessed there was a pretty
good chance that Delaine Lewingdon had been there and
taken off with them. Now he had to figure out what part
she and her brother-in-law had actually played in the
murders.

The search unit returned to Columbus at 11 A.M.

Steckman told the others to get some sleep, went
into his War Room, and flopped into a chair. Looking
around the walls where he had posted color photographs
of each murder scene and the ten victims, as well as a
map of Central Ohio with X's for the locations of the
crimes, he wondered if today, December 10, 1978—one
year exactly from the day of the murders of the two
women in Newark—he was really going to solve the .22-
caliber killings.

He sighed, rubbed his tired eyes, got back on his
feet. He had to get home for a few hours' sleep. It was
going to be a long, busy day—and, if his gut feeling was
right, a hell of an exciting one.

Ten

1

When Gary Lewingdon had been arrested in the parking lot outside Woolco, his wife, Delaine, had run to the yellow '67 Chrysler station wagon and driven directly home. She had gotten there at about 7 P.M., gone to the hall closet and taken out the brown satchel, checking to make sure the .22 Sturm Ruger, the .38, and Annick's wallet were there. She put the wallet into her purse, tossed the satchel into the back of the wagon, and shouted for the children to get into the car because they were going to Grandma Lewingdon's house.

When she got to Gary's mother's house, she left the guns in the satchel but went upstairs to the bathroom and shoved the wallet behind the metal cabinet propped against the door. Aside from the .22 Ruger and the credit cards, the wallet was the only evidence that could connect Gary to Annick's murder. No one would look for the wallet here.

At three-thirty Sunday afternoon, Officer Tom Davis, who had been briefed when he came on duty at the Columbus Detective Bureau, took a call from a woman who identified herself as Delaine Lewingdon. When he

learned who was on the line, Davis signaled his partner,
Mike Scudder, to listen in. Steckman had briefed them
earlier that she had implicated her brother-in-law in the
.22-caliber murders. During a routine record search,
Steckman had discovered four outstanding warrants on
Delaine Lewingdon/Dee Grumman for passing bad
checks and he wanted her arrested.

"What can I do for you, Mrs. Lewingdon?" Davis
asked.

"I want to know what my husband is being charged
with."

"Could you tell me where you're calling from? Before I give out any information, I have to be sure you are
who you say you are."

"I'm at his mother's home, Mrs. Florence Lewingdon, 1889 North Fourth Street."

While Davis kept her talking, Scudder radioed for a
cruiser to pick her up. Ten minutes later, a message
came in saying Delaine Lewingdon had been apprehended just as she was leaving her mother-in-law's
house. Scudder told them to keep her there until he and
his partner arrived.

When Davis and Scudder got to the house, they put
Delaine into the back of their car and told her she was
under arrest for the four bad-check warrants.

"Do you want to tell us about Joseph Annick's wallet?" Davis asked.

She looked up coolly, obviously used to dealing with
the police, and said, "I don't know what you mean."

"Your husband told the detectives last night that
they would find the wallet in the hall closet, and also the
.22 Sturm Ruger you bought him last February. But they
weren't where he said they'd be."

She sagged visibly and gestured towards the yellow
Chrysler station wagon parked across the street. "The
guns are in the brown satchel in the wagon."

"And the wallet?" asked Scudder.

She told them where to find it.

"Could you tell us why you took them?"

"I thought they were stolen," she said, "and I didn't
want the police to find them. I guessed you would search
the house, so I took them out."

Davis assigned the two uniformed officers who had

picked up Delaine to guard the house and the car while he and Scudder arranged for search warrants so that they could examine the contents of the car and get the wallet.

They brought Delaine back to the Central Police Station at five-thirty Sunday night, booked her, and turned her over to McMenemy and Womeldorf for questioning.

She signed a rights waiver, and the detectives asked some background questions she seemed eager to answer. Her former husband was Ed Grumman, and that explained the name on the Social Security card Gary had in his wallet, as well as the name on her receipt for the .22 Sturm Ruger.

She was in a vocational training program for nursing, she said. She had three children (ten, eight, and the two-year-old baby) by two of four previous marriages. Gary was very good to them. He had taught the older boy to play chess, and got him interested in reading science fiction. Gary also took the three on picnics, played games, and was a real father to them. The day of the arrest, he had been most concerned about getting them lots of presents for Christmas.

As soon as they started questioning her about the use of Annick's credit cards, she shut up. Nothing Womeldorf or McMenemy said could make her talk about it. They called Steckman at home, and he said he was on the way.

Steckman had already been notified by BCI that a .22-caliber casing taken from Gary Lewingdon's home matched one recovered from the Jenkin T. Jones murder scene. He phoned Detectives Sorrell and Cupp again and said he needed them right away. When Steckman arrived at the Detective Bureau and McMenemy told him Delaine was not cooperating, Steckman grabbed his .22-caliber file book and headed for the interview room.

He was upset when he learned how Delaine had been arrested. The uniformed police should have been told not to pick her up until she was inside the station wagon and thus in actual possession of the guns. All he had now was a car sitting on the street—possibly with guns in it. Now, even with a search warrant, and even if the guns were in the car, he couldn't legally connect them to her.

As he began to talk to her, it soon became clear that Delaine had consulted an attorney. Someone had obviously coached her on how to go to the police department, what to do to cover herself, how to make a deal.

"Delaine, let me tell you, you are subject to arrest right *now* for the credit cards and for possession of stolen property, because we've already recovered some of the things bought with Annick's credit card from your house. You're obstructing justice. You concealed evidence and weapons used in the commission of a felony. And that means *you've* committed a felony."

He watched her face go white.

Steckman knew he had to go on from there. He needed her information, her influence over Gary, and even though she couldn't testify against her husband, he would need her testimony on the brother-in-law.

To convict both men he would have to promise not to charge her as a conspirator or an aider-and-abettor. He suspected he might be attacked on his decision to make a deal with her, but it was a judgment call, and he had to make it now.

"We already know about Gary's involvement in the Annick homicide," he told her. "But what could you add to that if I told you I have no intention of charging you for withholding your knowledge of Gary's involvement in criminal activity?"

Her eyes searched his. "What do you mean?"

"We're aware of a lot of your problems, Delaine. We've learned a great deal about your activities. I know about your going to the Kirkersville Police and the Licking County Sheriff's Department—"

She glared at him. "Then why isn't my brother-in-law in jail?"

"Well, just hold on there a bit," Steckman said, opening the huge ring binder and pulling out some sheets. "That's what I want to discuss with you—about what you told Lieutenant Short. Now, I was led to believe you were implying that there were people in our department who had been paid by Mickey McCann for ignoring liquor violations and that they were the ones responsible for his death."

"No! I never intended to imply that," she said. "In fact I know for certain they weren't involved. When I talked to the officers in Kirkersville and Licking County I wasn't even permitted to discuss my brother-in-law Charles's involvement with the .22-caliber killings. All they were interested in was my personal life with Mc-Cann . . . and about Columbus police officers on the take."

"All right, Dee. I'll guarantee you now that we won't prosecute you on those charges, but if I ever find out you *were* involved in the killings, then you'll get no immunity at all. I'll charge you with those homicides."

"I wasn't there," she insisted. "I didn't do anything to anybody."

"All right. Are you ready to talk?"

"As long as I'm not going to be prosecuted for the things you mentioned, I'll talk to you."

Steckman reviewed the statement she had made to Short, and she repeated her charge that Thaddeus Charles Lewingdon had forced her husband, Gary, to accompany him on the killings.

Charles, she insisted, was the dominant one, his mother's favorite son. He was extremely violent, and controlled all the members of the family. He had a gun, she said, a black automatic pistol with a long barrel. It had threads on the end of it for a silencer.

"It looked a lot like the one I bought for Gary," she said.

Steckman sensed during the interview that two things were important to Delaine: that the blame should be put on Charles rather than Gary, and that she should be allowed to remain clear. He had to be very careful how he played his line. He had hooked a big one and had to be sure she didn't wriggle free. Just give her a little slack.

"Tell me, Delaine. Did Gary ever give you any positive information about Charles being involved in the .22's?"

"Oh, yes. Gary told me that Charles killed the girls at Forker's Café in Newark. It's true that Gary was with him, but Charles did the killings."

"Why were they killed? What was the motive?"

"I don't know about Newark. But Gary killed Mickey McCann to revenge me, because Mickey forced me into prostitution."

Aware of how much she was giving him, Steckman

hid his excitement behind a deadpan expression. He had to let her implicate both of them in a way that would stand up in court.

Under his gentle prodding, Delaine admitted she had told both brothers that Mickey carried a lot of money and that she thought Mickey had a safe in his house.

"You knew Mickey had a gun though, didn't you?"

She nodded. "I saw his snub-nosed .38 when I dated him."

"Do you know where that gun is now?"

"In the car. In the satchel."

"You've also got Mickey's gun in the station wagon along with Gary's gun?"

"Yes. Look, why don't I start at the beginning . . ."

She described the argument she'd had with Gary before he and Charles burglarized the Western Auto Store in September 1977 to get weapons. She'd been against it, she said, but Gary had gone along with his brother anyway. She talked about each and every homicide in detail: how they were planned, how they were committed, what was done with the stolen property, and how Gary and Charles behaved afterward.

"I'll testify against Charles," she said. "I insist on testifying against him."

"I'm sure you'll be called," Steckman said. "But we've got to arrest him first. If Gary will back up what you say."

"Can I see my husband?"

"I think I can have him brought over. While you're waiting, you might like to freshen up."

The interview had taken an hour and fifteen minutes.

While Delaine was in the washroom, Steckman called Detective Steve Martin at the Sheriff's Department and asked if he could bring Gary from the county jail to the Central Police Station. Since Gary was now Martin's prisoner, he could take him from the jail without red tape. Martin said he'd have Gary there by eight o'clock that evening.

Steckman then set in motion his strategy for taking Thaddeus Charles Lewingdon into custody. He knew it was important to get officers to the older brother's house as soon as possible because the news that Gary had been arrested would soon be picked up by reporters—and when it was released, Charles would probably run.

But at the same time, Steckman felt he had to proceed methodically. He'd reviewed the procedure with the Franklin County Prosecutor's office, careful to touch every base. He had to be sure of "probable cause" before picking up Charles without an arrest warrant. The most important case in his life was not going to fail in court because of a police blunder, not if he had anything to do with it.

He phoned Lieutenant Short in Licking County and asked him to go to Charles's house, but not to arrest him until the Columbus detectives arrived and he gave the order.

Then he called his men together and told them to meet Short's boss, Licking County Sheriff Max Marston, and his deputies at eight-thirty at the truck stop near the intersection of I-70 and Route 37. From there they were to drive to the State Highway Patrol garage.

"That'll put you close to Charles Lewingdon's house," Steckman said. "When I give the order, Short will lead you in. Before you arrest Charles, I need to hear Gary confirm Delaine's accusations that his brother was in on it. Call me every half hour, and I'll let you know when to take him."

After they left, Steckman went into the Homicide squad room to wait for Gary Lewingdon to be brought back for continued interrogation by McMenemy and Womeldorf. He put a new tape into the recorder hooked up to a mike in the adjacent interrogation room. Everything was ready, he told himself; all he needed now was a little luck.

2

McMenemy and Womeldorf led Gary Lewingdon back into the tiny interrogation room where Steckman had just finished with Delaine. McMenemy knew that as soon as he tapped his knee against the switch under the desk, the tape recorder set up in the closet of the adja-

cent Homicide squad room would go on, and dozens of
law enforcement officers packed into that room—who
had come from all over Central Ohio—would be listening.

He was not yet ready to turn it on. First he wanted to
settle Gary down and reestablish the rapport of last
night when Gary had confessed to killing Annick. He was
annoyed to discover later that someone had already
switched the recorder on from inside the squad room
and taped his opening remarks.

Womeldorf was pleased to see Gary's startled expression at seeing Delaine's purse on the chair. When
Gary pointed to it and said, "Uh . . . she was sittin'
there," Womeldorf just nodded. It was important for
Gary to realize that Delaine was in police custody and
had already been interrogated.

McMenemy leaned back in his chair and looked
Gary in the eye. "Boy, you hit it right on the money. You
said we'd be back to talk to you. You know, I didn't think
we'd have anything more to say."

Womeldorf joined in and laughed. "I thought he was
bullshitting us."

"We did," McMenemy assured Gary. "We really did.
We thought you were kidding us. You didn't tell us about
that silencer."

Gary asked if they were going to confiscate all his
guns, and McMenemy said they had to, except for the 30-
30 shotgun—unless there was a reason for them to keep
that too.

"What'd you find, as far as you know?" Gary asked.

"Well, you know I gotta advise you of your rights
again before I talk to you—just like before—I'm gonna
do that, and after I do I'll explain what we found and
maybe you can help out on a few things."

Gary hunched back. "I ain't saying no more."

"Okay," McMenemy said.

"I don't care what anybody else says," Gary insisted. "I ain't saying no more. Ain't working it out of me
either. I ain't telling you."

"Doesn't matter—" Womeldorf said.

"You can give me my rights or whatever, but I ain't
saying nothing else."

"Boy oh boy," McMenemy said. "You know you're

gonna be in all the papers. You're going to be . . . You remember that movie *Cold Blood*? Those guys . . ."

"No, I haven't seen it."

"They're famous," McMenemy said. "Jesse James . . . Billy the Kid—"

"I don't even wanna hear that shit," Gary said.

"They're famous."

"All I know," said Gary, "is you didn't have nothing till I fucked up."

McMenemy insisted he did have evidence against Gary, but was trying to give him a break. "I'd just appreciate you leveling with me . . . telling me the truth. And that's why I'm still cooperating with you and letting you talk to your wife. She wants to talk to you. That's why we brought you back. She's in love with you. Your wife's in love with you."

"What'd she say?"

"She said a lot."

When Lewingdon again refused to sign the rights waiver, McMenemy said, "You don't have to sign if you don't want to. If you want, I'll tell you this. Your wife has told us about the .22-caliber murders and about the relatives . . ."

"Good God!" Lewingdon stared at them and started to cry.

Seconds later, Steckman made the decision to allow Delaine Lewingdon to enter the interrogation room. He had realized during his interview with her that she was the dominant one in the relationship. He felt Gary would talk and implicate his brother if she told him to.

She entered the small room, smiled tearfully at her husband, and asked if she could kiss him. When Womeldorf said it was okay she threw herself into Gary's arms, crying and sobbing, "Honey, I love you."

The detectives allowed them a minute alone together, but their voices were picked up by the microphone as she whispered, "Did you tell the police anything about me? Am I going to be charged with anything?"

"I never told them anything," he whispered back.

When the detectives returned, Delaine was sitting on Gary's lap, kissing him. She got up, brushed her skirt, and sat in the chair beside him.

McMenemy brought out the rights form again. "We'll do this in front of your wife. We've talked to your wife and we're sure she'll tell you whatever you want to ask her—what Sergeant Steckman has had conversation with her about. But before we ask any questions—"

"That's all this is," Womeldorf added, "a rights waiver. You know that."

"Give me your ink pen . . ." Gary said. "Give me your pen."

Delaine said, "They have to read it, Gary."

When the rights were read and Gary had signed it, McMenemy noticed Delaine was shaking. "You feeling all right?"

"Get my brother-in-law."

"Pardon me, ma'am?"

"Just get my brother-in-law."

"Why do you want us to get him?"

"Because he is the cause of all this."

McMenemy, knowing that Steck was listening, waiting to hear Gary implicate his brother, pressed him. "Why is he the cause of it, Gary? Can you tell us that? Does he put you up to it? Does he threaten you?"

"Yeah, he's the main instigator."

"Did he plan this?"

"We both primarily did."

"Can he have a lawyer?" Delaine asked.

Gary shrugged. "It won't make no difference."

"Because you're still afraid of Charles and you won't tell them the truth," she said.

"We'll take care of Charles," McMenemy said. "Don't worry about that. There will be no way Charles can get to Gary."

"He can't bother me in here," Gary said.

"No," she snapped, "but he can bother me and the kids."

"Has there been anything in the news about me?" Gary asked.

"No," McMenemy said.

"Yes!" Delaine said. "This afternoon. That's how I found out what exactly the charges were and who was being charged, because nobody would tell me anything."

"Okay," Gary said. "If it's been in the news you better start getting on the radio—"

"And get Charles," Delaine snapped. "Because he'll take off."

"Not only will he take off," Gary said, "but you might have a hell of a hard time getting him. There might be somebody who'll die in the process besides him."

"Is he that bad of a dude?" McMenemy asked.

"Yes," said Delaine.

"Okay," said Womeldorf, leaning forward in his chair. "Is he armed?"

"Yes."

"With what?" asked Womeldorf.

"This is no time to kid us," McMenemy said.

Gary thought for a moment and rubbed his hand across his cheek. "A Struger," he said, combining the two names of the gun. "The one you're looking for."

"A what?" McMenemy asked. "The Stoeger Luger that's responsible for the .22-caliber killings?"

Gary said it was. Warning that Charles had promised never to be taken alive, he described several of his brother's weapons and gave directions to the house.

"All right," McMenemy said. "I'd like to go over the killings in sequence."

"Let's start with the one in Newark," Womeldorf said. "Was that the first one?"

"Yeah," said Gary. "First—"

"Excuse me," Delaine said, frowning. "I thought you had gotten bits and pieces last night from him. That's what the other officer told me."

Listening carefully, Steckman smiled when she said that. Street-smart Delaine was covering herself, pretending to have been tricked during her interview so Gary wouldn't realize she had volunteered everything.

"We've talked about another homicide, ma'am," McMenemy said, referring to Gary's statement the night before about having killed Annick. "Now you're going to have to . . . I'm going to be talking to Gary, okay?"

She nodded, and looked at the floor.

Gary Lewingdon described the killing of Karen Dodrill and Joyce Vermillion behind Forker's Café in Newark. It had been a Friday or Saturday night—December 10, 1977—exactly one year ago to the day. All their killings had been on weekends, he explained, because he and Charles worked during the week. The motive was money. They netted thirty-two dollars from the two women.

In recounting the McCann murders that followed, Gary said he and his brother had been out to the house three times over a two-week period—the first two times to look it over. On February 12, the night of the murders, they'd parked the car in a nearby vacant snow-covered field, backing off the road so it wouldn't be noticed. They wore boots, ski masks, and heavy parkas with hoods. They knew McCann's mother would be there, having observed her through the window the other two times as she'd watched television. Gary cut the phone lines while Charles worked on the side wooden door with a tire iron.

"She didn't hear you?" McMenemy asked.

"No. It was the way he worked on it," Gary said, "quietly . . . until the last moment when he knew it was going to make a noise . . . then he handed me his gun."

"What gun is that?"

"The Stoeger. When he popped the door open, I went in and hit her. I missed her once. That's the hole in the front window. I hit her in the arm. I think I hit her superficially one other place, and she came toward me and fell down."

"And then what?"

"He [Charles] took the gun, put in another clip, and shot her in the head, two or three times."

Gary told about their searching the house to make sure there was no one else there, finding a little money in drawers, in the mother's purse, in the counter, taking their time because they knew they had to wait for McCann. He described the rooms, the furniture, the waiting. He had stood at the back window, watching for two cars to come down the road.

"Why two cars?" McMenemy asked.

"Him and the dancer," Gary said.

"Okay, you're sitting there watching. What do you see?"

"I see two cars come down. They slow up. At this time in the morning—it's almost four—you can almost be sure that they are going to turn. Charles had the front bedroom window. He verifies . . . they do turn. Now the percentages has increased that it's them. We go out to the door off the kitchen leading to the garage—wait for them to come in. He pulls in. We didn't know if the dancer would pull her car in or not. I didn't know whether he would close the [garage] door either. But with Charles ready, I opened the door. Then we hear somebody opening the storm door on the other side of the wooden door. I got my hand on the knob."

"You're the first one out?"

"No, Charles is. When I open the door, I stand back. He fires and shoots the girl. . . . He continues to fire at her because she's moved aside. . . . She's screaming . . .

"I shoot twice to keep McCann from going out the open garage door. I try to bodily move around to the other side of the car. He's still on the driver's side. I try to move around to the open garage door fast enough to keep him from going out, but I don't want to fire again because I'm too close to the open door."

Both guns had silencers, Gary said, but he was concerned that the one on his .38 wouldn't muffle the sound enough.

"Then McCann goes out the door . . . and around . . . and he's out in front of the house . . . out toward the road from the garage . . . and Charles has only got two left in his clip after he finishes the girl. He follows him . . . comes out around the garage door and puts two in Mickey's back. Charles changes his clip, and we drag Mickey back inside and close the garage door. He's not dead yet. He begs, 'Don't kill me.' Then Charles finishes him with another clip."

They found two thousand dollars from cash bar receipts under newspapers behind the driver's seat. The first time they searched Mickey's body they found nothing, but the second time Gary felt a bulge at the back of his leg and found money in a sock tucked inside his knee sock—fifty-eight hundred dollars.

They took the dancer's boots off and opened her slacks. Gary said he could see the sequin bottom of her go-go outfit. When the officer asked why he removed the boots, he said, "To search."

They were interested only in money—not drugs or jewels.

After describing the McCann killings, Gary went through the other homicides in the same detailed fashion. When asked why they killed all the victims, he shrugged. "No witnesses."

After two and a half hours of Gary Lewingdon's interrogation, Steckman decided he had what he'd been waiting for. Gary had confirmed Delaine's statement and thoroughly implicated Charles in the .22-caliber murders.

Steckman phoned his detectives standing by at the State Highway Patrol garage. "Okay, we've got probable cause," Steckman said. "Arrest Thaddeus Charles Lewingdon and bring him here for questioning." Before he hung up, he added: "According to his brother, he's armed and dangerous. Be careful."

3

After Steckman gave the order, six cars—each with at least two officers—drove to Thaddeus Charles Lewingdon's house in Glenford, Ohio.

Licking County Sheriff Max Marston had earlier alerted the sergeant on duty at the office to stand by for further instructions. After Steckman's go-ahead, Marston called the sergeant and told him to phone Lewingdon at exactly ten-forty that night. The sergeant was to let the suspect know the house was surrounded and warn him to come out with his hands up.

When the sergeant made the call and asked if Charles was at home, a male voice answered, "It's him speaking."

"Now listen to me carefully—very carefully—and do exactly what I say. Your house is surrounded by police officers. I want you to go to the door and give yourself up."

There was a long pause, and then Charles Lewingdon said, "I don't have my jacket or shoes on. Can I put them on?"

"Yes, but come back to the phone so we can get the instructions straight."

Seconds later Lewingdon returned and said, "Okay, I'm going out the back door."

Then he walked out onto the porch with his hands on his head.

"What's this all about?" he shouted.

Sheriff Marston approached first, told him he was under arrest, asked him to assume the spread-eagle position, and patted him down. "Empty your pockets and put the stuff there on the ground."

Lewingdon did as instructed. "What am I under arrest for?"

Marston handcuffed him and Columbus Detective Bob Litzinger said, "For aggravated murder—homicides in Franklin, Fairfield, and Licking counties." Litzinger took him to the patrol car, and in the presence of a Licking County prosecutor who had joined the group earlier read Lewingdon his rights.

"Do you mind telling me who I'm supposed to have killed?" Lewingdon asked.

"We can go into that at headquarters," Litzinger said.

It was almost midnight when the detectives delivered their prisoner to the Central Police Station in Columbus. Litzinger went to report to Steckman, while Sorrell removed Thaddeus Charles's cuffs and Cupp read him his rights again.

"Are you gonna tell me who I'm supposed to have killed?" he asked.

"You've been implicated by your brother," Cupp said, "as being involved in the .22-caliber homicides."

Charles rubbed his knuckles across his chin. "I don't know what you're talking about."

"Well, Gary is doing a lot of talking right this minute," Sorrell said.

"Where?"

"Right on this floor," Cupp said. "He's in an interrogation room with two sheriff's detectives from the county, giving a full statement about his involvement with the .22-caliber murders."

"I don't believe you."

Sorrell slammed his hand on the desk. "Look, we're not going to lie to you, Charlie. If there's a question we can't answer, we'll tell you we can't answer it. But we're not going to lie."

Charles looked from one officer to the other, speculatively. "Could I hear that interview?"

"I don't see why not," Sorrell said, "but let me check it out with my supervisor."

After clearing it with Steckman, they led Charles into the Homicide squad room where the interrogation was being taped. From the monitor in the closet, they could hear the voices of Detectives Steve Martin and Tony Rich (who had taken over the interrogation for the Sheriff's Department) questioning Gary Lewingdon about the guns he and his brother had stolen from the Western Auto Store over a year ago. Although the theft record listed eight guns missing, Gary could describe only seven.

When they completed the list, Tony Rich asked Gary if he thought Charles would want vengeance after all this was over. "You think he'd kill you?"

"Yeah, if he had the chance he would."

"Are you willing to testify in court against him?" Rich asked.

"Yeah."

"Does that scare you?"

"It bothers me."

"How about your wife? Do you think she'll testify against him?"

"Yes, she's afraid of him."

"She's got good reason to be," Rich said. "How about any of these other people, Gary? Did *you* actually kill any of them?"

"No," Gary said. "Other than Annick, no. . . ."

"Claudia Yasko, you do not know?" Rich asked.

"Do not know," Gary said.

"Your wife does not know her?"

"I asked her and she didn't know her."

"How about Charles's wife," Rich asked. "Did she know what was going on?"

"No."

"Why didn't he confide in her?"

Gary paused for a moment. "Either of you hillbillies?"

When the officers said they weren't, Gary said, "She's a non-high-school-graduate hillbilly. She is very religious."

Martin said, "Do you think if Charlie would have mentioned it to her she would have immediately—"

"Flipped her lid," Gary said.

Charles Lewingdon listened closely to his brother for about ten minutes and said he'd heard enough. Sorrell and Cupp took him back to the office and asked if he wanted to say anything now.

"You'd better get a lot of paper and pencils," Charles said, "because this is gonna take a long time."

At twelve-thirteen in the morning, Thaddeus Charles Lewingdon signed a waiver of his constitutional rights, and for the next three and a half hours he poured out the details of nine murders to Sorrell and Cupp. He had nothing to do with the tenth murder—Annick—he said. Gary had done that one alone.

In response to questions about the McCann killings, Charles said they had gone to the house twice before the night of the murders to check the surrounding area. On the second try, they had planned to take Mickey, but his car had driven into the garage and the door had come down before they could get to him.

"Where did you park?" Sorrell asked.

"We parked different places at different times. Right where McCann's road comes out, across the street is a nursery or evergreen place. That's where we parked the third time."

"That's when it went down?" asked Cupp.

"Yeah, we got there and walked straight down the middle of the street he lived on, right up his driveway and around the back of the house. Then, let's see . . . we didn't leave no footprints in the snowbank 'cause we knew he could see them when he came in because his headlights would hit them."

"How'd you get up there without leaving footprints?" Sorrell asked.

Charles smiled. "Right before you get to the house there's a bunch of shrubs. Well, between them shrubs and the house there's about this much of no snow," he said, gesturing to show a measurement of about a foot and a half. "That's where we walked through. We jumped over the snowbank because the only path that was actually plowed out was to the big double door of the garage."

To help the officers understand his description of the McCann killings, Charles drew a diagram of the house. Speaking of the mother, he said, "The Luger was quieter so he [Gary] wanted to use it. She came through here, saw him and went to go back . . . The kill was here. As I came to here . . . she had come back and fell right in front of the fireplace."

Describing the death of Christine Herdman, he said, "The girl backed up to the freezer screaming. I told her to shut up. She wouldn't so I killed her . . ."

His recounting of killing Mickey McCann was consistent with Gary's, except when he said: "I told Gary, 'He's still alive.' So *he* took the .22 out of my hand and fired up through his . . ." pointing beneath his chin, "right here."

As Charles described the murders, he would stop periodically and ask if what he was saying coincided with what his brother had said. It seemed important to him to know that the accounts were consistent.

When Sorrell asked him about the location of the .22-caliber Stoeger Luger, Charles smiled. "You could search my place for twenty years and never find it." He told them it was in his green utility trailer and signed a consent for them to search the trailer and his Ford pickup.

Sorrell and Cupp finished with Charles at four o'clock in the morning, and Tony Rich and Steve Martin—now done with Gary—took over and interrogated Charles for another hour for the Sheriff's Department. In questioning him about how he and Gary had left the McCann house and gone back to the car, Martin said, "And you walked right back down the street again to your car?"

"Yeah."

"Weren't you afraid you'd be seen walking down the street that time of the morning?"

"Not really," Charles said, "not as late and as cold as it was."

Charles said it had been snowing hard when they left the McCann house about five in the morning and headed back to Gary's place.

Delaine, he said, had given them detailed information about Mickey's house, and when they returned and told her all about the murders, "She was just happier than hell."

Rich and Martin took Thaddeus Charles to the Franklin County Jail at five o'clock Monday morning, and a few hours later Gary and Charles were arraigned in Franklin County Court, charged with murder, and held without bond.

The chief of Columbus detectives, praising his department's accomplishment, was quoted as saying it was "the biggest arrest in the history of Columbus police."

Some of the other law enforcement agencies, including the Sheriff's Department, thought it hadn't been the result of great police work at all. As Howard Champ put it, "The arrest of the .22-caliber killers was just a matter of luck."

The afternoon of the Lewingdons' arrest, the ringing phone woke Claudia from a deep sleep. Pigman was on the road, hauling livestock to Indiana and Illinois, and she was alone in her German Village hideaway.

She had not been answering the phone recently, terrified that the killers might call her and learn she was at home. She knew that was foolish because her phone was unlisted, but her fear was so pervasive it reminded her of what Dr. Stinson had called it in his court testimony: *pan-anxiety—panic attacks.*

But now, half-asleep, she picked up the receiver and mumbled into it. There was a long silence, then heavy breathing.

Finally, a woman's voice whispered, "You'd better get out of Columbus. Maybe out of Ohio."

"Why?" Claudia asked, suddenly completely awake.

"Read the newspapers. They've caught the .22-caliber killers. You don't want to be around to testify at their trials."

Claudia screamed into the phone. "Who are you?"

"Isn't it a terrible thing that happened to that go-go dancer who was shot and put into a car trunk in Dayton and set on fire?"

"Why are you calling me?"

"It was a terrible thing. But she had a big mouth."

"Please, who—?"

The caller hung up. Claudia stared at the phone and then threw it down on the bed as if it burned her hand.

She was torn between joy at learning that the killers had been caught and terror that they feared she could identify them. They had friends, or relatives, or contacts who could reach her—who could kill her.

Her body was shaking so hard she had to grab the headboard for support.

If they could find out her unlisted phone number, they could find her address. They were probably watching her now, waiting for her to go out shopping for food. No . . . the .22-caliber killers murdered people in their homes.

Tears streaming down her face, Claudia used all her strength to push the dresser to barricade the door. Then all through the night she stayed awake and prayed and wept.

Eleven

1

The morning of December 11, 1978, the *Citizen-Journal* reported only the arrest of Gary with a front-page banner headline:

.22-CALIBER SUSPECT JAILED
LICKING COUNTY MAN CHARGED WITH LEGION
OFFICIAL MURDER

Gary was being charged at present only with the Annick murder, and was mentioned as being "a probable participant" in the .22-caliber slayings. They had no photographs.

The afternoon *Dispatch* headlined the later story:

TWO BROTHERS CHARGED IN
.22-CALIBER KILLINGS

A large front-page photograph featured a meek-looking Gary handcuffed and belt-shackled in custody of a Sheriff's deputy; a small inset close-up showed a scowling Thaddeus Charles.

On December 14, a Franklin County grand jury indicted Gary on twenty counts and Thaddeus on seventeen counts—all involving the .22-caliber killings.

The *Columbus Dispatch*, which on December 12 published an article about Delaine Lewingdon as a former go-go dancer for Mickey McCann, withheld the name of its informant, saying only "according to a former girlfriend and employee of McCann . . . who requested her name not be used for fear of reprisals . . . McCann fired Mrs. Grumman for becoming intimate with customers."

On December 14 the *Dispatch* revealed its source:

DANCER'S NAME APPEARED
ON EARLIER SHERIFF'S LIST

The name of Gary Lewingdon's often-married wife, Delaine, was on a list of persons who had grudges against Robert "Mickey" McCann, one of the 10 victims of the .22-caliber slayings.

The list was compiled by Franklin County sheriff's investigators, according to Mary Slatzer, an intimate acquaintance and former employee of the Sullivant Avenue bar owner.

However, sheriff's investigators refused any comment about the list and insisted they have never questioned Delaine Lewingdon, who also is known as Dee Grumman.

Mary Slatzer is the daughter of former auxiliary Franklin County Sheriff's Deputy Robert Slatzer. . . . Slatzer has volunteered information to *The Dispatch*, Columbus police, and the sheriff's office during the yearlong investigation. . . .

Mrs. Lewingdon is under Columbus police protection. . . .

When Detective Tony Rich saw the news article about Delaine Lewingdon's name having been on McCann's list, he was furious. He'd gone over that list with Slatzer, and the only name that was even close was a *D. Greenman*. There was no way he could have made any connection between a *Greenman* and the *Dee Grumman* that Paul Short had interviewed last July.

What bothered him most was that after he and Steve Martin had listened to the tape in Short's office in Licking County, both of them had told Short that they wanted to talk to her. And even after Short said Mrs. Grumman would have nothing to do with the Franklin County Sheriff's Department or with the Columbus police because they had "screwed her up before," Rich wanted to check her out.

He'd tried several times to reach her by phone in Kirkersville, but every time he called either there was no answer or else someone would get on the phone and say there was no one there by that name. When he'd asked Sheriff Berkemer if he should check her out, the sheriff said to let it go, because if the woman was talking to Paul Short it was Licking County's lead, and he didn't want to cause hard feelings between the two departments.

On the same day, the *Citizen-Journal* published a background piece on relatives of the confessed killers:

"PRIVATE" LEWINGDONS TELL FAMILY SAGA

The hard luck of the remote and private Lewingdon family began years ago, long before two Lewingdon brothers were arrested in connection with the ".22-caliber killings."

. . . Various other members of the family have been arrested on such charges as armed robbery, rape, kidnapping, vehicular homicide and others, nephew Joseph Lewingdon Jr. said.

But through it all the Lewingdons somehow have stuck together, he said. . . . "If somebody hurts one of us, the family protects you. If I would get hurt on the street my sister would be there," Joseph said. "Everybody would be there."

That afternoon, Claudia's phone rang at four-fifteen. "I've got an offer for you, honey," a woman said. "You leave Columbus and go to Dayton or Chicago, and you'll have all expenses paid. You got to leave town, honey, and you got to do it real soon."

"Leave me alone!" she screamed. "I won't do anything! I don't know anything!"

But the line went dead.

* * *

On January 26, 1979, the *Citizen-Journal* began the first of a two-part background article about the brothers, with a front-page headline:

"LEWINGDONS WERE LONERS: A Tale of Two
Brothers."

A childhood girlfriend said of Thaddeus, "He had the prettiest eyes. He was quiet, very gentle, almost a fragile kind of person. . . ." A boyhood friend of Gary's said, "Gary was a rather quiet, shy, withdrawn sort of boy. He was not the most friendly fellow."

The public record showed that the Lewingdon forebears had come to the United States from England, "probably early in the 19th century," and that an ancestor had served in the Union Army during the Civil War.

Thaddeus had gone to St. Thomas the Apostle Parochial School. Gary had been a choir boy. "Thaddeus was a good pupil, with mostly B's, but his grades began to go downhill during the two years before he dropped out [of school]. He got more C's, and toward the end received two F's." Later Thaddeus dropped out of high school and apparently joined the Army. After at least six months, according to the article, he reportedly received an undesirable discharge after going absent without leave.

Thaddeus moved to Chicago for several years. Gary joined the Air Force in 1958 and was discharged in 1962. Shortly following Gary's return to Columbus, their father died.

In the same edition of the paper, under a front-page banner headline, the *Citizen-Journal* published an exclusive interview with Delaine Lewingdon:

"WIFE OF '.22-CALIBER' SUSPECT TELLS HER
STORY—MRS. GARY LEWINGDON SPEAKS OUT."

She told reporters she believed McCann, his mother, and Christine Herdman were "victims of killing for hire," and that the same was true of the two women killed outside Forker's Café in Newark. The deaths of the two women, she said, were drug-related, and "the Cincinnati Syndicate," McCann's enemies, paid to have him killed.

Delaine said she had told Kirkersville police and Lieutenant Paul Short the previous summer that her brother-in-law was responsible for the .22-caliber killings. She didn't tell the Columbus police or Franklin County Sheriff's deputies, she said, because she did not trust them.

Setting dates and locations of the trials for each of the brothers became tangled in judicial red tape and state politics. Columbus prosecutors wanted the trials held in Columbus, but it soon became obvious it would be impossible to select an impartial jury anywhere in Franklin County.

Public Defender James Kura was appointed to defend Gary, and since the court felt to have both men represented by the public defender could result in a conflict of interest, the judge selected a private Columbus defense attorney, Gary Tyack, to represent Thaddeus.

Thaddeus would go on trial ahead of Gary, and Tyack fought to have the first of his trials, on three of the murders, moved outside Franklin County because of the prejudicial publicity. He succeeded in his motion for a change of venue, and Thaddeus's trial for the murders of Jenkin Jones, Joyce Vermillion, and Karen Dodrill was transferred to Newark, Ohio, in Licking County, to begin on January 29, 1979. (The trials for his involvement in the Fairfield County murder of Reverend Fields and the five Franklin County .22-caliber killings—the McCann and Martin murders—would be scheduled later.)

Tyack, a young dynamic attorney from a respected family of attorneys and a judge, asked also that the court order the Franklin County Prosecutor to turn over to the defense all evidence in the case. He specifically wanted the information that had been presented to the grand jury in March 1978, which had resulted in the earlier indictments against Novatney, Politis, and Yasko. Tyack made it clear that he intended to fight his client's confession with Claudia's confession.

On January 29, reporter Ned Stout, who had been covering the Lewingdon case for the *Dispatch*, wrote the inside story:

.22-CALIBER MURDER TRIAL BEGINS

. . . If the motions are resolved in favor of the
state, then a months-old blunder by the Franklin
County sheriff and the Franklin County prosecutor is expected to be made one of the chief defense arguments against Licking County
Prosecutor David Lighttiser's seemingly air-
tight case. . . .

The *Dispatch* has learned that Tyack would
like to put Miss Yasko on the stand. . . . But fearful for her own safety and a victim of frequent
harassment since she gained notoriety, Miss
Yasko, friends say, is attempting with moderate
success to retain her precarious mental balance.

She does not disclose the German Village address where she is living, and friends say that on
the grounds of her mental condition she will re-
sist any effort to get her into the courtroom at
Newark.

Thaddeus's Newark trial opened on January 29, but jury
selection was delayed as Tyack confronted Licking
County Prosecutor David Lighttiser and demanded more
time to consider his case after an erroneous *Dispatch*
story that Gary Lewingdon intended to make a deal and
plead guilty.

The jury of eight women and four men, selected on
February 8, were warned that they would have to look at
shocking photographs of the victims, and that Thaddeus
Lewingdon's confession would contain some rough language.

They were taken in sheriff's cruisers to Forker's
Café, where Joyce Vermillion and Karen Dodrill had
been shot to death in the early morning hours of December 10, 1977, and then to the now-boarded-up home of
Jenkin T. Jones, the seventy-seven-year-old man who had
been shot to death on April 8, 1978. Thaddeus rode along
in the back seat of one of the cruisers, but he did not get
out during the trip.

Prosecutor David Lighttiser drew a harrowing picture of the murders in his opening statement. He described the bodies and the location of each wound. Joyce Vermillion had bullet holes in her left chest, her left shoulder, her head, and her face. Karen Dodrill had wounds in her left breast, her abdomen, and several in her face. Jones had been shot many times in the back and in the head.

Mrs. Doris Williams, Jenkin Jones's daughter, testified that she and her husband had returned from an evening out before one o'clock in the morning. When they entered the house, she said, "The lights were on, the doors were open, and our little dogs were gone."

She found the body of her father on the floor near his bedroom door. She said his trousers had been pulled down around his legs.

When Larry Vermillion took the stand, he recalled that his wife usually worked three nights a week until the 2:30 A.M. closing, while he stayed with their young child. On the evening of December 10, his wife had phoned him at about 10 P.M. and told him she was getting a ride home after work. He asked her to bring some sandwiches for him to take to work the next morning. When he awoke and discovered that she had not returned home, he took their child to a relative and went to Forker's Café to look for her. He found both women's bodies on the back porch. Near his wife's body, he said, was the sack of sandwiches she had made for him.

Two weeks into the trial, the prosecutor unexpectedly introduced dramatic evidence in the form of Thaddeus's murder-scene sketches, drawn when he had confessed to the murders, indicating the positions where he and his brother stood and where the victims were when they died.

Columbus Homicide Detective Robert Cupp also introduced into evidence Thaddeus's taped confession as listeners in the packed courtroom strained to hear.

After listening to the tape, Tyack angrily accused Lighttiser of withholding evidence favorable to Thaddeus. Tyack said he had reason to believe there were major discrepancies between deputies' reports on the

McCann murder scene and Thaddeus's statements on
the tape. He demanded to see all the Franklin County
Sheriff's reports.

Judge Winston Allen denied the motion.

On Friday, February 16, with Thaddeus's trial nearing
its end, Tyack questioned Delaine as a hostile witness.
Throughout the trial Tyack had brought up her past as a
woman who often danced nude in sleazy bars, who had,
he said, "often hired out her body to men." He claimed
she had ties to the underworld, especially the Cincinnati
syndicate, and was involved with big-time traffickers in
narcotics. Mrs. Delaine Lewingdon actually had masterminded the chain of killings, Tyack charged, and plotted
with Gary to make Thaddeus Charles the fall guy.

Taking the witness stand in a dark coat and nurse's
uniform, Delaine denied having any ties with organized
crime, organized prostitution, or organized drug traffic.
She testified that Charles had done the killings and had
forced Gary to go with him. After they returned home
each time, she said, they would describe the crimes, but
she denied planning or participating in any of the murders.

She admitted having bought her husband the .22-
caliber Sturm Ruger automatic and ammunition shortly
after the McCann murders. And she admitted that when
she had worked for Mickey he had forced her to dance
nude. But she denied having told Lieutenant Short of
Licking County that she was forced to have sex with several Columbus police officers to keep them off Mickey's
back. Mickey had set her up, she said, to be raped and
beaten by two men.

In his closing argument to the jury, Tyack again accused Delaine of having masterminded the .22-caliber
killings. Referring to her demure appearance in a
nurse's uniform, Tyack said, "What did you expect from
Delaine? That she would come in here topless and in a
G-string? Did you expect her to say, 'Yes, I did it. Yes, I
did it. Send me to prison for the rest of my life'?" He
paused, and then said emphatically, "We have shown
that Delaine is responsible."

Nevertheless, on February 19, 1979, the jury of eight

women and four men found Thaddeus Charles Lewingdon "guilty on all counts."

Judge Allen sentenced him to seven to twenty-five years for aggravated robbery. For the murders of Joyce Vermillion, Karen Dodrill, and Jenkin T. Jones, he handed down a sentence of three consecutive terms of life imprisonment.

2

The press now turned its attention to the upcoming trial of Gary James Lewingdon. But on February 20, 1979, Franklin County Public Defender James Kura and his associate Gary Schweickart asked Judge George Marshall to delay the trial, and said they would request a change of venue because of the wide publicity. Kura pointed out that the newspaper coverage, especially the *Dispatch*, included such inflammatory phrases as: "bullet-sprayed bodies," "multi-county slaughter," "killing binge," and had referred to Gary Lewingdon as the "co-executioner." "I think Gary Lewingdon has already been tried and convicted by the press," he said, "and I believe that virtually no one in Franklin County believes he is innocent."

Schweickart and Kura asked Detective Steckman for access to the police reports and evidence about the case. Not only did Steckman feel confident that he had done his job well, but he also respected the skill and integrity of the two public defenders. He so believed in the rights of defendants and in the process of the law, that although he guarded his evidence tenaciously, Steckman took them into his War Room, unlocked the file cabinets, and said, "Look at anything you want to. Help yourself."

At the same time, Steckman's colleagues at headquarters began teasing him, dropping hints and digs, saying, "You won't win this one, Steck. You just can't beat Schweickart and Kura." They kept it up day after day—until it was no longer a joke—insisting there was no way he was going to get a conviction on the Lewingdon brothers, and that all his labors would be for nothing.

Steckman's friends put it down to jealousy, saying it obviously rankled some officers and detectives that he was getting credit for breaking the .22's.

On February 21, Claudia again received phone threats at two and at four-thirty in the morning. She called her mother and told her what was happening. Martha then phoned Steckman, who arranged for a police cruiser to be stationed outside Claudia's apartment. Despite this precaution, the following day when Claudia finally went out shopping, her place was broken into and ransacked. Only her address book and a portfolio of her photographs were taken.

Judge George Marshall turned down the public defender's request for a delay in Gary Lewingdon's trial and said he would try to seat a jury before considering a change of venue. Kura and Schweickart, determined to forestall the Monday start of the trial in Franklin County, responded with a storm of last-minute motions. Faced with a sudden change of plea by the public defenders on behalf of Gary Lewingdon to "not guilty, and not guilty by reason of insanity," Judge Marshall postponed Gary's trial until April 23.

As a result, *Dispatch* courthouse reporters attacked the public defender. On February 25, one wrote:

> If James Kura, a tax-paid defense attorney, had his way, he'd keep the citizens of Central Ohio in the dark. Or would he?
> . . . Kura spends much of his time as an administrator but has decided to step into the spotlight and represent Lewingdon. . . .
> In his motions to deprive the public of knowledge of the trial, or at least to delay information, Kura seems unmindful of his obligation to the public that pays his approximately $25,000 yearly salary. . . .
> . . . Some Courthouse observers say Kura is trying hard to be very diligent in his representa-

tion of Gary. Others say he is trying to trip up
the trial court so there can be grounds for appeal.

Others say he is just showing off.

Although Claudia tried to put the Lewingdon brothers
out of her mind, the constant media coverage placed
them before her again and again. Each time she walked
into the local supermarket she saw their faces staring at
her from newspaper dispensing machines. Each time
she turned on the television news she saw videotape re-
plays of them in handcuffs. She tried not to look.

In desperation to get out of her apartment, she went
to visit her sister, Nancy, at the large discount appliance
store where she had recently started to work. As Claudia
passed through the TV section, surrounded by sets all
tuned to the same channel, she heard the newscaster say
that Judge Craig Wright had—on the previous day,
March 2—released Thaddeus's confession to the media.

Suddenly, the two brothers surrounded her on fifty
or sixty TV screens. No matter which way she turned,
she saw their faces.

Claudia ran out of the store, screaming.

3

The postponement of Gary's trial meant that Charles's
second trial (for the McCann and Martin murders) would
take place before Gary's first. Franklin County Common
Pleas Judge J. Craig Wright granted a change of venue,
and to avoid the time and expense of a third trial for
Charles, Fairfield County agreed to consolidate their
charges on the murder of the Reverend Gerald Fields.

The second trial opened in Mansfield, Ohio, on
March 26, and once again the jury and courtroom ob-
servers heard the details of the nine murders with which
Charles was charged. Defense Attorney Gary Tyack
again brought up the subject of two women: Delaine
Lewingdon, who—he claimed—had masterminded the

.22-caliber killing spree, and Claudia Yasko, who had confessed to the McCann murders.

When Charles, in a surprise move, took the stand in his own defense, he disavowed his confession. His brother Gary, he said, had forced him into the murders. Though in his confession he had earlier said Delaine had masterminded some of the crimes, he now spoke of "a mystery man"—a friend of Gary's—whose blue eyes could be seen through his ski mask and whose upper-lip scar could be seen through the mouth opening of the mask. The man carried a Luger and had a German accent, Charles said, and threatened to kill his wife and children if he didn't go along with Gary's plans.

The German mystery man became a standing joke among the attorneys and courtroom hangers-on. There was talk of *The Kruger with the Luger* . . . and *The Kruger with the Stuger Luger* . . . and then *The Kluger Kruger with the Stuger Luger*. It became a competition to see who could tack on more rhyming words.

Despite Tyack's efforts, Charles's confession to the Columbus detectives was admitted into evidence.

After fifteen hours of deliberation, the jury found Charles guilty of all twenty counts of robbery, theft, and aggravated murder in Fairfield and Franklin counties. In addition to penalties of one to five years on theft, five to seven years on aggravated burglary, and fifteen to twenty years on other charges, Judge Wright sentenced him to six additional consecutive life terms.

On May 14, 1979, after judges in the three counties agreed to consolidate the charges, Gary James Lewingdon finally went on trial in Cincinnati for all ten of the .22-caliber murders. Steckman, who had been guarding the evidence at his home and never let it out of his sight, drove it down to Hamilton County in his van. He and several of the other officers who would be required to testify were put up at a downtown hotel.

Three guards brought Gary into courtroom 503, with his hands manacled behind his back. He wore a brown-and-white-striped shirt and brown slacks without a belt. His beard had grown fuller, and behind his black-rimmed glasses his face bore an expression of pained surprise. The guards removed the cuffs, and he seated himself with his attorneys.

Prosecutor Daniel Hunt, pacing up and back before the jury, slammed his fist into his palm repeatedly as he made his opening remarks. "They left no witnesses. They killed everyone. The State will prove that Gary Lewingdon is responsible for each and every killing. We're going to show you that Gary and Thaddeus started on a killing spree back on December 10, 1977, and when that spree was over it had covered three counties and nine people were killed. But Gary's thirst for money and blood didn't stop—he decided to do one himself—on December 4, 1978."

Public Defender James Kura told the jury that the entire case of Gary Lewingdon's guilt or innocence hinged on a mental question. He conceded that Gary had been with his brother at the times of the killings, but insisted that Thaddeus had been the trigger-man in the first nine killings, and that Gary should be found innocent by reason of insanity.

Thaddeus had bullied Gary, dominated him, terrified him, Kura said, and when he needed someone to help him rob, he forced his shy, quiet brother to go along. Gary had gone with him out of fear that Thaddeus would kill Delaine and her children. In desperation, Delaine had gone to the Kirkersville police and the Licking County sheriff early last summer and told them she thought Thaddeus might be the .22-caliber killer.

Gary feared his brother might find out and seek vengeance, Kura said, and then in a deranged state Gary went out and killed Joseph Annick in December. Gary used the credit card intentionally when he went Christmas shopping. He *wanted* to be caught.

Prosecutor Hunt called dozens of witnesses, including relatives of the dead, and showed the jury color photographs of the gunned-down victims and their ransacked homes. He carefully analyzed the planning the Lewingdon brothers had done before they killed.

"There's a direct tie-in of the defendant to that [Eldorado] bar. He'd been there. He knew Robert 'Mickey' McCann had gone to bed with his wife. He knew that she had prostituted for him. He had all kinds of motives and

revenge against that man. But the overriding thirst was
for money. So what did he and Thaddeus do? Act like two
insane men and run out and shoot him on the street?
That isn't what they did. They carefully planned. They
went to that house not once, not twice, but three times."

His voice filled with emotion, Hunt described what
Gary was doing while Thaddeus pried open the door.
"He did something that makes him as guilty as if he shot
every bullet and killed each person individually. He took
a pair of pliers, went to the phone lines, cut off their line
to the outside world of communication. It was like a
death box. . . ."

The defense began its case with character witnesses.
Gary's niece, Florence Ann Davis of Columbus, took the
witness stand and said Gary didn't have many friends,
but he was a good person. She told how he had encouraged her to complete high school though she had wanted
to drop out, how he'd tutored her, how they had often
walked in the countryside to admire the beauty of the
Ohio hills.

Delaine Lewingdon took the stand in a tailored two-
piece beige suit and a dark blouse with a high neck. She
testified that she'd met Gary in 1976 at Mickey's Eldorado Club, where she'd worked, and that Gary had been
a gentleman. She'd also met Charles there, she said,
"And he was like most of the other customers there. He
was all hands, and he scared me."

She had found Gary to be a shy and very quiet man
who accepted her for what she was and didn't push her
to make any changes in her life. The first night she dated
him, she'd gotten home late from work and found him
already at her apartment, which she called "a disaster
area." Smiling at the memory, she said, "When I walked
in, my apartment was all cleaned. I had never known a
man to clean a house before. So I thought I've got to date
him."

Gary didn't like to talk much about his father, she
testified, except to say that he'd been sick when he was in
the service. She knew his father had been institutional-
ized for mental problems. One time when they had visited his father's grave, Gary had cried.

When asked about her brother-in-law, Delaine said
she had been in deep terror of Charles. "On several occa-

sions, like right after they [the murders] started, Charles held a gun to my head and threatened that if I ever told anybody what was going on, he would kill me. And I knew he would."

She described his late-night phone calls, with heavy breathing and threats. It was after one of Charles's threatening calls at two in the morning that she'd gone to the Kirkersville police. She later told Gary about it, and though he was afraid, he said he'd back up her statement, talk to the police, give them any information they wanted. When Lieutenant Short had returned her call and asked to see her in his office, she had told Short what she'd told the Kirkersville police and asked him for protection.

"He refused," she said. "He wanted us to go out and get the gun . . . to bring it in . . . He wanted some sort of physical weapon that showed Charles was the .22-caliber killer before he would do anything."

Kura asked, "Did you ask Lieutenant Short to come out and talk to your husband . . . ?"

"Yes, on two separate occasions I did," she said, "and on two separate occasions he said he would be out. Because I knew if he would talk to Gary, that Gary would confess. There was no doubt in my mind that he would have just laid the whole thing out. But he never showed up when he was supposed to. Short didn't."

She described how, when the brothers returned from their forays, Charles would always order her to fix something to eat. "Particularly when he killed somebody he always would have a ferocious appetite." But Gary would be quiet, she said, sometimes physically ill, and he would usually cry.

Delaine described her migraine headaches and talked of the nightmares she'd had about Mickey McCann before he was murdered. He had once threatened to kill her, she said, and she would wake up screaming that Mickey was after her. Gary would console her and say that everything would be all right, she was safe and he would never let Mickey get her.

In the defense's summation, Gary Schweickart said to the jury, "You know you've got doubt based on reason, not passion. You must not seek vengeance for a community which was held in terror. . . . If going by the pound," he said, pointing to Steckman's evidence piled on the table, "they win hands down." Then, gesturing at the prosecutors, "But we aren't going by the pound. We're going by law and reason."

Daniel Hunt summed up briefly for the prosecution, and pointed out that almost all the evidence had Gary Lewingdon's stamp on it. "There are ten families and ten people crying out from their graves for justice and someone to speak for them, and only *you* twelve people can. Both brothers were equal partners. Both are robbers. Both are murderers. Both are guilty."

On May 26, 1979, the jury brought in a verdict of guilty on eight of the ten murders. They were unable to reach a decision on the slayings of Jenkin T. Jones and Joseph Annick.

After the verdict was read, Gary Lewingdon asked the court to provide him with three hundred cubic centimeters of Sodium Pentothal so that he could take his own life.

"Justice was not done by the jury," he read from a motion he'd prepared himself. *"I ask to go beyond the bounds of punishment . . . and by this motion to relieve the court of any obligation."*

Judge Marshall turned down the request, fined him $45,000, and sentenced him to eight consecutive life sentences. Though ordered to the Southern Ohio Correctional Facility in Lucasville, Ohio, where his brother was imprisoned, Gary later became psychotic and was transferred to Lima State Hospital for the Criminally Insane.

Claudia, overjoyed that the killers had been put away and relieved that she had never been called to testify, slowly came out of seclusion. Color came back to her cheeks, and she laughed again.

But when her fears returned, she knew it wasn't all over for her. The whole story hadn't been told. And much of it, buried somewhere deep in her mind, erupted in nightmares. She moved from German Village and began to toy with the idea of finding a writer who would tell her story.

*　　*　　*

With the Lewingdon brothers brought to justice and put behind bars and the .22-Caliber Murder Case closed, the people of Central Ohio felt safe in their homes again.

The Governor of Ohio and the Mayor of Columbus praised the Columbus Police Department, and the Chief of Police praised the officers and detectives who had brought the murderers to justice. Officials told Steckman that since the Sturm Ruger and the Stoeger Luger were no longer needed for evidence, the department would have the .22's mounted as a trophy of the case he had been instrumental in solving.

For Steckman that was reward enough.

But not everyone was satisfied with closing the case on the McCann murders. There were those who couldn't forget that Claudia had told Howard Champ details of the murder that could only have been known by someone who had been there.

And as Howard Champ had said more than once: "Before I go to my grave, I'd like to know how Claudia knew the crime scene, and what really happened that night."

Claudia before the murders, 1976.

Home of Mickey McCann.

Dorothy McCann, Mickey's mother.

Go-go dancer Christine Herdman.

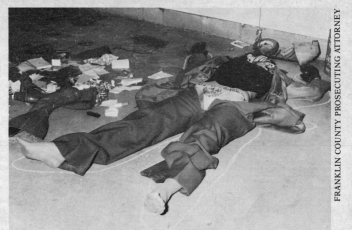

Mickey McCann.

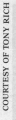

COURTESY OF TONY RICH

Detective Howard Champ (top)
and Detective Tony Rich (left),
the first detectives on the scene

Robert "Ray" Novatney.

Deno Constantin Gregory Politis.

Lew Dye (left), Claudia's attorney,
and *Playboy* investigators.

Claudia being released from Franklin County Jail,
with Lew Dye.

PHOTO BY DANIEL KEYES

Prosecutor George C. Smith.

Assistant Prosecutor James O'Grady.

PHOTO BY DANIEL KEYES

Detective Paul Short,
who interviewed Delaine Lewingdon.

Detective Sergeant William Steckman,
in charge of the .22-caliber task force.

Gary James Lewingdon, arrested December 10, 1978.

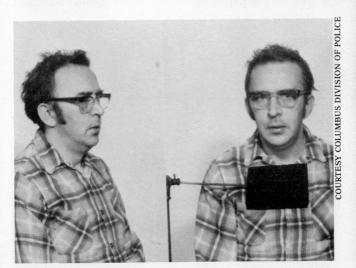

Thaddeus Charles Lewingdon, arrested the same night.

Newspaper photograph of Delaine Lewingdton.

PHOTO BY DANIEL KEYES

Home of Gary and Delaine Lewington.

Taping closet in Columbus Homicide Detective Bureau.

Saddlebag with ski masks,
gloves, and .22-caliber
Sturm Ruger.

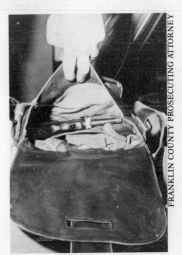

The guns: .22-caliber
Stoeger Luger (left) and
.22-caliber Sturm Ruger
with homemade silencer.

Detectives Jerry McMenemy (top) and Charles "Sam" Womeldorf (bottom) in interrogation room where Gary Lewingdon confessed.

PHOTO BY DANIEL KEYES

Mary Slatzer, Mickey McCann's
former girlfriend.

COURTESY OF ROBERT SLATZER

Auxiliary
Deputy Robert Slatzer,
Mary's father.

Claudia, eight years old, 1959.

Claudia in 1962 with Mary Yasko, grandmother (left), and mother, Martha Yasko.

Return from Hawaii: Claudia with father, George Yasko (left) and younger sister Nancy (center).

Four years after charges were dropped.

PHOTO BY DANIEL KEYES

Claudia today.

II

Unveiling Claudia

Twelve

1

Two weeks after Gary Lewingdon was found guilty and sentenced to eight consecutive life terms, Claudia, through her new attorney, David Long, began a lawsuit against Sheriff Harry Berkemer and the detectives involved in her arrest (Howard Champ, Don Champ, Tony Rich, William Davey, and Ronald Herdmann), and against Prosecutors James O'Grady and George C. Smith and the commissioners of Franklin County.

Long filed the civil suit on June 8, 1979, in the United States District Court for the Southern District of Ohio, Eastern Division, charging that Claudia's civil and constitutional rights had been violated and that Franklin County officials and officers had been guilty of unreasonable search and seizure, illegal arrest, and negligence, and that she had suffered humiliation, emotional pain and suffering, embarrassment, and loss of reputation in the community.

The complaint also charged:

All of the acts described in the foregoing paragraph were undertaken by defendants [James] O'Grady and [George C.] Smith solely for politi-

cal gain and constituted an abuse of the authority vested in them by the laws of the State of
Ohio and Franklin County.

Long was suing for half a million dollars in damages
plus punitive damages of two and a half million dollars.
In preparing his case with the help and financial support
of the Playboy Foundation, Long amassed hundreds of
documents, including copies of Claudia's taped confession, transcripts of the suppression hearing, police
records, bills, Martha's notes and records, and everything connected with Claudia's past. The cases against
O'Grady and Smith were dismissed in July 1981, and
Claudia soon dropped the lawsuit. At Claudia's request,
David Long later turned all his records over to me. When
Dr. Byron Stinson refused even to meet me, saying over
the phone: "I'd rather keep out of the line of fire,"
Claudia went personally to Upham Hall and picked up
her medical records.

Her providing me with those documents, and helping me arrange interviews with many of her friends and
associates, showed me that Claudia was being open and
cooperative. I didn't feel she was hiding anything, and I
was convinced, as most people who spoke to me were,
that she had indeed been the innocent victim of police
bungling and political opportunism.

So during that first year, in addition to interviewing
Claudia almost every Thursday, I spent the rest of my
time studying those documents and tracking down many
of the people who had, in one way or another, been involved with her. Thus I was able to reconstruct the story
of her arrest for the McCann murders as well as the investigations and trials of the real killers.

But tracking a cold trail in 1983, I began slowly to
discover another story behind the facade of the public
story.

Psychologists speak of "screen memories" which
people sometimes create—false memories to hide
behind—to blot out experiences too painful to remember. When I discovered that's what Claudia had done to
hide from herself the pain of what had really happened
on that terrifying night, I faced a dilemma. My work, it
seemed, was only half done. I did not yet have the answer

to the key question: "Where was Claudia on the night of the triple homicide?"

To get the answer, I would have to break through Claudia's screen memories, and to do that I needed to learn more about her past, the history of her mental condition and, above all, the pattern of her relationships with the men who had helped shape what she had become.

But as I dug deeper I discovered—despite her constant assurances that she had nothing to hide—that Claudia was becoming afraid of what I might find.

The second year and a half of my work was an unending struggle against Claudia's fears, fantasies, and evasions. I found myself caught up in the search for answers that seemed always within my grasp, only to vanish as I reached for them. Claudia not only blotted out scenes from the past, but she would often forget what we were doing in the present. Time and again I swore I had to give it up before I was overwhelmed by frustration. But it was too late for me. The story had taken on a life of its own.

Howard Champ's comment about wanting to know how Claudia had known the crime scene, and what really happened that night, had made me aware then that although the Columbus police had solved the case of the .22-caliber killings, they had never solved the mystery of Claudia.

Now, I realized, neither had I.

Until nearly the end of our working relationship, Claudia withheld from me—as she had from the detectives, her attorneys, and her psychiatrist—the heart of her secret.

It was only when I stopped asking what she was hiding from me, and began asking what she had all along been hiding from herself, that I was able to peel away the layers of lies and illusions that had screened the terrible answer for five years.

2

Try as I might to help Claudia fill in some of the gaps in her memory, she could recall almost nothing about the six months between June 1978—when she had been released from jail and was living in seclusion in German Village—and the time the Lewingdons had been arrested that December. But then one afternoon, after we had been working together for about seven months, she greeted me at the door excitedly.

She had run into someone in Columbus that week, a friend she'd made when she had been living in German Village, and the woman told her she would be pleased to talk to me. Claudia insisted that I should interview her to find out about their relationship during that period.

I called the woman, who agreed—reluctantly, it seemed to me—to meet me at the Beck Tavern in German Village near where both of them had lived.

When I arrived, she put off talking to me. She had changed her mind, she said. She didn't want anyone to know about her association with Claudia. When I offered to protect her identity by using a pseudonym, she made me promise not to do even that. No name. No description. No way she could be traced.

All I can say is that she was young and attractive. We sat at the bar. I bought her a drink. The rock music and shouting voices surrounded us so loudly that I had difficulty hearing her words. But I feared if I suggested we move I might lose her.

I asked if she had known Claudia before she'd been sent to prison.

"No, I didn't meet her until after she was released."

"How'd you come to meet?"

She paused, and I saw her eyes flick around her. "Through a friend," was all she would say.

"Okay. No names."

She was silent for a long while, stirring her drink and looking around her. "Claudia and I met here—at this bar—just after she moved into German Village. We sat and talked, and she was so funny. She was so sweet. She was so innocent. So wonderful."

"How did she show that sweetness?" I asked.

"You can just tell by her smile," she said, "and she just looks at you and taps you on the hand, you know."

"Yes," I said, smiling. "I know."

"It was the first time I'd met her, and we got along real quick. Sometimes you like somebody, or you don't like somebody. We liked each other immediately. She was supposed to meet a lawyer here, and she had this stuff with her to show him. She was flipping through the pages of it, you know, what they give you when they let you out of jail, and they tell you what you're up for—pages and pages of this, and I'm just sitting there, saying '*You?* C'mon, who in their right mind would believe it?'"

"How well did you get to know her?" I asked.

"Claudia and I spent a whole lot of time together at a period when she really needed people. We lived six or seven blocks away from each other. She'd call me, and we'd both leave our apartments at the exact same minute. We'd meet halfway, and then we'd walk and just giggle and do silly things on the way to the tavern."

I asked if Claudia lived alone. As far as she knew, Claudia did, but she remembered a trucker who took them out to dinner one night and she figured he was the one paying Claudia's bills. "He drove an eighteen-wheeler," she said, "and he was very nice, and very, very kind."

"Pigman?"

She laughed. "Yeah, now I remember. Once he left his rig parked out in one of those tiny winding German Village streets, and a policeman came into the tavern and said people were complaining about all those pigs squealing, and the stink. The officer gave him a summons, and he had to pay a big fine."

When I asked if she knew anything about their relationship, she shrugged. "I'm the kind of person, if I don't want to know the answer I don't ask the question."

"In my line, I have to ask, whether or not I want to know the answer."

She winked at me. "I remember one evening Claudia and I were sitting right here at the bar talking, and a friend of mine came up and said, 'There's a guy over in the booth who's really interested in Claudia. He wants to take her out to dinner.' It turned out he was a new young assistant prosecutor, and I figured I'd better tell him who she was. When I did, he got up and ran out of the place. I think he nearly had a heart attack."

She grew quiet, musing as she stared into her drink. I sat quietly and waited.

"We spent a lot of time together for a while," she said. "That was what we used to do, meet each other halfway, walk to the tavern. She would drink grapefruit juice, because she didn't drink, and I would drink alcohol. Sometimes we'd go to have dinner out—a pizza or something—but first Claudia would always stop at the bakery and buy the biggest cookie you've ever seen in your entire life. I mean, this cookie had to be a foot wide. She was in absolute heaven. She'd eat it, and we'd talk. She was somebody I loved. God—"

"What do you think Claudia was feeling at that time? What was she going through?"

"What she went through was sheer horror," she said.

"Tell me about it."

"I don't even know how to put it," she said, shaking her head. "She was seeing some doctor or a psychologist or something, and he had her under such incredible amounts of sedation that I would cry watching the woman try to walk up the steps. It was ridiculous—absolutely ridiculous—I told her to stop taking the stuff. I don't know what medication they were giving her but it was just really sick. I mean, they took her whole personality away. They took her *a-way*."

"Was Claudia fearful of being harmed?"

"In the beginning, no. After that, it got a little strange."

"Do you recall when it changed?"

"A few months after I met her," she said. "When they were looking for those people—the .22-caliber killers—she was afraid. She was very afraid of somebody coming after her. And she never really told me why. Somebody needs their hand held, all you can do is give 'em a big hug and tell 'em not to worry, and do what you can for 'em."

It was obvious that she was torn between her deep feelings for Claudia and her fear of talking.

"There's nothing else I can tell you," she said.

I could see by her expression that she meant to end the interview.

"Can or will?" I asked.

She shrugged.

"Okay," I sighed. "But, really. Isn't there a pseudonym I can use for you?"

"You promised."

"How about something like Madam X?"

"You can do better than that," she said, getting up to go. Then she paused and turned back to me. "I'll tell you what. Just refer to me as *Australia*."

3

When I told Claudia of my interview with Australia, she laughed. The memory pleased her. "Yes, I remember those big cookies. They were gigantic! I loved them. I wish I had one now."

She said it so happily, I wished I had brought one for her.

"Australia gave me the feeling of what you were going through then. I wish we had more background like that."

"Well, you've got to talk to lots of people besides me. Too bad you can't talk to Bobby. If someone hadn't murdered him, he could tell you a lot about what happened."

"He wasn't murdered, Claudia."

"Oh, yes he was. Bobby was found dead on his couch on Thanksgiving Day, 1981. I told you someone put strychnine into his heroin."

"And I believed that until I saw coroner's report. You're the one who went and got it for me. Don't you remember? The toxicologist indicated no foreign agents in the blood besides alcohol."

She shook her head.

Fortunately, I had my notes from the coroner's statement with me, and I read part of it to her:

"Victim was apparently in good health until his death. Brother relates that deceased was at one time a heroin addict and believes that reinvolvement with drugs is a possibility here."

She giggled. "Possibility? God, he was a doper. I still think someone put strychnine in his heroin."

"The report lists *heroin abuse* as part of Novatney's medical history but lists the cause of death as due to *cardiopulmonary arrest as a consequence of chronic intravenous narcotic abuse.*"

"Well . . ." She flicked her wrist as if to show me what she thought of coroners' reports.

"It's a good thing I was able to interview his mother and brother," I said. "Without some insight into Bobby, there'd have been a hole in the story big enough to sink it."

She agreed.

"If only I could talk to Deno Politis about what happened during that time. Any idea where he is?"

She shook her head vigorously. "No, Dan. Deno would never talk to you. He hates me. And he's very, very dangerous. Keep away from him."

"We'll see," I said, not committing myself. As we were nearing the end of our first year of work, Claudia was becoming more adept at diverting me from probing areas she had obviously intended to leave untouched.

The good mood her memory of the cookies had brought on was now dispelled as she recalled Bobby. I decided to get back to the question she had parried for so long.

"What I need now, Claudia, are answers to questions I've asked before, but never got."

I could see her bracing herself.

"How did you know that Mickey ran outside that night and was shot in the snow?" I asked for what must have been the hundredth time. "How did you know about the hazelnuts on the floor and the snow blower in the garage?"

"I don't remember!" she insisted. "Why do you keep asking me those things?"

"Because without the answers to how you knew those things and what you did that night and why—we've got nothing."

"I'm trying to help."

"Let's work from what we've got," I said. "We know your alibi was that you were at breakfast with Ginger and Pigman."

4

It took me another week, in between other interviews, to track down Mary Slatzer. When I finally reached her by phone, in mid-August 1983, I told her what I was working on and asked if she would talk to me about Mickey Mc-Cann.

"Why?" she asked.

"The papers and the police painted a pretty negative picture of him," I said. "I'm trying to find out the truth of what happened that night, and I'd like to learn about him from someone who knew him well."

"Yeah," she said. "I'll talk to you about Mickey."

She suggested we meet the following Thursday at five in front of a downtown Columbus restaurant called the Clock. I was so delighted to have arranged the interview that my hand was trembling as I jotted it down.

On August 25, I had one informant not show for a noon meeting; I interviewed Columbus police officer Brinkman at 3:30 P.M. and I arrived at the Clock on High Street at five. As I started inside, I noticed a man standing in the entrance, eyeing me. He had a copy of my last book under his arm, and when he was satisfied I was the person in the picture on the dust jacket, he introduced himself. He was Bob Slatzer, he said, Mary's father. Mary had phoned him and told him about our appointment, he said, but she had changed her mind and wouldn't be coming. He had taken two buses all the way from his east-side home to come downtown and let me know so I wouldn't be left standing outside for hours.

My disappointment must have shown. I invited him to have a beer and soon discovered he was eager to talk about the now six-year-old case himself.

Robert Clinton Slatzer was a short, thin, feisty man of fifty-one, with narrow eyes and a gruff voice. Although the name Slatzer descended from a remote Dutch great-grandfather, he said, his parents had been born in Ireland. He had five sons, and Mary was the eldest of five daughters. At the time of the McCann homicides, he pointed out, he worked as an auxiliary deputy for the

Franklin County Sheriff's Department and had assisted in the investigation.

But he seemed bitter towards the detectives of what he referred to as "the county," and vehemently told me of their incompetence. They had convicted the Lewingdons, he admitted, but that was only part of it. "There's a lot of unanswered questions," he said. "You're wasting your time on doing a book about Claudia Yasko," he insisted. "She just knew what everyone else on the street knew. There's people who know a lot more than she does."

"Who would that be?" I asked.

"My daughter Mary."

"I do want to talk to her," I said.

"Well, she's like me," he said. "Both of us were damned upset the way the newspapers pictured Mickey. He was really a great guy, you know. The way they wrote about him, you'd think he was the perpetrator instead of a murder victim."

"I'd like to know more about him," I said.

"Mary could tell you everything," he said with a wink. "She lived with him for five years."

"I don't know what made her change her mind about meeting me, but it's important for her side of the story to be told—if Mickey was the good guy you say he was, that should be made part of the record."

Slatzer assured me he could get me an interview with his daughter. Our meeting was over, and I drove him home.

One fall afternoon after I finished another fruitless interview with Claudia, I phoned Bob Slatzer from her place at a prearranged time. He told me to come to his house right away. He had lured Mary there on a pretext, he said, but if I showed up she would surely talk to me.

When I arrived at Slatzer's house I saw him standing in the doorway with his back to the street. As I got out of the car, he waved at me with a gesture warning me to remain out of sight. A few minutes later, he led me inside and introduced me to his daughter.

Mary Slatzer was a small, attractive, but hard-looking woman with short dishwater-blond hair, a bitter laugh, and a tough attitude. She gave her father a glance of disgust when it became apparent he had tricked her into coming to his house just to meet me.

I had stepped into the middle of a very strange family relationship, and it made me nervous.

As guilty as I felt at the way Slatzer had manipulated his daughter, I told her it was important for her side of the story to be made public, and for her knowledge of Mickey to correct whatever injustice she felt the Columbus press had done to his memory.

She settled back in the couch, looked at her father, studied me for a few moments, and then said, "What do you want to know?"

I hardly dared to breathe as I pulled out the tape recorder and turned it on. "How did you meet Mickey?"

"Oh, Lord, how did I meet him? I was staying out on the west side with my cousin, and we went into his bar one night, and she introduced me to him—she knew him before I did. And he asked me to come back. That was on New Year's Eve. I never went back for six months. Then I ran into him in a restaurant and I started working for him."

"What was your job?" I asked.

"I was a dancer first . . . well, I lived with him from that time on and I just did a lot of everything."

"Were you the manager of the place?"

"When I turned twenty-one I ran it. He was hardly ever in there. I helped manage the club, including all the hiring and firing."

"What was Mickey like?" I asked.

"I thought he was a great guy. He'd give you the shirt off his back. He had a lot of friends . . . and he had a lot of people who owed him money. Only thing was he didn't believe in banks, because he got caught by the IRS for income-tax evasion. He was on probation for four years."

"He was a little crooked," her father said. "Was he a little crooked?"

"No!" she snapped. "He paid the price! He had to pay back ten thousand dollars!" She glared at me too, as if daring me to criticize the dead man. "You asked what he was like . . . well, he was good to me. He gave me anything I wanted."

Her father interrupted again. "Would *stormy* be the appropriate word to describe your relationship?"

"Stormy?" she mused.

"Sometimes stormy?" he insisted.

"Sometimes . . ."

"Is that a term you would use?" I asked. "I don't like putting words into people's mouths."

She shook her head. "No. We had more good times than bad."

When I asked why she had stopped living with Mickey she said, "Oh, I was living with him—off and on—up until the time he was killed."

I couldn't hide my surprise. "I thought there was a breakup."

"No. As a matter of fact," she explained, "we had been busted. He had to close the bar down for six months, and we were going to go down to Florida together."

She told me McCann had been married once, long before they'd met, and had a daughter he'd never seen.

"Marriage ever come into the question?" I asked.

"No. It was easier that way. You see back in seventy-three I became pregnant with Mickey's child and I lost it. He took it pretty hard. He wanted to have kids but it just never happened."

"But you were living with him?"

"Off and on."

"What about Christine Herdman? What was her role at that time?"

"She didn't have a place to stay. He was good that way—letting people stay there. She'd only been living there a couple of months. In fact I introduced them. She came in the bar as a customer and said she was looking for a job. I told you I did the hiring and firing. Well, I'm the one who hired her."

"Still, it seems kind of unusual," I said, "to take a stranger into your own house."

"He always did. A lot of Mickey's dancers would come out and live with us. He was just that way."

"The impression I get from the papers is that he and Christine were lovers."

"No," she said, simply, "I wouldn't think so."

"The truth is he fooled with a lot of women," her father said.

"Sure," she said, "if he could get away with it. He was in the bar every night."

I said, "So you and he were still living together as—"

"Off and on."

"Was that an *on* time or an *off* time?"

"That night I was going to go home with him, but my dad picked me up."

I couldn't hide my surprise. "That sounds like an incredible stroke of luck."

"I guess . . ." was all she said.

Her father broke in again, as if interrogating her on the witness stand. "Were you working with any law enforcement agencies?"

"Yes, I was."

"While you were there?"

"Yes."

"Before he—?"

I cut him off and turned to Mary. "Tell me about it."

She said she had been working with law enforcement officers to get Christine Herdman busted for selling narcotics at the club.

"Were you working with someone from the sheriff's office?" her father interjected.

"Yeah," she said. *"You!"*

"How did that get started?" I asked. "In your own words."

"I seen Chris selling some dope in the bar . . . pills."

"What was the sample you turned into the sheriff's office?" her father asked.

She looked at him in annoyance. "They said it wasn't nothing."

"That was the other time," he said. "I mean the PCP."

"Oh . . . the PCP."

"As long as we're talking about dope," I said, "was Mickey involved in selling drugs?"

"No," she said. "He did not believe in it. He was strict on that. He did not believe in it at all."

"Was he involved in prostitution?" I asked.

"No."

"Was he involved in gambling?"

She looked surprised. "Gambling?"

"Did he run a poker game?"

"He played poker in the bar after hours. I didn't see nothing wrong with that."

"I didn't say there was anything wrong with it," I said. "I'm not judging it. Did he have a regular high-stakes game going?"

"No."

"Oh, come on, Mary!" Slatzer said. "We know he had three- . . . four-thousand-dollar poker games there—"

"He did not, Dad!"

"—and you served bar then."

"No!"

"That's reliable information."

"That's a lie, Dad. He played cards maybe once a month."

Slatzer persisted: "And the conclusion that all the law enforcement officers got was that he was being protected by someone high up."

"That's a lie!" she snapped.

"What police officers hung out at the bar?" he asked.

"There was a *lot* of policemen come in there . . . *off duty*."

"Was he afraid of anyone?" I asked.

She gave me an odd look. "The Friday before he was killed he asked me, 'Do you think anyone hates me bad enough to kill me?' and I said, 'No.' Which I . . . you know, I didn't think anything . . ."

"What made him come up with that question?" I asked.

Mary said that a week or two before the murders, when she and Mickey arrived at the house, they spotted some men on the back porch who fled at their approach. From that time to his death, Mickey had been suspicious of everyone and started carrying a .38 pistol.

Her father interrupted again to ask if she had gone out to eat with Mickey on that fatal night. Yes, she said, they'd gone to White Castle for hamburgers. He asked if she knew how much money Mickey was carrying on him the night of his murder.

"Twenty or thirty thousand," she said. "Maybe more."

She hadn't helped him count his money that night, but a man had come in and paid six thousand dollars that he'd owed. And Mickey—as he had a habit of doing—counted his money right at the bar.

I asked what her reaction had been when she learned of the murders. She'd nearly fainted, she said. She'd been at home in bed when a friend called and told her about it, and after she pulled herself together she called the sheriff's office on her own because she figured they'd want to talk to her.

"Deputies came to my apartment," she said, "that Monday night."

Confused, because I knew it wasn't possible, I pulled out my calendar and said, "Let's get the date straight."

"Let's go back and get the *money* straight," her father insisted.

Mary's head snapped up. "What are you, Dad? Are you writing this book?"

He laughed and nodded towards me. "He knows I was in on the investigating end of this."

"What's that got to do with anything?" she demanded.

The last thing I wanted was a fight between them. "He's just helping me out if I miss some things," I said. "I'm not interrogating you, just—"

"I know, but he makes me feel like I'm on trial!"

"That's my style," Slatzer said.

I referred to the calendar to break the tension. "The bodies were discovered on Monday, the thirteenth of February. Did you have an alibi for the day of the murders?"

"Yes, I did." She chuckled, pointing to Slatzer. "I was with my father."

Robert Slatzer confirmed that he had picked up his daughter after work for the last three nights before the murders. The person who usually picked her up had car trouble at the last minute, and the weather was bad.

"Yeah, I didn't go in to work that Monday," Mary said. "The next day, Tuesday afternoon, is when I called the sheriff. They picked me up from where I was living at my brother's house. They took me downtown and asked me if I did it. Asked me if I knew who did it. They wanted to know about my taxes. Prostitution. They wanted to know if Mickey was queer—he wasn't. My where-abouts."

Bob Slatzer leaned forward and pointed an accusing finger at his daughter. "Nobody ever knew why you left Mickey. Why did you leave his home? Why did you move out?"

She squirmed. "Why did I move out?"

"Nobody ever heard that story of why you moved out," he pressed. "Did he throw you out? Or did you move voluntarily?"

"I moved out on my own."

"Why?"

She became flustered at what had again become a cross-examination, and she glared at her father. "Be-cause . . . I was . . . I was at that time seeing someone else."

"Did he know it?"

"Yeah."

"Did he care?" her father asked.

"Sure he did."

"And he was seeing somebody else?"

"At that time, yeah."

"Who was he seeing?"

"Uh . . . her street name is Sunshine . . . she's from Kentucky. She lived with Mickey for about six months and she got pregnant by him and she went and had an abortion. It upset Mickey and she left. That's when I moved back in with him."

"You didn't like Sunshine," her father prompted.

"No, I didn't."

"In fact, you didn't like any of the girls he went with."

"No. I'm not going to lie about it. I didn't like Chris-tine, but I didn't want to see anybody die."

"What about the story that I've told you—that you've heard—"

"There's so many stories you told me, Dad—"

"The one main one! That everybody has said, *'Mary has never told everything she knows.'* Is there something you know that you haven't told?"

"No," she said, now definitely acting like a hostile witness. "I don't know anything I haven't told. What else am I supposed to know?"

"That's what people are wondering," he said. "That's what I'm wondering."

Her voice became soft. "I've told everything I know."

"Were you told by officers in Columbus, people I worked with who were on intelligence: 'Mary, if you hold out on us you'll go to jail'?"

"Yeah, they did. They were talking about the stolen TV's in Mickey's bar."

"What's that about?" I asked.

She faced me and held her hands out, palms up. "They told me if I didn't tell them everything, they'd indict me to the grand jury."

"For what?" I asked.

She laughed. "I don't know. Ask my father. *He* put them up to it."

"We wanted all the facts and all the truth," Slatzer said. "This was a murder investigation."

"Excuse me, Bob," I said, "but now I want Mary's opinion of the real reason for McCann's death. What do you think, Mary?"

She seemed relieved at the interruption in the grilling she was getting from her father. "Money," she said.

"You feel it was strictly a robbery? Of course, you've seen all the other things in the papers: *professional killing, organized crime, love triangle . . .*"

She shook her head aggressively. "He had a bad habit of flaunting his money. And worse, he would tell people where he lived. And I warned him about it."

"That seems pretty naive," I said. "Except for those things, he doesn't sound like a stupid man. How do you explain it?"

"It was psychological," her father said. "Mickey was raised poor, and never had anything, so if someone put him down he'd pull out his money and count it for 'em. It was like saying, 'Here, see what I've got.'"

"The only strange part about it," she said, "is that we were always very cautious when we went home. Before we went in, we always looked for things that weren't safe. We'd check to make sure the doors and windows were still locked. I can't understand him pulling in and not noticing the back door or anything."

"You're saying that normally before he went in he'd go and check the side door."

"No. The first one to go in would be *me*."

I couldn't restrain my laughter. She smiled sheepishly.

"I was always the first one in. Probably only because I was on the passenger side, but that was the way he was. He was cautious. That's why I can't understand."

"There's another irony," her father said. "Mickey had a security-system label in the window, but he wouldn't spend the money to have it installed."

"He did have the floodlights," she said, "but it wouldn't have made any difference. Mamma McCann would have let anybody in."

I asked her if she ever heard details of the murder scene, and she said that Keith Walker, the club manager who had called the Sheriff's Department, told her that the thermostat had been turned up all the way and the heat was up to a hundred degrees. Keith had arrived at the scene later and identified the bodies.

"He took Mickey's death very hard," she said. "He complained of having constant nightmares about the murders, and his hair turned completely gray."

"So Keith knew the position of the bodies," Slatzer said, "the way they were shot and everything." He looked at me and shrugged. "Don't you know the people on the street had more details than the murderers *or* the police? Would you believe the sheriff's office questioned a lot of people?"

"No," Mary said, her gaze distant. "I think their main concern was me."

"Why?" I asked.

"Because they thought I did it."

"How do you feel about that?"

"I think they treated me rotten. I've never been treated that way before. I think it was wrong for them to make me go to the Shamrock Bar the day Mickey's body was being viewed and lock me in a room to question me. Howard Champ called me a liar and said I wasn't telling him everything."

"What did you think," I asked, "when you read in

the papers that the deputies thought it was organized crime and a professional killing?"

"I thought it was a lot of bull," she snapped. "You know, I went through Mickey's notebook with the city police."

I hadn't known that. "What notebook?"

"Mickey had a list of names of people who owed him money and that were trouble. Seven hundred and fifty names."

"Seven hundred and fifty?" I echoed.

"A lot of them were past employees. People he even had come out to the house for dinner."

I couldn't hide my surprise. "He invited his employees to his home?"

"Yeah, for dinner or for breakfast."

"Sounds like a very sociable guy."

"To a degree," she said. "If he liked you he would give you anything you needed."

Bob Slatzer said, "He wasn't as bad as they printed in the papers. He wasn't that way."

"Not too many people would agree with you," I said. "From the newspaper accounts and from what others have told me, I figured he was a monster."

"No, he wasn't," Mary said. "I think he died a horrible death. He was little, but he was tough, and if he'd had any chance and he could get out of that garage he'd go. Once a long time ago he'd been shot in the knee, and he kept going."

I asked her if Mickey had special places to keep money around the house.

"Yeah, behind the big velvet picture hanging over the dresser in the bedroom. He just stuck it behind there. And he was very forgetful. He'd put money in places and forget about it. In the back seat of the car under the mat, in the trunk."

Bob Slatzer was obviously growing impatient with the direction of the interview. "Let's get back to the *narcotics*," he said. "I think she's missing the big one. Before you were talking to Christine Herdman—"

"Right," she said, frowning as if wondering what he was leading up to now.

"I'll do this like an attorney would do, or somebody

investigating: Do you remember the guy who gave the sixteen-year-old an overdose? The one that you gave me the drug paraphernalia from what was turned in to the sheriff's office?"

"Right," she said.

"The one I had to go to the sheriff to get permission to work with the city on?"

"What about it?" she asked.

"Well, he was a big dealer, traveled all over the country. Tell him about that."

Mary shook her head, confused. "What do you want me to tell him? They told me it wasn't nothing. That it was sugar or flour—"

"That was another time. Wasn't he busted?"

"Dad, I don't know."

Slatzer finally gave up trying to lead his witness and turned to me. "The truth of it is this guy gave an overdose to a sixteen-year-old and he was busted. He traveled from state to state and picked it up."

"What's the connection to McCann?" I asked.

"He came into McCann's bar," her father said.

"What's that got to do with anything?" Mary demanded.

Slatzer said sarcastically that it had to do with Christine's drug connection.

"Ohhh," she said, getting the point. "Well, Mickey never did it. He didn't believe in it."

"What they didn't know," her father said, "what Mickey didn't know—because he would have thrown her out of the bar—was that Mary was working undercover for the narcotics squad."

"Ohhhh. . . . No . . . no . . ." she moaned, agreeing with her father. "Mickey didn't know it."

"No one knew this except for the people she was working with."

"You had this good relationship with Mickey and you cared a lot about him," I said. "How'd you feel operating as an undercover agent in his own place without telling him?"

"I didn't feel bad," she said, "because I didn't think it was right for them to be doing it—Christine and that guy. I'm strictly for the law."

"Christine was dealing drugs in Mickey's place?" I asked.

"Yeah," Mary said, "and he didn't know it."

"Why didn't you just tell him?" I asked. "Why didn't you just say, 'Mickey, get rid of her. She's dealing drugs'?"

"I don't know," she said with a nervous laugh. "I think I wanted to get her busted."

"Mary's got a close relationship with police officers," her father said. "She's got as many sweethearts on the police force as Mickey had girlfriends."

"Sure, I dated *a few* of them."

"She had a thing where she loved policemen."

"No, I don't *love* 'em."

"Out of all the majority of men on the earth, she's dated more policemen than she's dated any other type man."

"Well, sure," she said.

"That's the way it is," her father said. "If you asked half the policemen on the hilltop, unless they transferred them now, or around the south end or something, they know Mary. She's always been close to policemen. Maybe that's because of my relationship with 'em, but she's been close to policemen."

She made a face at him and became silent.

"Did the Eldorado Club have girls dancing?" I asked. "Go-go dancing?"

"Right."

"Were they clothed, or topless, or . . ."

At this point she laughed and blushed. "That's what we got busted for—*topless*."

"Just *topless*, not *bottomless*?" I asked.

"Well . . ." She giggled again and shrugged.

Then I saw her father pointing his finger at her. "Right there." He laughed. "Indecent exposure."

I looked at her. "You danced nude at the bar?"

"Sure I did. And I don't see anything wrong with it."

"I didn't say there was anything wrong—"

"One of these days they'll legalize it."

"It's legal now," her father said.

"No, I'm talking about with liquor," she said angrily. "Someday this hick town will legalize it." She pursed her lips, frowned at her father, and then turned her attention to me. "Anything else?"

Slatzer took over again. One of the things that bothered him, he said, was that the Sheriff's Department hadn't sealed off the bar after the bodies were discovered. "There could've been a lot of money in that bar that was never discovered, but you'd have thought they'd seal the bar to search for evidence in a murder investigation. After they found Mickey's body, they closed down the bar, but they never sealed it, and people came in and out of that place."

I asked Mary if she knew where in the bar Mickey used to hide his money.

"Yes, in the back room, in a hiding place over the furnace in the basement, in the beer coolers. The money he kept on him, he went to bed with. He slept with it under his pillow—all the hundred-dollar bills—forty or fifty thousand dollars. Never put it into banks. Never trusted banks. But he also kept large amounts of money in a sock, which he then stuck into one of the stockings he was wearing. Thousands of dollars kept on his person at all times."

That explained the detectives' description of the knee sock on McCann's right leg having been pulled down to the ankle.

"Tell him about running up the double tapes," Slatzer said.

"We never rang up the girls' drinks," Mary explained. "We kept track of them separately. Week by week we would redo the tapes. He'd call out figures to me, and I'd ring them up."

"So he was skimming," I said. "And you knew about it."

She shrugged.

She hadn't done anything illegal, she said. She was on the side of the law, and pointed out that she had worked with the sheriff's detectives, going over lists of people who had a grudge against Mickey.

"Like Dee Grumman," her father said.

"Tell me about Dee Grumman."

"She worked with me," Mary said. "She tried to say that somebody set her up and that she was raped. Well, that's a lie. She picked up all kinds of guys in there. I mean, not for prostitution, I mean just picking them up. When she left, she quit on bad terms. She owed Mickey three hundred dollars and we went to her house."

"You went with him?" I asked.

"I was with Mickey. Yes. And Mickey asked for his money. But Gary Lewingdon, who was living with her at the time, told Mickey if he didn't get away that he'd kill him. So we left."

"Did Mickey take that seriously?" I asked.

"No, he had a lot of guys threaten him."

"Did you take it seriously?"

"No."

She went silent.

The newspapers had reported that under the terms of his will admitted in Probate Court, Mickey had left his entire estate to a woman named Thelma Hoffman. I asked Mary what she thought of that.

"She was his friend in earlier years," she said. "I was told by Mickey that there was a second will—a later will that would take care of me—but it was never found."

"So what did you get?"

"Nothing. But I don't care. When he was alive, I was happy. That's enough for me. The hardest thing is to believe he's gone."

5

The first thing Detective Sergeant Bill Steckman said when I phoned him for a second interview and told him I was still researching Claudia and the .22-caliber murders was: "You have really bought yourself a circus."

He had put it just right. It's exactly what I had been feeling for the past fifteen months.

I had interviewed Steckman for the first part of the book three months earlier, after he had gotten clearance from his supervisor. We had met at the Central Police Station, not his own office, because he was no longer on duty with Homicide. He had been transferred to the Vice Squad.

For our second interview he told me to meet him at

his post in an auxiliary depot in an out-of-the-way part of town. He was on duty after midnight. I got lost, had to phone him, and he came to get me and led me in.

I really wanted to follow up on our discussion about Delaine Lewingdon, to understand why she had gotten off completely free, but I decided to lead up to it slowly. We talked about other aspects of the case, and after about an hour of filling in details, I said, "The .22-caliber murders must have taken a lot of your time."

"I worked on the case eighteen hours a day and lived it twenty-four."

"What effect did that have on you?"

"It brought out the intensity of homicide-detective work," he said. "And I didn't realize how much it was affecting my relationships, on the job and off, and it put a drain on my social and family life. It never occurred to me that I was hardly ever with my wife and children."

After the Lewingdons were convicted, Steckman was divorced from his first wife and had since remarried. His new wife was in law enforcement, he said, and that made things a lot easier. I sensed he didn't want to say any more about it, so I changed the subject.

"What's Deno Politis like?"

He shook his head as if warning me. "Deno is hard. He's nail-hard. Dino is much harder now than he was at the time of the McCann homicides. Then he was vulnerable to interrogation—or some other things maybe— much more so than he is now."

I asked if he knew where I could find him. When he said he had no idea, I saw him smile. The relief I was feeling must have shown on my face.

We talked for another hour reviewing the capture of the Lewingdons, and I asked his reaction to Howard Champ's remark that it wasn't the Columbus Police Department's work that had solved the case, but just a lucky break.

"That's very true," Steckman said. "I can't say that it never would have been solved [otherwise] because there is a possibility that Delaine Lewingdon, who was the only person who had the key—that was willing to turn the key—would have approached us or the county or somebody else again. But absent that ever happening, had Gary Lewingdon not been so greedy that he had to take those [Annick's] credit cards and use them and get caught, he'd still be out there wandering around with a .22."

"That's something that bothers me," I said. "How was it possible? Those two guys don't strike me as being extremely bright. The killings are kind of sloppy. How do they get away with something like that?"

Steckman looked me directly in the eye and shook his head. "Talk to Delaine Lewingdon—different picture. The person at the top that's telling them what to do is the brightest one of the three—Delaine. . . . In street smarts, she's got a Ph.D. Thaddeus was smarter than Gary, from the standpoint of refusing to let him take anything that could be traced back to the victims. . . .

"Delaine was concerned about her connection with the credit-card use, the fact that she knew where they came from. . . . She was convinced that she could be charged with being a conspirator in that homicide. . . . Probably an hour into the interrogation it came indirectly from her that she had been talking to an attorney for over a year. This attorney knew who the .22-caliber killers were. I could never get anything out of her that would make him be involved. But he was involved as far as telling her what to say when she went to the police. If she ever got caught, 'Here's what to say. Here's what to demand. You get your end of the deal before the policeman get anything.' And she knew it. It was almost like she'd practiced it."

"What's the attorney's name?"

"Wouldn't tell me what day it was until I guaranteed her what her position was. Now, I knew at that time that I didn't have the authority to plea-bargain, but it was important enough that we find out who was responsible for these homicides that I would put my job and my position and reputation on the line by doing that. And if a prosecutor at a later time resented it, then I was willing to go through the heavy cross-examination. I knew at that time what I was walking into . . . they're going to eat me alive. And they tried. But it never worked. And nobody to this day can prove any more on Delaine Lewingdon than we could prove on the day she walked in there. . . ."

I asked again, "Do you remember the name of the attorney Delaine was seeing?"

"I do, but I wouldn't disclose his name."

"I think I know who he is."

"I'm sure you do."

We talked awhile longer, and as the interview came to an end I asked him what I feared might be a delicate question. "How come you're no longer on Homicide? What are you doing on the Vice Squad?"

He shrugged as if he didn't want to talk about it. But when we were outside, with the tape recorder put away, he told me he felt he'd been transferred because of a political cover-up in another homicide case—not the .22's. He sounded bitter for the first time since I'd met him.

"How did you feel when you were transferred?"

"I felt my career was shot down."

"Do you think you'll ever get back to Homicide?"

"I wait for the day . . ."

Then as he got into his car, and I was turning to get into mine, he said, "You know I had both .22's— Thaddeus's Stoeger Luger and Gary's Sturm Ruger— and there was talk in the department about having them mounted as a sort of trophy. Like they have in collections of weapons used in notorious crimes . . ."

"What happened?" I asked.

He shrugged, and started his car. "People lost interest, I guess."

Then he drove away.

Thirteen

1

A few weeks later, when I'd almost given up all hope of any kind of breakthrough with Claudia, she turned to me and said, "The spirits now say I should have faith in you."

"I see. I appreciate their vote of confidence."

"I'm serious, Dan. They say you're not going to do anything to hurt me, and that I won't be put back in jail for anything you write about me."

"I've been telling you that for over a year."

"I'm going to trust you. I have to. This book means everything in the world to me."

She waited for my reaction, but I listened quietly, not trusting myself to speak.

Claudia studied my face as if evaluating me. "I know you're going to find this hard to believe, but I'm a superb actress. We actresses put together bits and pieces of things that happen around us, and then give a performance. That's where the details of my confession came from. When Deno Politis was arrested the sheriff's detectives questioned him about the .22's. After he got out, he came to our place and told Bobby everything he had learned about the bodies, the apartment, the clues. As I heard him talking I must have become convinced he did it out of jealous passion because Mickey was sleeping with Chrissie."

"Claudia, I've heard the tape of your confession, I find it hard to believe—"

She gripped my wrist to silence me. "I'm not finished. There's more. You don't know this, but after the bodies were found the word got around on the street about what the death scene looked like. The things I heard were burned into my brain. And when Howard Champ was questioning me, leading me, giving me hints, all those things came together with the things Deno talked about, and I acted out a fantasy of myself as a murderer. Dan, you know I'm incapable of hurting anyone. I can't even swat a fly."

I agreed I didn't believe she could ever have killed anyone, but I had heard that explanation before, and I didn't buy it.

"All right," I said, "then I'd better interview Deno."

"Oh, no!" she gasped, and gripped my wrist. "He's dangerous. He once killed a man. I spoke to his former girlfriend the other day, and she said he never would talk to you. She told me he's forgiven me, and she said she would meet you. But you can't talk to him."

Driving home that night, I mulled it over in my mind. The thought of tracking down someone as tough as Politis worried me, but if I was going to understand what had really been going on in Claudia's life at the time she implicated him and Bobby, Claudia's point of view wasn't enough.

Despite Claudia's and Steckman's warnings, I had to try.

I decided to approach Politis's girlfriend first, so that if I did find him later and he turned me down, he would not be able to prevent her from talking to me.

In September 1983, I finally reached Elsie May Benson and she agreed to see me. We arranged for an interview at her apartment on the southwest side of Columbus. When I pulled into the parking area outside her place, I just missed a pair of legs belonging to someone doing a repair job underneath a car. I parked, stepped over the tools strewn on the walk, and pressed the bell to her apartment.

Tall, buxom, and attractive, Elsie May welcomed me inside. She seemed eager to cooperate and spoke freely about her memory of events surrounding the murders.

She had met Claudia four years before the murders when they had both been working at a cocktail lounge called Sangria North. Two years later Elsie May met Deno—and started dating him—while he was living with Claudia and Bobby Novatney.

"At first, I just fell head over heels for him," she said. "I had a crush—a big one. We started living together, and it was a very stormy relationship, very."

"What do you mean by *stormy*?" I asked.

"We fought a lot," she said. "He's very bull-headed. He's gotta have things his way . . . you know, very independent. We just went through a whole heck of a lot. I guess gradually I started drifting away from him. I just couldn't take it. We lived together—off and on—for maybe three years."

"What's your relationship now?"

"Just friends. He's trying to help me get my car fixed. We see each other every once in a while. He comes over here from time to time."

"I saw someone out front under a car as I came in," I said. "You don't mean—"

"Oh, no. He's not out there now." She laughed. "I wouldn't do that to you."

I laughed with her. "All right, if as you say he's bull-headed and the relationship was stormy, what did you see in him?"

"I think it was just a physical thing. 'Cause he's such a big, mean-looking guy."

"Is that what you like?" I asked, teasing her. "Big, mean-looking guys?"

She giggled. "I guess. Back then. I don't know, I was really attracted to him. But he's jealous. Very, very, very jealous, and I just couldn't handle it."

I asked her opinion of Claudia.

"I like Claudia," she said, "but she's not all there."

"What leads you to that conclusion?"

"She'll say one thing, and then a minute later she'll

contradict herself. I think she lives in a fantasy. But she helped me out a couple of times. Deno and I had a hell of a fight one night. I was drinking and I went over there and she helped me by talking to me."

"Did Deno ever talk to you about the McCann killings?"

"Well, he knew McCann and Christine Herdman. And he's interested in that kind of stuff anyway. He was driving around and wanted to show me Mickey McCann's house. I didn't really care, but he wanted to show me the house on Ongaro Drive. I guess the police had been following us that night, because they asked me why Deno drove past McCann's house. It was that very night they arrested him."

I asked how she felt when Claudia, Novatney, and Deno were arrested for the McCann murders.

"I just couldn't believe it. I was shocked. I knew he'd been with me every night around that time and he couldn't have done it."

"So you were Deno's alibi?"

"Yeah."

"Did they take you in for questioning?"

"The day they arrested Claudia—before Deno was arrested—they came to Dyer's Trailer Court where I was living. Deno wasn't there. They showed me their badges and said they wanted to know if I'd go down and talk to them about some traffic tickets Deno had. I said, 'Yeah, if I can help you any I'll go down with ya.' Then on the way going down they told me they were homicide detectives and I got to thinking why did they want to talk to me about traffic tickets. And when I get down there they tell me, 'We've got Claudia Yasko in the next room and she's confessed to the McCann murders along with Deno and Ray.' My mouth just dropped. I was shocked."

She said the deputies kept her there for eight hours, questioning her about her relationship with Deno, what they'd been doing, where they'd been. "At one point they asked me if I'd like to go in and talk to Claudia, and I said sure."

I hadn't heard that before. "What did you say to her?"

"The first thing I said to her—I'll never forget this—

I went in there and I said, 'Claudia, what in the world is goin' on? What have you done?' and she says, 'Elsie May, I don't know why I did it.'"

"Were those her words? *'I don't know why I did it'*?"

"Yes, and she had this faraway look in her eyes—you know, scary."

Elsie May said she had been called to testify before the grand jury and told them about the time Deno had taken her to visit Novatney and Claudia, and they'd been talking about the things they'd heard on the street about the murders. "Over and over again I swore to Deno that from the moment I walked in there I said to the grand jury that he didn't do it, but Deno always blamed me for testifying."

At that moment our interview was interrupted when the front door opened and in walked a tall, muscular, sandy-haired man wearing jeans and a grease-spattered sweatshirt. He looked at the two of us sitting on the couch, at the tape recorder on the coffee table, and his heavy-lidded hazel eyes stared at me for a moment filled with menace.

"Just wanna get something to drink," he said, walking through to the kitchen.

Elsie May's eyes opened wide with fear, and I knew before she mouthed: *"It's him,"* that the legs I had seen sticking out from under the car had indeed belonged to Deno Politis.

As he passed through the living room on his way out, I decided it would be best to tell him who I was and why I was there. I stood up and he glared at me for all the world like a hungry lion. All I could think was that, finally, Daniel had blundered into Deno's den.

"I'm Professor Keyes," I said, using the title as a shield and trying to ignore the pounding in my chest.

His eyes flicked from Elsie May's to mine in an unspoken question.

I said, "I'm writing a book about Claudia Yasko, and—"

His glance changed into one of disdain, and all he said was, "Hah!" and stalked out, slamming the door behind him.

"I'm sorry if I've caused you any problem," I whispered to Elsie May. "I couldn't have known—"

"Well, usually if he comes to work on my car he doesn't get here till eight o'clock."

"You think he's sore?" I laughed nervously. "I don't want to get him angry at me."

She shook her head. "He just won't talk to you. I told you he's bull-headed."

I decided it was best to leave at that point. I wound up the interview, packed my papers and tape recorder, and said good-bye. "You going to be all right?" I asked.

She shrugged. "You can come out again anytime."

When I got outside, I saw his legs sticking out from under the car again. I headed towards my own car parked beside it, put my bag and recorder into the trunk, and stood there a moment thinking about what had happened. If ever I was going to have a chance to interview Politis, I had to approach him now. Foolhardy, stupid, dangerous, but I had to try.

I knelt beside the car he was under, bent my head, and called out to him, "Deno, I just want to let you know one thing. If you want to tell your side of the story—let the world know what you suffered—I'd be pleased to talk to you."

He slid out from under the car, took a rag out of his pocket, and wiped the grease off his hands.

Talking rapidly to keep him off guard, I said, "I'll tell you this. After today, I won't make any attempt to get in touch with you. But if you want the truth of what happened to you told—instead of just Claudia's version and Detective Champ's version—you have my promise that I'll include that in the book. Since Bobby Novatney is dead, you're the only one who can help balance out Claudia's memories of what happened."

"I always called him Ray," he said.

"I beg your pardon?"

"Ray was Bobby Novatney's middle name. I was one of the few people who called him Ray."

"I see . . ."

"Are you wired?" he asked.

I patted my chest. "Oh, no. I put my tape recorder into the car."

"Well, if I ever talk to anyone it won't be just for my health."

"I understand, of course—"

"Because nobody knows what I know," he said.

To my astonishment, he talked about how they had come after him the night of his arrest with a sheriff's car trailing him, and then flashing bright lights into his eyes, blinding him, expecting him to run so they could shoot him. Claudia was the cause of Ray's death, he said. Politis talked emotionally for about three minutes. This tough, taciturn man, who had been silent for all these years, really wanted to pour it out.

"I think your side of it should be told," I said again. "So the world won't think—"

"I don't give a shit what the world thinks."

"Of course not," I said.

"You got a card?"

"What do you mean?"

"A business card. With your name and phone number."

I dug into my wallet, came up with one of my cards, and handed it to him. "As I said, Deno, I won't call you or make any attempt to contact you. If you want to talk, you can phone me collect anytime."

"I'm gonna check you out," he said.

"Yes," I said. "Of course. But don't forget if you decide, call collect."

I got into my car and sped away, my adrenaline still working. Maybe I should have offered to buy him a beer somewhere in a local bar. No, that would have been foolish. I had no idea if he was the type who got violent after a few drinks. On the other hand, I had no way of knowing if he'd ever call me, and after what I'd said, I couldn't ever try to contact him.

After a few weeks, I gave up all hope of ever interviewing Deno.

2

I called an out-of-town attorney, not originally for an interview, but to ask if he knew the whereabouts of the statement Delaine had given to Steckman. A verbatim transcript of the tape existed, I knew, because in one of the trial transcripts a prosecutor refers to it, saying to a

defense attorney, "Well, you're holding it in your hand."
I had an official paraphrase of it, with indirect quotes,
but I wanted to verify it with the original.

The attorney told me that at the prosecution's request, the trial judge had sealed the Delaine/Steckman
interview along with other documents. That judge had
since died, he said, and suggested I ask another judge to
unseal the records. I considered it but discarded the
idea. The paraphrase would do the job.

Our conversation finished, I was about to hang up,
when he let drop the comment that Delaine had more to
do with Gary's arrest than anyone knew.

Then, unexpectedly, he kept talking.

"In fact," he said, "I was the one who told Gary to
rob the Woolco Department Store as a way of getting
himself caught."

"He *wanted* to be caught?" I asked, unable to hide
my astonishment.

"Oh, yes . . ."

At that point I suspected he was the attorney Steckman had been referring to—the one whose name he
wouldn't disclose to me—not at all the one I had suspected originally.

The man obviously wanted to talk about his role in
the case.

He agreed to meet me for a taped interview, but
when I drove over a hundred miles to meet him, he didn't
show up. That happened twice. After that, I couldn't
reach him and whenever I got through to his secretary,
she said he was in court or taking depositions. Though
she assured me he was not avoiding me, she had no idea
when he would be available.

Twenty long-distance phone calls later, I reached
him at home at ten o'clock one night. He was just having
his dinner, he said. Could I call back in half an hour? For
the next two hours his phone was busy, and I imagined
he'd taken it off the hook. I kept trying.

Finally, I heard ringing and he answered, but now he
seemed reluctant to talk. When I offered to use a pseudonym instead of his real name, he told me what he knew. . . .

On Saturday evening, December 9, Harry Boles said,
five days after the shooting of Joseph Annick, he had
been hosting a party at his rural home. The house was

filled with twenty-five friends and professional associates, mostly defense attorneys, prosecutors, and a judge. The phone rang at about eight o'clock.

It was an agitated Delaine Lewingdon.

"This is a bad time, Dee," Boles said. "I've got a house full of guests."

"It's got to be now," she insisted. "I've told you what this is all about. You sent me to the Kirkersville Police Chief and then you said to listen to him and go to Sheriff's Deputy Paul Short, but no one's done a goddamned thing."

Boles, who had known Delaine for many years, felt he understood her pretty well. "Why don't you come into my office tomorrow?"

"No, Harry. My husband's here with me, and he wants to talk to you. He wants to turn himself in, but he's scared Charles will kill me and the kids. Talk to him, Harry. He'll listen to you."

"All right, Dee," Boles said. "Hold on. I'll hang up here and take it in my den." He moved quickly into his den and picked up the phone. "Dee? I can talk now. Put him on."

He heard muffled conversation and then a soft voice said, "Mr. Boles, this is Gary Lewingdon. Dee has talked to you about this situation. What do you think I should do?"

"You really want to turn yourself in?"

"Yes. It's the only way to stop it."

"And what she has told me is true?"

"Every word of it."

Boles thought for a moment. "I know you're both worried that if you turn yourself in, your brother will take it out on Dee and her children."

"That's right."

"I've got an idea. I read in the papers that Joseph Annick's wallet was missing with his credit cards and driver's license. Do you have it?"

There was a moment's hesitation, and then Lewingdon said, "Yes."

"This is what I'd do, if I were you. I'd go out to department stores and use Annick's credit cards to buy things—Christmas presents for the children. Keep at it. Go from store to store until someone catches you using a

stolen credit card. That way, it will look to Charles as if
you did something dumb and got caught. He won't suspect you're turning yourself in, and he won't hurt Dee or
the children. When you're arrested, and they let you use
the phone, call me. Now let me talk to Dee again."

Delaine took the phone, and Boles said, "Go with
him, and stay with him to make sure he does it. Until he
and Charles are in custody, you and the children aren't
safe."

Harry Boles told me that what he had done was
probably enough to get him disbarred. As an officer of
the court, it had been his duty to turn Gary Lewingdon in
to the authorities. But, he said, he knew damned well
that what he had been told by Delaine would never make
a case against either of the brothers. There was not
enough to indict anybody. And she had told him enough
about Gary's brother Thaddeus Charles to put his own
life and his wife's in jeopardy, if Thaddeus ever discovered that he knew.

When Delaine had first come to him and told him
she was certain Charles was the .22-caliber killer, he
hadn't believed her. But unlike Chief Wes Anderson and
Lieutenant Paul Short, he gave Delaine credit for being
no fool. She was a tough, streetwise woman.

"Knowing Delaine," he said, "I feel it's unlikely that
she was an innocent bystander. Delaine Lewingdon was
always a woman to take seriously."

After I hung up and checked to make sure that my telephone taping mechanism had worked properly, I sat
there limp for a few moments. Neither Steckman nor
anyone else connected with the investigation had known
that the night before Gary Lewingdon was picked up, his
wife had called her attorney and set in motion the plan
for the arrest of the .22-caliber killers. Catching the .22's
hadn't been a lucky accident at all, as Champ had said,
nor just greed, as Steckman had said. Gary had used Annick's credit cards on purpose because his wife's attorney had talked him into it.

A lucky phone call had filled in one of the missing
pieces of the .22-caliber puzzle. What I needed now was
the same kind of luck with Claudia.

3

When I called Russ Million in Austin, Texas, on November 10, 1983, to talk about his recollections of working on the case for *Playboy*, one of the people I asked about was Deno Politis.

"You know, he's a real rough guy," Million said. "Apparently, everybody knew that. Officers were telling me, 'Be careful with this guy.'"

"Did you ever meet him?"

"Well, Dye put him in touch with us through some other guy and we were going to meet him someplace at four. Then he calls and says, 'Well, I can't make it at four. It'll be more like seven.' And I said, 'Well, call me, I'll be at Dye's house.' And he calls me at seven and he wants me to meet him at some bar in the Bottoms at midnight."

Million chuckled. "At that point, I said, 'Look, I want to talk to you if you want to talk to me.' But I told him, 'I'll meet you at McDonald's at ten o'clock in the morning, but I'm not meeting you in the Bottoms—on your turf—at midnight. No way.'"

"What happened?" I asked.

"We never got to meet him."

"He wasn't buying that?" I said.

"No."

When Deno Politis phoned me early in January 1984, four months after he'd walked in on my interview with his girlfriend, I was caught off guard.

"You still interested in talking to me?" he asked me. I said I was.

"Well, maybe we can get together," he said, "but I'm not promising anything."

Recalling Million's caution, I was determined not to meet Deno at midnight at a bar in the Bottoms. "Where are you calling from?" I asked him.

"The main branch of the Columbus Public Library."

I figured that was where he had gone to check me out as he had said he would. "Hey, that sounds like a great place to meet," I said. When I told him I'd never been to the Columbus Public Library, he described the location and agreed to meet me the following Thursday at six o'clock.

"There's some benches in the main lobby," he said. "I'll find you there."

After he hung up, I tried to imagine what it would be like trying to interview Deno Politis in a library. If it turned out to be awkward, he might suggest we go somewhere else. What the hell, I thought, if a seasoned private investigator like Million wouldn't confront Deno on his own turf, I sure as hell had no intentions of doing it.

I phoned the Columbus librarian, told her I was working on a book, and asked if there was a private conference room I could use to interview an informant.

There was, she said, and I could.

I drove to Columbus an hour before our appointed time on a freezing January 12, 1984, to scout the location and find a safe place to park. I checked out the room, and when I learned that the library closed at ten, I asked one of the guards to look in on me a few minutes before closing time. At six o'clock, I went downstairs to meet Deno, telling myself not to be too disappointed if he didn't come.

He surprised me.

Deno showed up looking well-groomed and neatly dressed, wearing a full-length black leather coat. When I took him up in the elevator to the private conference room, he looked at me quizzically. "For someone who don't know this place, you sure got around fast."

My hands were sweating.

For nearly half an hour Deno wouldn't let me turn on the tape recorder. Suspicious, nervous, demanding, he wouldn't let me touch it before he laid down a number of conditions for the interview. First, he insisted that I not use the real name of his girlfriend. I agreed, and we decided I would use the name Elsie May Benson.

I would have to use everything he told me, complete and without editing, he insisted. I told him that was impossible because as the writer, I had to make the decisions about what to write and what to cut.

He told me he had arranged for a friend of his to meet us, and before I could tape he would wait for his advice.

As we waited, he asked what kind of things I wanted to know. I mentioned that some things in Claudia's confession dovetailed with things Mary Slatzer had told me and clarified parts of the Lewingdon confessions. I wanted to check some of them out.

"Like what?"

"For example, Claudia tells Champ that before the murders you and Bobby went to case the McCann house because you planned to burglarize it."

"That's right," he said. "We did."

"And Mary Slatzer said that a week before Mickey was murdered someone broke in through the basement window. That was why Mickey had it boarded up and why—according to the Lewingdons' confessions—they couldn't go in, as they'd planned, through the basement window but had to pry open the garage-side door."

"Yeah?" Politis said.

"So you say you and Bobby went out there. Did you break in through the basement?"

"That's right. We busted in to rob the place."

My fingers were itching to turn on the tape recorder. I had no assurance he would repeat this for the record. I told myself the important thing was to keep him talking.

"Tell me about it," I said.

"I'll tell you. You know what I'll tell you? Nothing! Why the hell should I talk to you at all?"

"What do you mean?"

"That crap about me and Bobby going into Mickey's house—I just said that to see where you'd go with it. And you just proved to me that you got your mind all made up. You showed me you think I'm a common criminal."

I was stunned. He had laid a trap for me and I'd walked into it. I apologized. I rationalized. I explained. I was damned embarrassed. I don't remember what I said to him, but I didn't want him angry at me, and I wanted to keep him from walking out.

Luckily, when Deno's friend finally showed up, he encouraged Deno to stay and talk to me. Even so, every time I turned on the tape recorder, Deno made me shut it off. I toyed with the idea of interviewing him off tape, but decided I needed the protection of having his actual words in case he ever changed his mind and denied his statements.

He demanded that I send him the tapes to listen to. I promised to send him copies. He asked for huge sums of money and a percentage of the book's royalties. I told him it didn't work that way—that I never paid for interviews. When all of his arguments and demands were either explained away or met, he finally let me turn on the recorder.

"All right," I said, beginning the interview as I usually did, "tell me a little bit about your background. Where are you from?"

He looked at the recorder. "Is that on?"

"Yes, you see that little red light is—"

"Turn it off."

I did and he told me he didn't want to talk about his background. We would limit ourselves to the events connected with Ray and Claudia and his own arrest for the triple homicide.

"Okay," I said, turning it on again, "tell me how you first found out you were going to be arrested."

"Before this came down," he said, "when they first pulled Claudia in on it, her lawyer, Lew Dye, came on television. I seen it with my own eyes. He was even accusing me of being the trigger-man. And this is why I say Lew Dye was in it for the publicity."

He glared at the red light on the recorder and shook his head. "Right after that they went out and picked up Elsie May. They had her trying to describe guns I had in my possession—which she had no knowledge of at all—and they was pinpointing a gun, showed her. 'Could this be it?' 'Was it this one?' There's a gun that I gave a friend to keep for me, which was a .32-caliber pistol, they had her describe as a German Luger . . . that this was the [murder] gun . . . The morning of the indictment they reminded her of the gun she pointed out, and they told her if she didn't repeat this that she was going to go to Marysville for perjury. They used her in front of the [grand] jury on account of she was a sane person, whereas they could tell that Claudia was stone nuts."

I finally got him to tell me a few things about himself: born and raised in Columbus, west of the Scioto River in the Bottoms, Deno admitted to having a reputation as a tough street-fighter. After he divorced his wife, he'd tried to build a new life. He was doing well in his home-siding business. He had his truck and his tools, and the jobs came up often enough so that he could send money for his eleven-year-old daughter and help support his aging father—the only two people in the world whose opinion of him mattered.

"I never trusted or cared for anyone else," he said. "The rest of the world can go to hell for all I care."

He told me about the lamb-chop theft, embarrassment showing clearly in his face. He'd been drinking too much after getting paid for a home-siding job, happy about having two checks totaling eleven hundred dollars in his wallet. The way he told it was similar to the way Tony Rich had described the episode, but listening to Deno, it seemed obvious it had been an impulse about which he was still upset.

Then he shook his head. "I don't want this put down."

"This is a matter of public record," I said defensively, "because you were arrested for it."

"No . . . that's embarrassing. I even tried to pay for it but they wouldn't let me." He pointed at the recorder accusingly. "You snuck that thing back on, didn't you?"

"No, I turned it on before. I didn't sneak it on. I showed you I had it on when we were filling in."

I appealed to his friend for corroboration, that I had openly showed him when I had turned the machine on. Fortunately, the friend nodded, Deno's anger subsided, and he told me the rest of the story.

"It was foolish," he said, shaking his head when he finished. "That's more embarrassing than this damned [murder] charge."

I asked him to tell me about meeting and dating Christine Herdman.

"I met Christine Herdman one afternoon in a bar, about three years before her death, in the Point Lounge. We was sitting there, there wasn't too much going on. We got acquainted, and I asked her what she was doing later. We were going to make a date for later on that night. Then the subject was brought up, 'What are we gonna do in the meantime?' I asked her, I says, 'Would you like to go do it?' She says, 'That sounds like a good idea.' So we went and done it."

"What did she look like?" I asked.

"Very beautiful build. Beautiful complexion. Long dark hair. Face was, uh, rough look, hard look. Medium height."

He'd been out with her three times, he said.

When he talked about his arrest for the murders, the anger showed in his face. "That was after ten days of harassment, being followed, knowing that I was going to be arrested for it."

"How did you know that?"

"I knowed it because Claudia was already arrested, and they told Elsie May I was going to be arrested. They made sure I knew it. And by being followed. I even hid my truck, and my tools got ripped off. That made me mad, so I didn't care . . ."

They took him to jail, and booked him for murder.

It had turned out that he'd had a pretty good alibi. Deno had been playing cards that night, with about eleven people, including a bar owner, his wife and children, and one police officer. I could see why the judge had let him out on his own recognizance.

"What went through your mind?"

"It made me angry. . . . When I did that [gave them his alibi] Howard Champ slammed a book down and said, 'Why wouldn't you tell us that with your lawyer a couple of days ago?' And I told him, 'Cause that takes money, to get a lawyer, and I didn't have no reason to do it.' And he says, 'Well, O'Grady says we got enough evidence to try you on, and I've done my work. I'm going home.'"

"What were you feeling in the county jail?"

He looked at me. "Well, okay now, this is where your work comes in about the mind, right? It took me three days to realize I wasn't dreaming. I felt what it was like to die in the death chair three times . . . waking up full of sweat . . . dreaming of going to the chair. See, now this is where I feel like a crybaby. I don't like to be that way."

"That's all right," I said. "It's important."

"I worried about my child. I worried about my aging dad's health . . . how he was taking it. As far as my close friends, I knew they wouldn't believe I did it. I even asked myself if I was drunk and did do it . . . not remembering."

I asked him about the polygraph.

"The night before I took it," he said, "I couldn't sleep thinking about it. Then when I did take it, I passed all the questions except one. They said I'd been in Mickey McCann's house at the time of the deaths.

"I thought I was going to have a heart attack," Deno said. "I was thirty-one years old, and a strong man, and I had to be helped . . . I was weak . . ."

Deno poured out his memories and his bitterness for two full hours. At one point, he said, he finally realized why the sheriff's cruiser had driven up to his trailer that night about an hour before the deputies came to arrest him. They were setting him up.

His friend, who had been listening quietly, occasionally encouraging Deno to talk, now expressed his own opinion about what Deno had just said. "I often suspected—you know I was a friend of his at the time— that the whole purpose of their surveillance was to catch him . . . to get him to retaliate in some manner on some petty offense and shoot him. [They've got] Claudia's testimony. He's dead. Can't defend himself. They had him. Case is closed."

"That's what they tried to do," Deno agreed excitedly. "That's the reason for the headlights coming on at night. See, I was drunk, and I give them the—"

"They knew he was aggressive," his friend went on, "especially towards police. And I think they were trying to set him up. It's just an assumption—"

"That's right," Deno insisted. "That's what they did."

"To clarify," I said. "You feel they wanted you to run and if they shot you down they had Claudia's statement—"

Deno slammed the table. "That's what they wanted."

"Let's put it this way," his friend said. "When they arrested the people that actually did it, they didn't follow them around for a week—drive by their trailers. They had every law enforcement man in the county picking up this man's history and as soon as his credit card showed up . . . that was it. . . ."

Whether Deno had felt this at the time of his arrest and indictment, I had no way of telling. But, obviously, in the years since, both of them had become convinced that the sheriff's deputies had planned to make him the scapegoat.

I wished I knew more about Deno's articulate friend but decided against pushing my luck by asking him questions about himself.

I went over passages in Claudia's confession in which she'd described him holding the gun and killing people. I wanted his reaction.

"It's— It's— You know— It's outta sight," he said.

"I just want to know how you feel. Your reaction."

"How I feel—how I feel—it's the police work of our fine Sheriff's Department . . ." he said bitterly. "The *Dispatch* was even in on that stuff too."

"Tell me."

"Just the way they worded it . . . They convicted me before—you know—the way they wouldn't let me say my story when I went to 'em."

"Tell me about going to the *Dispatch*."

"After we was out, Claudia was interviewed. Ray was interviewed. *But I wasn't interviewed.* I called the *Dispatch* when I was out on bond. There was things that . . . I didn't like, that the paper was still mentioning, that wasn't true. And I called the paper up, and I asked to speak to the person that was writing these things. Well, she wasn't in and the guy says, 'Who is this?' and I says, 'Well, I want to talk to her private.' He says, 'Tell me who you are and what you want to talk to her for?' I says, 'This is Deno Politis, and I want to let her know how those sons of bitches really arrested us—that you're not printing down.'"

He shook his head, as if still frustrated by the memory. "So the next day I check in with my lawyer—call him up. I had to check with my lawyer every day, okay? He asks me, 'What's goin' on?' I says, 'Nothing.' He says, 'Anything happening?' I says, 'No.' And he says, 'You stupid fucker, you're gonna end up in prison or you're gonna end up dead.' And he repeated back [to me] the exact words I told that newspaper person."

It was obvious to Politis what had happened. "So the only thing there was—the person I talked to had called the prosecutors and the prosecutors called my lawyer and told him, 'Keep your boy straight.'"

As he recalled the events, his anger was so strong, I began to feel angry too.

"What were your feelings when the Lewingdons were arrested?"

"My feelings was bitter towards the police department because if they reacted the way they should've seven other people would still be alive."

"The police department?"

"Uh, the Sheriff's Department," he said, correcting himself, "not the police department. I don't feel bitter towards the police department at all. It was just the Sheriff's Department . . . and the prosecutors . . . because they were the ones that masterminded it."

Deno smiled, and when I asked him what he was thinking, he said he remembered that he had been so happy when George C. Smith lost the election for Ohio attorney general in 1978, that he spent his last few dollars to send him a telegram of congratulations.

The door opened and the library guard looked in to tell us the building was closing.

When I asked Deno how he felt towards Claudia now, he shrugged. "I seen Claudia after that," he said, "and I told her I didn't have a grudge against her. Ray did. Ray didn't understand. Ray hated her. I kept telling him that she didn't do it. She's sick. She didn't know what she was doing. The police did it."

The interview was over, and the three of us walked down the stairs together and through the lobby. Before I pushed through the front door to go out into the icy January night, Deno reached over and straightened out my trench-coat collar and then moved ahead of me and held the door open for me. As we walked off in opposite directions to our cars in the library parking lot, he turned, smiled, and waved good-bye.

Fourteen

1

From the beginning, Claudia had avoided talking about her childhood and adolescence. Most of it, she insisted, she couldn't remember.

I later found out (from a young social worker with the public defender's office who recalled having been in junior high school with Claudia) that because Claudia was so much taller than all the boys, and had developed full breasts much earlier than the other girls, she was in a constant state of embarrassment. Her short attention span and her unpredictable lapses of memory led her schoolmates to mock her and call her retarded.

I had already met and talked to Claudia's mother, but Claudia's older brother, David, absolutely refused to see me. According to other members of the family, there had been a break between Claudia and David in 1970, when after her nineteenth birthday she had quit high school and gone to live with him near the Army base at Fort Bragg, North Carolina. That was all anyone would say about David.

A few days after my interview with Deno, George Yasko, Claudia's father—who had been divorced from Martha shortly after Claudia turned eighteen—agreed to talk to me. I arranged to pick him up in front of the downtown Columbus apartment building in which he lived with his aged mother.

The six-foot-two now semiretired shoe salesman squeezed himself into my compact car and suggested we drive to an east-side bar where we could talk.

Referring to Claudia's confession and arrest, he insisted he'd never been told much about Claudia's problems. "Martha and I were this way," he said. "I tried not to burden her by telling her bad news, and she reciprocated by not telling me any bad news."

As far as he'd known, Claudia was a very quiet child, and it was difficult to tell whether or not she was happy. She loved to draw and she loved music.

"Claudia never did anything memorable when she was growing up," he said. "In other words, she never broke a window. She never spilled ink on the rug, or anything like that."

As far as Claudia's mental condition was concerned, he said, "Sometimes she has her light on and sometimes it's off." He had gotten to the point now where it was difficult for him to accept what Claudia said. "There's such a gray area there, that I can't pick out and say this is black and this is white. There's no way I can tell anymore. At the beginning I believed everything she said."

"Was Claudia a beautiful child?"

"She was a nice-looking girl . . . but I always have to preface all my remarks," he said, "with the fact that she was tall. And that bothered her when she was in school. Like when you're nine years old, and you're in the third or fourth grade, and you're a good head taller than *any* boy . . . it's a problem. We had a miserable time fitting her in shoes and in clothing appropriate for her age. At the age of two or two and a half, I was already having to buy her women's size shoes."

On the other hand, dark-eyed, black-haired Nancy, he said, being only five-foot-two, had been a surprise to him and to everyone else in his tall family. When I asked him what he thought about that, George said that Nancy—seeing how Claudia suffered towering over everybody in school—had prayed to be short, and her prayers had been answered.

George paused as if deciding whether or not to say

something, and finally leaned across the table confidentially. "Claudia has fantasized two different things. I don't know whether she told you . . . Incest?"

I didn't answer. I was beginning to see why Claudia couldn't talk about her childhood.

"Now this is fantasy," he said. "We discussed this. Martha said she knew it wasn't true on *my* part. And I said, well, it certainly wasn't. You know, it wasn't true. And Nancy said that she was interviewed about that some time ago. She knew it wasn't true."

"What was the other thing?" I asked.

"I'm trying to think. . . . Oh, she [Claudia] said that Martha was a prostitute. Well, that was completely erroneous. I got that from Martha, and somebody else told me that. . . . At about the same time, Claudia was going around telling the police that I was with the Mafia, so they'd better watch out."

We both laughed.

"Yeah," he said, "and that goes over like a lead balloon. Luckily . . ." he said, pulling out of his wallet a card from the Fraternal Order of Police. "I got that from Number Nine, and that's signed by Dewey Stokes, who's president. That's Ohio, and I also have the national. I don't think one out of a hundred police carry the national. So they kinda *know* me, and know that stuff isn't true."

"Claudia never told me you were with the Mafia, or that Martha had been a prostitute."

He nodded, relieved. "I was always a perfectionist," he said, "and I've tried to bring up my children to do the best possible job. We have a saying in the family: *He who makes the mess, cleans up the mess.* And we carried that over to everything."

When I interviewed Nancy a couple of days later, she said she felt most of Claudia's problems stemmed from the fact that Claudia had "stronger feelings [towards David] than brother and sister, and when he didn't reciprocate, the problems began."

Claudia's problems with her sexuality, Nancy suggested, might also have stemmed from a time when Claudia was in her teens and had worked in the neighborhood pharmacy. She had phoned home one day, Nancy said, hysterical, saying she had been sexually

abused by someone who had come into the store—
someone she knew.

Nancy told me that at fourteen, she herself had become pregnant by a classmate and felt she couldn't deal
with her own mother's ultimatums. She had gone to live
with the Steckmans, she said, confiding to Mrs. Steckman that she would never have an abortion or give the
child up. That was when Bill Steckman had offered to
adopt her and her child and had become her "Pop."

As I interviewed Claudia's parents and her sister, I
began to understand why she didn't want to talk about
them. Claudia had apparently grown up in a tense and
complex household, and the roots of her problems went
deep.

The following Thursday, I visited Claudia for our regular
session, surprised as she greeted me at the door smiling
slyly.

"What . . . ?" I asked, taking off my coat.

"I got a call the other night."

"From your spiritual adviser?"

She shook her head. "Elsie May Benson."

I slumped onto the couch. "Oh, no!"

"She thinks it's very funny. We had a good laugh
about Deno not wanting you to use her name and your
giving her a pseudonym—*Elsie May Benson*? At least
Australia was unusual."

"I wonder why he told her."

She shrugged. "To show her who's boss, I guess."

She offered me coffee, but I declined. My nerves
were edgy enough without making things worse. My goal
for tonight was to get her to recall what Nancy had told
me about Claudia's experience at the pharmacy.

When she came back, cradling the coffee mug in her
palms, I asked her about it.

She frowned, shook her head. "I don't know what
you're talking about."

"But Nancy said—"

She slammed the mug on the table, splattering coffee. "I can't imagine what she might be referring to."

By the emotion with which she reacted, I guessed
she had blocked the painful experience deep in her memory.

"Would you hate a man who abused you sexually?"

"I couldn't hate anybody. I'm not a vengeful person."

"Claudia, I believe that."

"I didn't even hate the three men who gang-raped me."

I knew what she was talking about.

Although Claudia's psychiatrist, Dr. Stinson, had refused to meet me, leaving me to portray him only through court testimony and her memory, Claudia had—after many delays—obtained and turned over to me her medical records. I recalled the entry in which Dr. Stinson had written:

"At the age of sixteen [sic: actually at nineteen] *she had moved to North Carolina* [to be] *with her brother who was in the Army at the time. While in North Carolina, Claudia was raped by three GI's . . ."*

I had avoided bringing it up, and this was her first allusion to the rape.

"Will you tell me about it, Claudia?"

She stared at me as if trying to see behind my eyes.

"Why do you want to know about it?"

"Because I'm searching for events in your life that will help me understand you."

"I already told you about it."

"No, you didn't."

"I did. I remember telling you. Why do you want to hear it again?"

"Claudia, when I saw that notation in your medical record, I was astonished. I knew nothing about a gang rape."

"I told you."

It went on like that for almost an hour, when finally I said: "All right. Have it your own way. You told me, and I need to hear it again."

"Why?"

"Because I can't find any tape with that on it, and I don't remember the details. I need it, because it could explain something about your personality and your behavior. Tell me."

She glared me at suspiciously, but she finally described what had happened to her one night in the summer of 1970, after she had moved into a mobile home

near the Army base at Fort Bragg, with her brother
David and his friend Paul from Indianapolis. . . .

Earlier in the day, she recalled, the temperature had
been 104 or 105 degrees, and the air conditioner hadn't
been working. Though she knew her brother was on duty
that night, when the banging on the door woke her, she
thought Paul was asleep in the rear of the trailer and
wondered why he didn't get up to see what was going on.
She didn't learn until later that he'd gone to the enlisted
men's club to escape the heat.

She staggered out of bed, went to the door, and
asked who it was.

"It's an emergency," a man's voice said, and for a
moment she thought it was David. "I've got to use the
phone to call for help."

She opened the door.

Three men in Army uniforms burst into the trailer.
One grabbed her from behind, the second one punched
her in the face. When she started to scream, the third
one—she thought she recognized his face—turned up the
stereo loud. Then they held her down on the floor and
took turns raping her. Each time she struggled, one of
them would hit her again. She knew they were high on
drugs and alcohol. The first one threw up all over her,
and from then on, whenever she heard or read about
someone being raped, it would bring back the odor of
whiskey-smelling vomit. And whenever she smelled vomit,
she relived the rape.

When they were done with her and left she heard the
sound of a car starting up and driving away. She grabbed
a tablecloth, wrapped it around her, and stumbled
across the path to where her brother's sergeant lived.

He took her to the hospital and sent for her brother.
David nearly went berserk when she told him what had
happened. He reported it to the Military Police, and the
next day she gave a statement to the officer in charge.

It wasn't hard to find the rapists. Neighbors, who
had complained about the loud stereo, described the
three G.I.'s who had run out of her trailer and identified
the make and year of their car. Claudia described the one
who had looked familiar. Witnesses at the enlisted men's
E/4–E/9 club had seen the three men together.

They were arrested, and Claudia was brought in to

sign the complaint. But when she heard that because she
was under twenty-one, the gang rape might result in the
death penalty, she was horrified. As much as they had
hurt her, she didn't want to be the cause of their dying in
the gas chamber. She knew some women might demand
the ultimate revenge, but she couldn't do that.

She refused to press charges.

The officer in charge of the investigation tried to
convince her it was the right thing to do, but she shook
her head and said, "Forget it. That's not the way to handle this. Somebody should talk to them. They need help
. . . counseling . . . they're sick. I don't want them to die
for what they did to me because I have never believed in
the death penalty."

Then she looked up at me, shaking her head. "You
know, when those guys knocked on my door and asked to
come in and use the phone, I must have forgotten that we
didn't even have one."

Poor, mixed-up, vulnerable Claudia. Her refusal to
press charges because it might result in the death penalty for her three attackers moved me deeply. I was glad
she had finally told me about it. Her compassion and
mercy towards others—even the three men who had
harmed her brutally—confirmed what others had said
about her, that Claudia couldn't harm a fly.

And it was painful to realize that now, five years
after the .22-caliber murders, she was still haunted by
the memory of McCann and his mother and Christine.
Bringing those memories out into the open, she had felt,
was the only way to banish those ghosts.

But I could see she was going to fight it all the way.

2

Claudia told me she met Bill "Smoky" Ham a few weeks
after she'd been gang-raped. She'd gone—as she usually
did—to the enlisted men's club where David was playing
bass with a rock group. Because she had been stopped by
a police officer who warned her against hitchhiking, she
said, she missed David's performance.

"Weren't you afraid of hitchhiking?" I asked her,

still trying to get used to the new picture I was getting of her.

"No. I did it everywhere I went," she said. "I used to be really foolish. I was bold, but it was stupid. You wouldn't believe some of the things I did. I could have been killed."

Smoky, a helicopter mechanic with the 82nd Airborne Division, asked her to dance. He was six-foot-four and very handsome, she recalled. As they clung together on the crowded dance floor, she found herself strongly attracted to him.

His family was in Hawaii, he told her, where his father was a member of the Honolulu Police Department. Smoky planned to go back to Hawaii after his discharge at the end of the year.

The following week, though she had minor surgery for a blood clot under a toenail, she hitchhiked on crutches to the club, where she met Smoky again. They went to a house he was renting in the Bonnie Dune area, and that night she decided he was the man she wanted to marry.

"I was doing a lot of drugs then," she explained casually, "hallucinogens, mescaline, LSD. And cannabinol too."

I was shocked. Despite the fact that by now I'd interviewed her for nearly a hundred hours, it was the first time I'd heard her talk about ever having used street drugs. She had led me to believe she'd taken only medication prescribed by doctors for her mental illness.

"Do you know what cannabinol is?"

"I know almost nothing about street drugs," I said.

I could have added that up to this point I also knew very little about her past. The impression I had formed over the past eighteen months, of an innocent, mentally ill woman victimized by society, began to fade. It worried me to discover how much she had hidden from me, and that I was only now beginning to know her.

"It does something to the equilibrium and affects your sense of balance," she said.

"What does?"

"Cannabinol. Why anyone would want to take it, I don't know."

"So why did you?"

"I wish I had the answer. Why did I hitchhike? Why did I confess to killing three people? How do I explain these things? I've tried to figure it out, but I can't." She paused and looked up at me suspiciously. "What are you going to put into the book as an explanation for my behavior?"

"I don't give explanations," I said. "I just describe what happened."

"Ohhhh . . ." she sighed, relieved. "The readers will draw their own conclusions?"

"Of course."

"I've always had strange, unexplainable behavior. As far back as when I was six."

I was upset but tried to keep a passive expression on my face. I was anxious to hear any memories of her childhood.

"Ohhh . . ." she gasped. "I lost it! I just had a whole scene in my head and it went away. I don't even know what it was. It was something about my mother enrolling me in school."

"Kindergarten?" I prompted.

"No, they had it in those days, but I didn't go."

"First grade?"

"Mmmmm . . . well, anyway, Sister Antoinette knew something was wrong with me. She wrote letters to my parents. She asked them to come to the school to talk to her. I do remember my dad going over to talk to her and to the Mother Superior, and the Monsignor. They just knew something was wrong with me. They kept sending me to the guidance counselor. They believed it was a spiritual matter."

"What did you—?"

"In fact, a Catholic priest came over to the house and anointed all the doorways and doorknobs with oil and then he sprinkled holy water into all the stuff. He was exorcising the house. It was haunted. Definitely haunted."

"Okay."

She laughed. "That reminds me of the house I lived in with Smoky in the Bonnie Dune area the time the Cumberland county sheriff came to the door. My God, I'll never forget this. Knock on the door. We were in the kitchen eating. Not Smoky—he wasn't there. But I can still picture some other guys in uniform. They were eating in a hurry—they had to go to a meeting or something for the military, and one of them looks out the window and sees the sheriff's hat. Oh, did we scramble to throw the drugs away! Trying to flush them down the toilet, but they were coming back up because there was too much. And somebody got a stepstool trying to reach the attic and threw some of it up there. Do you know what the problem was? It was my collie—I called him Speedy because he was a speed-freak. It turned out he bit a little girl next door. And here we threw away hundreds of dollars' worth of drugs."

She was laughing as she described it.

"We were on some of those drugs, I know. We had something called salicy . . . something . . . I can't pronounce it. We nicknamed it Simple Simon because it made you very simple. And when the deputy told us the little girl got bit, and she was crying and everything, instead of having compassion for her we were hanging on to each other and just laughing hysterically. The deputy got very angry. We ended up having to pay her emergency-room bill. They came out to investigate the dog, and he didn't have rabies but they found drugs in his blood."

"How did that happen?"

"The previous tenant of the house had gotten it addicted to speed. You should have seen Speedy. Lost all his hair. People thought he was real old." She laughed. "He was a mess. It was really sad. Our bald dog named Speedy."

What saddened me was her smile when she described the bitten child. Even knowing that inappropriate laughter or weeping was one of the symptoms of schizophrenia, I couldn't help being upset by it. When I learned she had told Howard Champ she didn't take street drugs, only medication, I'd built up a picture of Claudia as an innocent victim. Now I felt as deceived as he had been. But I had to struggle to control my reactions as she described her experiences. I was here to listen and write—not to judge her.

3

After Smoky received his discharge from the Army in January, Claudia told me, she went with him to Hawaii. She was nineteen.

"When we arrived at Honolulu International Airport," she said, "his whole family was there. There must have been, without exaggeration, fifty people. And they were giving us all these leis and they were happy to see us.

"We went to his parents' ranch in Waimanalo—on the windward side of Oahu, and we were married on March 13, 1971. Since Smoky's mother was half Portuguese and half Hawaiian, we had to follow the Hawaiian custom of newlyweds living in the parents' home for the first year."

If most of Claudia's childhood was a blank, her memories of Hawaii were a blur.

A few months after her marriage, she recalled, she was arrested in a drug bust at the apartment of a friend in Honolulu. She spent the next three days in the women's prison on Oahu, and later learned it was only because of Smoky's connections with the Honolulu Police Department that she hadn't been prosecuted—on condition that she leave Hawaii and enter a drug rehabilitation center on the mainland.

In the fall of 1971, they returned to Columbus, and Claudia entered an adult psychiatric day-care center. They lived at her mother's house for a few weeks until they were able to rent a place of their own nearby. But the winter cold was too much for Smoky. The following January he went back to Hawaii, and a few weeks later Claudia followed him. On their first anniversary, March 13, 1972, they moved from his parents' home to their own apartment.

Claudia said she knew her behavior had been strange in Hawaii: wandering about the place at night, unable to sleep, depressed, nervous, jittery, with attacks of agoraphobia. The Catholic priest who had married them suggested she see a psychiatrist friend of his, Dr.

Tanaka, who was the first to diagnose her as a paranoid schizophrenic with acute hysteria.

Her marriage to Smoky went downhill. She could not, or would not, tell me much about him. Most of 1972 was a blank, though she admitted that life had been a constant round of bars and nightclubs and strange men. She vaguely remembered being beaten severely in January '73 by someone who broke her cheekbones and knocked out most of her front teeth. She recalled the plastic surgery and the months it took for her face to heal, and how—when the bandages were removed—her friends said her face had become even more mysterious now, more alluring, more sensual.

Smoky and she were divorced on March 7, 1973. A week later she took an intentional overdose of her medication and was rushed to the Queens Medical Hospital in Honolulu.

Released in a few days, she discovered she'd lost all sense of time. Her cognition deteriorated, and she drifted from job to job, one bar or nightclub to another—singing, dancing, tending bar.

She worked as a topless waitress at the Green Spot and then at the Lemon Tree, feeling sorry for the men who gawked at her breasts, trying to touch her. She again began abusing street drugs regularly to make life bearable. Especially cocaine—so easy to get in Hawaii—injecting it into the veins in the back of her legs, behind her knees. She quit the Lemon Tree and went to work at the Royal Lanai, where she met Thalia Loman. They decided to share an apartment, moved in together, and became lovers.

"That was my second bisexual relationship," she told me.

I sensed she put it that way to see if it would shock me. I kept a straight face, showed no reaction. I knew if I revealed even a hint of disapproval, she would never again confide in me.

"My first affair with a girl was in junior high school," she said. "Helena and I tried to keep the relationship secret, but somehow the other kids found out and taunted us by calling us lesbians. It bothered Helena more than me," Claudia said, her eyes misting. "Then on Valentine's Day, when we were supposed to meet, she took her father's revolver out of the closet and killed herself."

Claudia's pain showed clearly as she looked at me. "It still hurts me deeply that people can't understand that love between women is as important as between men and women. The cruelty of people who can't understand that made Helena die because she loved me. If not for Thalia, I would probably have destroyed myself too."

She said that when she first learned her new friend was a *Kahuna*—a witch—she was repelled. But then Thalia took her to the Occult Bookstore on Kapiolani Boulevard. Upstairs in the School for the Occult Claudia took courses in palmistry, astrology, and reincarnation. She learned how to read faces, and palms, and minds. She said it reminded her of the time her parents had bought her a Ouija board when she was in first grade, and she had taken that gift as a sign of her destiny.

Thalia helped her with her studies, and Claudia was excited by the mystical powers she had acquired. When she was given a certificate of graduation, it somehow made up for her lack of a high school diploma.

"I was proud to be a Kahuna," she said, gazing into my eyes.

I had to look away.

I dug into my briefcase and brought out a letter I'd found among her mother's records, dated June 4, 1974, in which she had written Martha that she and Thalia were busy sewing blouses to sell at the Independence Day "Who" Rock Festival in Honolulu's Diamond Head crater. That brought back her memory. . . .

They had rented space for a booth, she recalled, not only to sell blouses, but to read palms, minds, and tarot cards. Claudia expected to make a lot of money.

"The night before the festival, we were too excited to eat or sleep. We stayed awake and talked all night. So before we left for the crater, knowing I needed a stimulant, I snorted cocaine."

At the Diamond Head crater, with the help of two men, they built a booth. Claudia tied bamboo, nailed up shelves, and used watercolors to paint a bright sign.

Throughout the morning she and Thalia read tarot cards, palms, and minds. Claudia recalled that before lunch Thalia slipped away for a few minutes, and when she returned, she smirked slyly. "Those guys are great," she said. "Look at the present they gave us—Hawaiian Hash—guaranteed to celebrate the day with fireworks."

Claudia explained that meant they had laced the marijuana—as serious island pot smokers always did— with opium.

"With no food or sleep for twenty-four hours," Claudia said, "I sure as hell needed something."

The drugs quickly began to disorient her.

As she emptied her mind to receive images from the tarot cards or the customers' minds, her mood swings began to frighten her: from hysterical laughter to black sorrow. She wanted to stop, but as long as people needed her, she knew she had to stay. She could never refuse to help anyone.

She recalled a shadow falling across her. A young dark-haired American woman stopped in front of the booth and whispered, "I'd like you to read my mind."

They sat facing each other, and as Claudia gazed into her dark eyes, oddly clouded, the tension and fear mounted. She saw an aura about the woman . . . and the merging images of violence, blood, and death.

Unable to tolerate it, Claudia screamed and fainted.

She regained consciousness at St. Francis Hospital. She had collapsed, Thalia told her, screaming that what she saw in the young woman's mind was too terrible to bear. What it was, Claudia couldn't remember. The doctors kept her for observation.

She'd been at the hospital for two weeks when she had a visitor, a short, pockmarked Hawaiian from the Oahu chapter of the Recovered Souls Christian Fellowship.

He asked if she wanted to leave the hospital to join a program of Independent Transitional Living. It was a place, he told her, for people who didn't have anywhere to go. They would provide clothing, three meals a day, a place to sleep, showers—everything she would need.

Claudia agreed to go with him. He explained that the best way to avoid bureaucratic red tape would be for her to say she was signing herself out in care of her father.

She signed the release on July 20, 1974, and was taken to a temporary house in Honolulu. She would have to spend a short time there, the stranger said, before being transferred to the main center—a house with twenty-two rooms. There were counselors for people from prisons, mental institutions, and hospitals. Most fellowship members, she learned, were court referrals. She stayed at the house for three days before they flew her to the Big Island—Hawaii.

The Reverend Harry Wilson and his wife, Tess, who ran the Recovered Souls Christian Fellowship, had her picking coffee beans and cutting sugarcane. They gave her a small allowance. Later, when she became weak they let her work in the health-food store, weighing beans and flour. She felt happy there and at peace.

All the buildings and gardens of the compound in Kealakekua had biblical names: the house she was assigned to was "The Upper Room," and from her window she could look down at "The Garden of Gethsemane."

Reverend Wilson taught her that her infant baptism in the Catholic Church, with its mere sprinkling of water, meant nothing, that salvation required adult conscious acceptance of Jesus and complete immersion. Claudia prepared for her participation in a mass baptism in the waters of Black Sand Beach. Three hundred and fifty people showed up from the neighboring islands, from California, Washington, and Oregon, and the guests joined in singing.

"I smelled a beautiful fragrance in the air," Claudia told me, "but I never saw any evidence of incense. And they were singing in tongues. All these different languages, but still in perfect pitch, perfect harmony. And suddenly I noticed, above their voices were super-high voices, much higher than first soprano, and I didn't understand it. I didn't see a record player or tape recorder anywhere, and I couldn't understand how my ear could even hear something like that. And I wasn't the only one who heard it. So I know it wasn't a hallucination."

"What did you think of all that?" I asked.

"I don't *know* what it was. But I believe it was an angelic visitation."

Reverend Wilson submerged her in the ocean three times, saying, "Claudia, I baptize you in the name of Jesus Christ." She dried quickly in the warm sun, and then she joined the prepared feast, filled with a greater joy than she had ever known.

On July 27 she went with a group of people to an audience with Sister Vanita, who, she was told, had the power and authority to give the Gift of Tongues.

She was instructed to speak aloud the words from Acts 2:4.

"And they were all filled with the Holy Ghost, and began to speak with other tongues, as the Spirit gave them utterance."

If she was sincere, Reverend Wilson assured her, she would be given the Divine Gift. If not, she would get nothing. As the line of aspirants moved closer to the holy woman, Claudia feared she wouldn't get a heavenly language.

But suddenly, as she spoke the words she felt the power of the Holy Spirit with all its energy, and found she had received an even greater gift. She had been given Diversity of Tongues. She couldn't understand the words that came out of her mouth, but they assured her she was speaking Spanish and Turkish as spoken in the first century.

Martha's correspondence file contains a letter from Claudia dated August 7, 1974: "It is the first real spiritual high I've ever experienced," she wrote. "I live with a gentle holy man and his family and another girl about my age. For the first time in my life, I feel clean inside and have peace of mind."

But Claudia became upset at the restrictions placed upon her. She resented not being allowed to go to the movies or to listen to rock music. And when Reverend Wilson told her to convince her mother to sell her house and possessions and donate them to the "Fellowship" because that was the way to prove her sincerity about regaining the path to Christ, she became suspicious.

Martha's memos show that Claudia called her collect from a pay phone on August 16 and told her she had written the letter praising the Fellowship only because she knew that all mail was tampered with and Reverend Wilson would read it. Actually, she said, the sanitary conditions were deplorable, and she was guarded even when she went to the rest room. Everyone was forced to work hard, and something was put into their food to make them dazed so they would stagger around everywhere. Those who tried to escape were sent to a building in the jungle.

When she called home again on September 25, she told Martha she was sick and weak because they wouldn't let her have the medication her doctor had prescribed.

"I'm being held against my will, Mamma. If they find out I called you, they'll take me to another building that's hard to find, and I'll never be heard from again."

Martha called the Kona Police Department and notified the officer in charge that she was prepaying an airline ticket for her daughter. She asked him to get Claudia and put her on the plane. The officer told her that the Fellowship was currently being investigated because of other complaints against it, and there would be no difficulty in getting Claudia out.

At eight o'clock on the evening of September 27, 1974, the Kona police helped a weak and wasted Claudia into a wheelchair and onto a Hawaiian Airlines flight to Honolulu, where she made connections for the United Airlines flight to Columbus.

4

Though Martha was relieved that Claudia was safe and delighted to have her back, during the next four weeks the hallucinations and bizarre behavior began again. Claudia was admitted to Mount Carmel Mental Hospital on October 22, and was then transferred to the Ohio State University Hospital psychiatric ward at Upham Hall, where she met Dr. Stinson for the first time.

Stinson's "Confidential Medical Summary" records her remarks. She told him she had been kidnapped in Hawaii and was being pursued by the Mafia.

"Why would they be pursuing you?" he asked.

"Because I'm a singer, and I'd be worth a lot of money to them."

"How do you feel about being here?"

"I feel good. I feel safe here."

"How do you think we can help you?"

"I want to wipe out all my thoughts of suicide."

The interviewer wrote his impressions of her into the file:

"The patient is a tall, averagely built, attractive, seductive 23-year-old white female. She is wearing a red turtlenecked sweater, a gray pant suit, nylon stockings and dress shoes. She has good rapport during the interview and good eye contact, but manifests a flat facial expression and voice. . . . She assumes reclining positions and repeatedly tosses her hair and engages in playing with nearby objects with her index finger. The speed of her activity is appropriate and normal. The character of her speech is normal. This patient related an intricately woven, lengthy story involving a religious cult, the Mafia, her kidnapping, torture, and the FBI, which occurred several months before admission. . . . She was plagued by increasing daily thoughts of suicide and claims to have been intermittently *hysterical*.

"The patient describes hallucinations and delusions. She is presently concerned with her recent '*kidnapping and with trying to find a place to live when I leave here.*'

"She displays little understanding of her problem. She is not actively suicidal but retains suicidal ruminations."

Claudia was given the Minnesota Multiphasic Personality Inventory, and the results were entered into the record: "MMPI reveals that the patient is probably psychotic with mixed hysterical and schizophrenic symptoms. The test suggests a permanent thought disorder with regression as the characteristic defense."

Treated with occupational, recreational, group, and individual psychotherapy, Claudia proved to be a cooperative patient. Since she was an excellent hypnotic subject, Dr. Stinson used hypnotherapy.

By early December, under the treatment team's supervision, Claudia made arrangements to leave the hospital and planned to move into an apartment with another patient.

Stinson prescribed Haldol 5mg. and Cogentin 1mg. and reported that she responded well to treatment. His first diagnosis was: *Hysterical neurosis, dissociative type*.

At the time of her discharge, on December 6, 1974,

arrangements were made for follow-up care at the Adult Psychiatric Clinic.

After Claudia left Upham Hall, she found and lost several jobs the following year, and finally went on welfare. She met an intensely religious woman who convinced her that a religious movement called "The Way" was the answer to all her problems.

"The Way International," boasting a hundred thousand members nationwide, is structured as a tree, its roots and trunk in Knoxville, Ohio, where it had been founded, its branches in different states, with each cell—meeting in individuals' homes—called a "twig." As each twig grows too large to meet in one home, a leader takes part of the group into his own home and the offshoot is a new twig.

It was a function of her mental illness, I decided, that led Claudia—again and again—to search for answers with fringe religious groups, with cults, with practitioners of the occult. Her suggestibility made her an easy target for these groups.

Claudia was awed by The Way—the preaching, the speaking-in-tongues, the mental and physical healing—and she declared herself born again. She moved into a three-bedroom house on Summit Street with two women members of the movement and felt safe. She was happy and eager to live her reborn life, determined to stay out of trouble. She swore she would be careful about whom she got involved with.

"That's when I met Jim Stahl," she said. "Even though he's an ex-convict, he's a wonderful guy. I hadn't seen him for years, and then a few months ago I called for a cab to take me to work and guess who was driving it? Jim Stahl! It's fate! Pure fate! I asked him if you could interview him, and he says he'll talk to you."

The weariness must have shown on my face because she touched my arm reassuringly and whispered, "I really think you should."

Fifteen

1

It had become apparent to me that one clue to Claudia's confession to the McCann homicides was somehow connected with her involvement in exotic fringe religions. The other was her obvious attraction to criminals. To solve the mystery of her knowledge of the death scene, to learn more about the forces that influenced her, I was going to have to find out more about both.

The section of Parsons Avenue where Jim Stahl lived was a seedy area of run-down boardinghouses and empty stores. I suspected that it, too, was a high crime area.

As I climbed the narrow staircase to Stahl's rooms, he came to the door to greet me, a short, swarthy man in his thirties, with a dark mustache and slicked black hair. He led me to a tiny kitchen, and we sat at a table near the window overlooking the street.

I took out my tape recorder, and he glanced at it nervously but shrugged. "Claudia wants me to talk to you. I'll do anything I can to help her."

Stahl said they first met in February of 1976.

"Are you sure?" I asked. "Claudia said 1975."

Stahl shook his head. "I was paroled from the Marion Correctional Institute on December 5, 1975. I met her about two months later."

I decided to trust his memory. If there's one thing an ex-convict remembers, it's the date he got out of prison.

"Tell me what you recall of that meeting."

"I was living on Summit Avenue at the time. It was a cold Friday afternoon, and I was heading downtown for emergency welfare and food stamps. When my bus came, I got on, paid my fare, and looked around. I glanced carefully at all the faces—a habit you get into when you've been in prison for so long. It was nearly empty, just five people. But then I spotted the most beautiful woman I ever seen looking at me, smiling at me, motioning for me to sit beside her."

Smiling, Stahl said, "I *knew* I was supposed to sit there, but I don't just jump into things. I always test fate. I passed her by and sat down at the rear of the bus. I figured, either she thought she knew me or else she was about a hundred-dollar hooker."

Stahl said he'd spent seventeen of his thirty-four years in detention homes and prisons, for forgery, robbery, and carrying concealed weapons. He knew he had to walk a tight and narrow line while on parole, be very careful about his behavior.

"Still . . . she was so beautiful. I told myself, if she turns and smiles once more, I'll try. Then she does it, she turns and smiles. Real seductive but still innocent, you know. Okay, I figured, what the hell . . ."

He went to sit beside her, introduced himself, and they began talking as if they'd known each other for years.

"Claudia tells me she had her purse on the seat next to her," he said, "and before the bus stopped she picked her purse up and put it in her lap. She tells me she knew I was getting on this bus and we'd meet. That proved to me she was a psychic. I read a lot in prison about people with mental powers, and now I'd finally met one. We talked about reincarnation, and the possibility we might have known each other in a former existence. And I was wondering in what other life could I ever have had anything to do with someone so innocent, so vulnerable. And yet there we were, like old friends meeting after a long separation."

"Did she tell you where she was headed?" I asked.

"She was going to her grandmother's house to borrow ten bucks. We exchanged phone numbers and addresses, and it turned out we lived near each other on Summit Street. And then—it was very strange—as I stood up to get off at my stop, it just popped out of my mouth: 'I'll see you tonight. We have a lot to talk about.' Just like that."

Later, when he left the welfare office, Stahl said, he remembered he had no money to take a woman out on a date. He hung around outside and sold his food stamps for fifty-five dollars.

That evening, Stahl took the bus to her place and was surprised to see her apartment was just as poor-looking and tiny as his. He met the two women she lived with and could tell they didn't like him at all.

He splurged on a cab, and he and Claudia went to the Ohio State University campus area to have a few drinks and to dance. When they got on the dance floor, the college kids who had crowded the floor just moments earlier stayed off and watched the short man and the tall woman who danced so beautifully together. He'd often been told he looked like Sonny Bono and with her height and long dark hair she could pass for Cher. Most of the students thought they were Sonny and Cher, and he found it fun to pretend he and Claudia were celebrities.

Afterwards, they walked across the campus and shared confidences. He told her he was out on parole. He had run away from home at seven, he said, had been in and out of detention homes and had just grown into a life of crime.

She told him of her aspirations to be a model and an actress. She spoke of her mental problems: how her medication had temporarily stopped the voices and hallucinations, leaving her shaky but determined to make it again on her own.

They took a cab back to his place, and Stahl could hardly believe he was going to bed with her, but as he moved to take her, he saw the faraway look in her eyes.

"I'm a minister," she said. "I should have told you."

He rolled off. "What the hell are you talking about?"

She told him that when she had gotten out of the

mental hospital she'd joined The Way. "The two women I live with are from the group, and I'm considered a minister."

"Well, that's another thing we have in common," he said. "When I told you I knew I would make it this time and stay out of prison, it was because I was born again too."

After they made love, Stahl felt sad. If only there was some way he could help her. But with no money of his own, no job, and a prison record . . .

He decided to help her spiritually. Her description of The Way bothered him. He found himself doubting the group, and he didn't like the idea of Claudia being ripped off by a religious cult. He offered to go to one of the twig meetings with her, to check these people out and learn what was going on. He went with her one evening, and afterwards when they were alone at his place he told her she was placing her faith in false prophets.

"What do you mean? How can you say that?"

"Look, Claudia, The Way says they believe the Bible is the direct word of God, right?"

She nodded, wide-eyed and defensive.

"And you heard the group leader say that when Jesus was crucified, four thieves were crucified with him. *Four.*"

"Yes, I was wondering about that. I always thought there were two, but The Way says four."

Stahl pulled out a Bible and thumbed through it. "As you can imagine, I've always been interested in what the Good Book has to say about thieves. I got to studying it a lot when I was in the slammer. Here, read that aloud."

She read the line his finger pointed to, Matthew 27:38, *"There were two thieves crucified with him, one on the right hand, and another on the left."*

He flipped to Mark 15:27, *"And with him they crucify two thieves; the one on his right, and the other on his left."* Luke 23:32 put it slightly differently: *"And there were also two other, malefactors, led with him to be put to death."* John 19:18 said, *". . . they crucified him, and two others with him, on either side one, and Jesus in the midst."*

Stahl slammed the Bible shut and held it up. "If The

Way people say they take the words of the Gospel like they're written, and if they report the Word of God so different than it's set out by Matthew, Mark, Luke, and John, how can we be sure they aren't wrong about their way of healing and salvation? Maybe you've put yourself into the hands of a group that will lead you straight to hell!"

He spoke with an earnestness and a fervor that frightened her, and she cried and thanked him, and said she believed him and would have no more to do with people from The Way.

I could see the memories were painful for him. He smiled sadly.

"For the next few weeks, we saw a lot of each other. I loved to be with her. She was so innocent, and yet I got a kick out of the way she could freak people out by telling their fortunes. I liked the way people looked at me when she was with me. But I knew it couldn't last because I had nothing to offer her.

"I began checking the 'help wanted' ads for models, figuring if I could get her started on the right road, it would be enough for me to know I'd helped her."

Stahl said that the first week in March 1976, about a month after they'd met, he saw an advertisement for women to model and to do TV commercials. He phoned the National Video Corporation and spoke to Phil Gary, the president, who said he would like to meet Claudia to see if he could use her. Stahl passed along the information to Claudia, who agreed to go for the interview on the north side of Columbus.

"She got the job," Stahl said softly. "And then she moved in with the guy who hired her."

"Did you have contact with her again at that time?"

"I phoned her once at Phil Gary's place to wish her a happy birthday. She seemed okay. That was the last I knew about her until I read the story in *Playboy*. I said to myself, those people who think she murdered someone are crazy. I even wrote a letter to her lawyer, Lew Dye, and told him I knew Claudia couldn't have killed anybody because she couldn't hurt a living creature."

"Did you try to see her or visit her?" I asked.

Stahl shrugged. "After Claudia moved out, I went down to Florida and robbed a bank. At the time she was arrested for the murders, I was in the federal penitentiary. That's where I was when I read *Playboy*."

As I left Stahl's apartment and went down the stairs, I felt I was coming back from the dark side of a world I'd known about only from headlines and the evening TV news. Not that I was naive about crime and criminals. For earlier books, I'd visited jails and hospitals for the criminally insane, and I'd interviewed law enforcement officers and convicted felons. But now, talking to people like Stahl, who took crime for granted as a way of life—as the easy, natural way of doing things—was beginning to get to me.

Still, I was touched by Stahl's memory of his great romance with a beautiful woman. Because he cared about Claudia, because he felt she was too good for him, he gave her up to someone he hoped would give her the advantages that were beyond him. He passed her on to Phil Gary.

2

Phil Gary (Scianamblo), a short young man in his mid-twenties with hair down to his shoulders, always wore a railroad engineer's cap to hide his balding top. A self-styled hotshot promoter, Phil explained to me that, several months before he met Claudia, he had created a company known as World Wide Socials, Inc., "for liberal-minded adults who wanted to party together." He printed stationery and ran an ad, but it didn't work out, he said, because as a single he didn't like partying with the couples his ad had attracted. Columbus, he decided, was the wrong city for swingers.

After that, in addition to taping commercials for local TV stations and running poker games at his apartment, he had set up a company called the National Screen Test Modeling Agency as a subdivision of his National Video Corporation. He found attractive women to work for him.

When he interviewed Claudia for a modeling job, he said, she was so desperate for the chance to be a model and an actress that she told him she had been "Miss Hawaii" and had appeared in a *Hawaii Five-0* TV segment. If she photographed as beautifully as she looked, he told her, he would use her as a TV model, but what he needed right now was someone to replace his receptionist, who was getting married.

Claudia took the job, and that evening she and Stahl went out to dinner and celebrated.

In the next few weeks, in addition to working as a receptionist, Claudia did TV spots for Dyna-Gym, a Chrysler-Plymouth dealership, and Rent-A-Carpet. Thrilled to be on television, she called all her old friends and told them to watch. She was sure that success was almost within reach.

At the end of April, when Phil's roommate/photographer moved out of his apartment to go back to her parents, he suggested Claudia move in and share his place.

He showed her his duplex in a town house at the Continent apartment development, behind the French Market—a shopping center laid out in imitation of Paris streets. Her share of the rent would be much more than she was paying now on Summit Street, but with her new job and the modeling opportunities, he assured her she'd be able to afford it.

"She loved the place," Phil Gary said, "and she liked the idea of becoming my roommate. But there was one problem. She told me she was afraid this ex-con, Jim Stahl, was going to kill her, and she wanted me to go with her and protect her while she picked up her stuff at the apartment. When I got over there, I found out it was quite different. Stahl didn't say anything. He just sat quietly on the sofa and watched us. I noticed that when we left, she didn't even bother to say good-bye."

After Claudia moved in, Phil said, he transformed his modeling agency into the Video Date Escort Service. Both Summer 1976 issues of *Good Times in Columbus*— a local magazine distributed to hotels, restaurants, and night spots—feature ads with a sensuous photograph of Claudia, and beneath it, the suggestive ad:

*Enjoy the town with one of our
beautiful girls.
See your date first on videotape . . .
Pick the girl you like best . . .
We try hard
TO SATISFY ALL OUR CUSTOMERS!!!!*

Claudia was booked on two or three dates a week. Of the seventy dollars the customer would pay for a three-hour dinner date, Phil would keep forty and the women would keep thirty. He made it clear, he told me, that Video Date was *just* an escort service, and the women were expected to go straight home afterwards. Of course, whatever they did after that, he said, was their own business.

Later, when I confronted Claudia, and asked her if she'd been a hooker, she denied it vehemently. "I only did it for money once in my life."

She explained that one of Phil's customers, a wealthy businessman they called "Tennessee," flew her and one of Phil's new "models"—Vicki Hancock, a go-go dancer with the street name of "Patches"—to a Knoxville motel. After a night of sex with the two of them, including watching Claudia and Vicki perform together, Tennessee paid them five hundred dollars each. Later, Claudia said, he sent for them on several occasions, and she and Vicki decided to keep the money for themselves and not let Phil know about it. By the time their customer tired of them and broke off the arrangement, Vicki and Claudia had become lovers.

Phil Gary stopped the escort business after two months. "Everybody thought I was running hookers . . ." he said, "so I passed." One of the things that bothered him, he said, was the dumb things Claudia was doing, like the time she brought a customer who wanted his money back to the apartment. "I got to thinking, this is stupid. I could send her out someplace, and she'd get killed. So that was it for the escort service."

After the Video Date Escort Service, Phil decided to use his TV equipment to make erotic movies. *Far-Out Fantasies* was planned as a soft-porn video featuring Claudia and Vicki Hancock. Each episode would open with a beautiful model reading imaginary letters from viewers who had written in asking to see their sexual fantasies acted out on the screen.

Although Claudia insisted that Phil had promised to make her a movie star and would pay her ten thousand dollars after the films were sold, Phil denied that. The titles she had given me: *Right Body, Wrong Grave*, and

Baseball, Apple Pie, and Thirty-Nine Naked Ladies, he denied ever having filmed. He explained that the only one he had taped, *Far-Out Fantasies*, was just an amateur home-video experiment that he never sold or released.

To prove that Claudia was wrong, he played the videotapes for me in his apartment.

They were so terrible, they were funny.

In the first segment Claudia acts the part of a woman being picked up at the Chic gay bar by a beautiful bisexual woman (portrayed by a female impersonator in drag, playing the part of a bisexual transvestite).

In the second segment Claudia is seduced by Vicki and another lesbian. In both episodes, Claudia is drugged and unconscious throughout.

The amateurish pornography was hilarious, yet I felt guilty as I laughed. Seeing Claudia this way saddened me. Phil explained that after he finished directing *Far-Out Fantasies*. Claudia seemed to change. She began taking amphetamines, and he found her quarrelsome behavior and her love affair with one of his other women intolerable. After Vicki Hancock left Columbus in July, he realized Claudia was becoming very paranoid, and he told her he'd had enough of her and wanted her to leave.

She talked of killing herself.

Hysterical and hallucinating, Claudia called her mother for help. Two of Martha's friends came to Phil's apartment, packed Claudia's things, and moved her to Upham Hall in a psychotic state of collapse.

3

Dr. Stinson's "Confidential Summary," dated October 6, 1976, describes Claudia's second admission to Upham Hall:

"Ms. Yasko is tall and slender, quite seductive, wearing heavy makeup and jewelry. Her speech and actions are very dramatic, and she makes very good eye contact. She is cooperative with the interviewer but appears restless at times. Her mood is somewhat elated and anxious and she plays with objects in the room as she talks.... Thought process and speech are within normal limits. Associations are close. She shows no delusional thinking and reports no history of hallucinations. ...

"Ms. Yasko attributes her condition to a long history of homosexual relationships dating back to the age of 10 years. The past year she has lived with a woman with whom the patient played the 'male role.' Their relationship was broken last July and since then Ms. Yasko has become increasingly anxious, unstable at work, and suicidal.

"She feels compelled to rid herself of her homosexual tendencies and to live as a woman all the time. ...

" *'I don't want to be bisexual anymore,'* she said. *'I want to become a woman 24 hours a day.'*

"Ms. Yasko showed some improvement during her stay. She was engaged in one-to-one, group, occupational and recreational therapies as well as in a social skills group. Her socialization with staff and other patients was very good, but she showed little indication that she could establish meaningful relationships with people on the outside."

Dr. Stinson discharged her on October 23, 1976, changing his earlier diagnosis of: "Hysterical Neurosis, Dissociative Type" to *"Schizophrenia, Latent Type."*

At the suggestion of another psychiatrist, Claudia entered a drug rehabilitation group called Outreach for Youth in Pataskala, Ohio. A strict religious regimen, her mother and the Outreach directors agreed, would enable Claudia to regain her strength and solve her drug-abuse problem. For the next four months, she lived isolated from her friends, her past, and drugs. In a letter to her mother on March 1, 1977, she wrote:

> ... You see the devil will try everything in his power to discourage you. He will tell you lie after lie. Satan will use a son or mother-in-law as a weapon. Anything to break a heart or cause sorrow. But I am telling you Satan is the father of all liars, hate, anger, jealousy. I rebuke him now ...

Phil Gary told me he had been concerned about Claudia's welfare, and a few weeks after she was removed from his apartment he tried to find out where she was. He got the number of the Pataskala group and phoned.

"The woman at the other end of the line told me Claudia was not allowed to receive phone calls from men," Phil said. "So I asked if I could leave a message. When I told her my name, there was a silence and then the woman says: 'Oh, then you must be the man Claudia says is trying to kill her.' The same thing she said to me about Stahl."

And, I thought, the same thing she later told the police about Bobby Novatney. For all I knew, she might be telling everybody that *I* was trying to kill her.

The way Claudia saw it, almost every person she attracted—man or woman—ended up using and abusing her and after every encounter she retreated into the shadows of mysticism and mental illness. For Claudia, it seemed, every sexual relationship with a male became a threat of death.

Well, I had no intention of ever giving her the slightest reason to tell anyone that she was afraid I would try to kill her.

Going into Columbus for interviews was beginning to tell on me. In more than two years, I had made ninety-five trips, often staying one or two nights at motels when I planned several interviews with different people. On the edge of a burnout, I warned myself again that I was a fool to go on, but the answer was always the same: I had to know what had really happened. I had to solve the goddamned mystery.

Sixteen

1

The records show that Claudia spent about five months in the drug rehabilitation program of Outreach for Youth, and after she was released early in March 1977 she stayed a week at the Salvation Army. She remembered moving in with a couple who provided a halfway house after Outreach, but not being able to stand the confining rules and restrictions, which reminded her of the Recovered Souls Christian Fellowship in Hawaii, she had to get away.

After two weeks at the halfway house, Claudia received an invitation from Julia Kelly, a young woman who had also been a patient at Outreach, to stay with her and her husband in their trailer in Lancaster, Ohio. Claudia accepted.

One morning, the last week in March, Claudia rose before dawn and packed her blue suitcase, taking only her clothes and leaving everything else behind—papers, letters, knickknacks—as she always did. Whenever she moved, she started fresh again, wanting nothing to remind her of the place she was leaving. Each move was like being reborn.

When the taxi got her to the downtown Greyhound

terminal, it was still dark, but she had missed her six o'clock bus to Lancaster and would have to wait five and a half hours for the next one.

She decided to get some coffee from the vending machine, and as she passed the game arcade in the lobby, she saw a tall handsome man with dark hair and a neat goatee playing pinball. He wore beltless jeans, and though it was cold for the end of March, he wore no shirt under his open denim jacket but carried it rolled up under his arm.

When he looked up at her, she saw he was perspiring. "Got change of a dollar?" he asked.

She found change in her purse, and as she handed it to him she noticed his nervous, dilated blue eyes.

"What's a beautiful girl like you doing around here this hour of the morning?"

"Missed my bus to Lancaster. What about you?"

He yawned and wiped his nose on his sleeve. "Meeting some people on business. What's in Lancaster?"

She recognized the symptoms of someone in need of a fix.

"I'm going to stay with some people there."

"If you like, when I'm done with my business I'll drive you," he said. "Better than waiting until noon."

Claudia accepted his offer and joined him in the pinball arcade.

His name, he told her, was Robert Raymond Novatney, but she could call him Bobby. He didn't much care for the name Claudia, so he was going to call her Laudie.

After about an hour, a short, bald man came into the terminal lobby, looked around carefully, and went into the men's room. Novatney excused himself and followed him. A few minutes later the man came out and left, and when Novatney rejoined her he had his shirt on. The calm expression on his face and his pinpoint irises told her he had just shot up.

"I'll drive you now," he said, "but first I've got to see a guy who owes me money." He led her outside to a beat-up tan Volkswagen. "It's my brother's. I don't believe in wasting money on cars."

They drove to a house on the near east side of Columbus, and she waited in the car while he transacted his business. When he returned ten minutes later, he slipped behind the wheel and sang out, "Next stop, Lancaster!"

As they headed southeast on route 33, Novatney talked continuously, and she could tell he was intelligent and read a lot. Now that he had his fix, he looked hard and strong, like a man who could take care of himself. She felt he was attracted to her, and she found him fascinating.

He dropped her off at the Kellys' mobile home, but when they saw Newfoundland dogs in a wired-in run and heard more dogs barking from inside the trailer, he jotted down two phone numbers on a slip of paper. "Laudie, if you don't want to stay here, call me at one of these numbers. I'll come and get you." Then he turned the VW around and drove off.

After dinner—when Claudia realized that in addition to the two children, three of the dogs would be sleeping inside—she asked to use the phone.

There was no answer at the first number (his brother's), but the second turned out to be the downstairs neighbor, who agreed to call Bobby to the phone. After a long wait she heard his voice.

"This is Laudie," she said. "Come and get me."

He picked her up two hours later.

Novatney took Claudia to his apartment on Wilson Avenue and explained that his close friend Deno Politis lived with him. "Deno's girl Elsie May drops in sometimes to visit. But if it gets too crowded, I'm sure Deno will move out."

That night, as Claudia hung her clothes in the bedroom closet, she saw a hypodermic, a rubber strap, and empty glassine envelopes on the shelf. There was also a gun.

When they went to bed, though she was physically and mentally exhausted, she responded when he made love to her.

In the days that followed, Claudia began to realize that because she would forget things, because she would lose the thread of a conversation, Bobby and Deno thought she was stupid and spoke in front of her as if she were a child.

She learned that Deno ran an aluminum-siding business, and that sometimes Bobby would work for him.

She also discovered that Bobby couldn't go longer than eight hours between fixes and understood why he didn't believe in wasting money on cars.

But Deno was against drugs. He would never let Bobby go out with him to work on house-siding installation when he was high. She respected Deno for that.

Bobby became increasingly concerned with the lack of money. He insisted that her welfare checks weren't enough, and he helped her get a job as a go-go dancer at the Latin Quarters. There she met Pigman, who would come to watch her dance every time he was in Columbus and would always take her out for breakfast. Bobby was jealous at first, but she assured him that her relationship with Pigman was platonic.

A month after Claudia moved in, Deno Politis moved out, and it was about this time she learned that Vicki Hancock—her costar in Phil Gary's *Far-Out Fantasies* and her former lover—was dancing at the Sly Fox. She arranged a meeting, and they renewed their love affair. It was easy to keep Bobby from finding out.

But Claudia was bothered that Vicki had gotten a reputation among the other go-go girls as a big-mouth. Vicki would have a few drinks and threaten to talk to the police about some of the bar owners connected to the Cincinnati/Dayton syndicate. The word was out that she was digging her own grave.

One night, while they were having dinner at a Chinese restaurant on Broad Street, Vicki passed out and fell to the floor. Only half aware of what was happening, Claudia sat in a trance as the manager called the Emergency Squad. She knew she had to say something, do something, but it wasn't until they took Vicki outside and lifted her into the ambulance that Claudia shouted hysterically that she wasn't letting them take her friend away alone.

"She's unconscious!" she screamed. "How do I know you bastards won't rape her?"

They finally let Claudia ride with them in the ambulance.

Claudia saw Vicki a few times after she was discharged from the hospital, and then Vicki disappeared. No one at the Sly Fox knew where she had gone.

A month later, Claudia heard on the evening news

that a charred female body the Dayton police had discovered in a remote area the previous Friday, June 10, 1977, had finally been identified. Twenty-six-year-old Vicki Hancock—street name "Patches"—had been shot dead, stuffed into the trunk of her own car, and set on fire.

Claudia stood there in shock. She visualized Vicki's beautiful body now charred black. They probably identified her by dental records. There had probably been an autopsy, and they had cut into Vicki's skin. Claudia ran into the bedroom and cried.

Street talk was that Patches had left Columbus because she was afraid. Though her boyfriend—Gary Wayne Cooper, alias "Cadillac"—was arrested, everyone said he was just taking the fall. The women speculated that one of the owners of the go-go bars in Columbus had called in a hit from Dayton. Claudia knew that the people who ran the go-go bars wanted it to be a warning to the other dancers and waitresses to keep their mouths shut.

There were tears in her eyes as she told me of Vicki Hancock's murder.

I decided not to mention that Phil Gary told me the Dayton police had discovered that Vicki Hancock had once worked for him and asked Howard Champ to interrogate him. Phil said Champ watched the same videotape I had seen of *Far-Out Fantasies* featuring Vicki, Linda, and Claudia in the lesbian love triangle, and that Champ borrowed it to make a copy for the Sheriff's Department files.

That had been nine months before he met Claudia and arrested her.

2

The stress of living with Bobby grew daily, and Claudia didn't know how to handle it. The summer heat was unbearable, and there was no money for air-conditioning. It bothered her that her eighty-three-dollar-a-month welfare check went to pay his eighty-dollar-a-month rent. The rest of her income, salary and tips, went to support him and his drug habit.

Her life had fallen into a routine of working at the

Latin Quarters, sleeping for twelve hours because of the Haldol and Cogentin, then dragging herself out of bed, and moving in a daze for hours until she came fully awake. Bobby's friends came to the house frequently to drink beer and talk.

One evening, during the last week in August, Claudia was awakened by screams from the back of the house and went to look out through the venetian blinds of the dining-room window. She saw two men holding a young woman with honey-colored hair, saw them stab her, put her into a car, and drive away.

When she told Bobby about it, he said it was none of her business. "You don't want to get involved. You don't want to go to court."

But the vision of the stabbing haunted her. Without telling Bobby, she went to neighbors two doors away and asked to use their phone to call the police. They said the same thing Bobby had: "Forget about it. It's not your business." But when Claudia described the young woman, the wife—worried about her own runaway daughter, who fit the victim's description—let Claudia call the police.

The officers finally arrived, but the neighbors wouldn't let them into their house. Claudia had to talk to them in the backyard.

Nothing was ever found—no blood, no body.

Everyone said Claudia had imagined or hallucinated the scene.

Bobby demanded to know why she hadn't minded her own business. "With your goddamned Good Samaritan attitude, you're going to get into real trouble one of these days. Your big mouth will get you killed, just like Vicki Hancock."

That shocked and depressed her, and in the days that followed, her voice grew hoarser and hoarser until she lost it completely. She couldn't eat or sleep, and three days after the "stabbing" she went to the emergency room at the Ohio State University Hospital and was admitted to Upham Hall.

Since she couldn't talk, she wrote a note on a piece of paper: "I lost my voice after witnessing a stabbing."

Dr. Stinson's "Confidential Summary" of her August 26, 1977, admission corroborated the story she had told me:

"The patient was first admitted to Upham Hall at age 14 for hallucinations and delusions. She has been hospitalized three times since then with diagnosis of 'hysterical personality' [sic]. . . . Three days prior to admission the patient reports having witnessed the stabbing of a woman in the alley behind her home. She reported the incident to the police even though none of the neighbors corroborated the story, saying that 'if you talk you'll get in trouble.' Since the 'stabbing' her voice has become progressively more hoarse, disappearing altogether by the day of admission.

". . . MMPI [Minnesota Multiphasic Personality Inventory, August 29, 1977] indicates very little change from a previous profile, 'a psychotic pattern with severe emotional disturbance. Thought disorder with fluctuating level of reality testing and paranoid mentation is frequently found.' IQ estimate by the Shipley-Hartford scale is 110 with a conceptual quotient of 104.

"The patient is of average appearance, wearing dark eye shadow and clothing to heighten her superficial female image. There is evidence of cultural deprivation. . . . She speaks in a dramatic way, quite animated, with frequent exclamation and gestures as she chews her gum vigorously. Her mood is matter-of-fact as she tells her hair-raising stories. She is oriented and her thinking is coherent, frequently irrelevant, with rambling associations. Simple calculations, serial 7's, and recalling the presidents is done with some difficulty. Interpretation of proverbs was more concrete than abstract.

"She relates hallucinations of seeing 'auras around any living or breathing thing,' and has delusions in which 'things look distorted to me, as if they are farther away.' The 'stabbing' may also be a hallucination. She relates no recent suicidal ideation.

"The patient received no medication while in the hospital. She became involved in ward activities in a friendly, outgoing manner and regaining her voice within three days."

Pigman visited her at Upham Hall and told her that when she was released from the hospital this time, she had to get away from Columbus, out into the fresh air, see new sights, meet new people.

"When you're better," he said, "I'm going to take you on the road with me. You can keep me company."

"I'd like that," she said, feeling good about him. Though he was old enough to be her father, she thought, he really cared about her.

Dr. Stinson terminated her third stay at Upham Hall on September 2, 1977, repeating his second diagnosis: *"schizophrenia, latent type."*

Bobby came with his brother's car to take her back to the apartment. He said with Deno's help he was kicking the habit, and he was going to get a job and take care of her.

She believed him.

Claudia had forgotten to tell me about meeting Bobby's new friends, and she became upset when I questioned her about them. One was a light-skinned mulatto Bobby called "Joker" because he couldn't let a line pass without making a joke about it. Claudia felt bad when Bobby explained that Joker had to stay drugged to keep laughing at life because he had sickle-cell anemia. Dope, Joker said, was the only thing that kept the grim reaper's sickle from mowing him down.

Bobby's other new friend was also a doper. Bisexual Rickey was tall and thin, with bright red hair and a full red beard. He had a cold quality about him that made her very nervous, and she had the feeling he would do anything—hurt anybody—who stood in the way of his getting Delaudids.

One Sunday, while she was washing dishes in the kitchen, she overheard the three of them discussing the front-page story in the *Columbus Dispatch* of December 11, 1977.

Later, when she was alone, she read it:

2 WOMEN SLAIN: MOTIVE UNKNOWN

Newark, Ohio—Police are investigating the shooting deaths of two women whose frozen bodies were found Saturday outside the rear door of a bar. . . .

The dead women are Mrs. Joyce Vermillion,
37, a barmaid at Forker's Café . . . and Karen
Dodrill, 33. . . .

Because Claudia worked as a waitress, the story
touched her. She felt terrible at the thought of the dead
women's bodies frozen in the icy night. She shivered in
the cold as she went to work again, and as she danced,
moving and bumping her body to the rock music, she
glanced into the glazed eyes of the men and hoped none
of them would want to kill her.

When she got home that night, she knelt beneath a
sacred plaque of Jesus praying in the Garden of Gethsemane she had mounted above the door between the living room and the dining room, and she prayed for the
two dead women.

She had no way of knowing at the time, she said, that
these were the first of the .22-caliber murders and that
their deaths would change her life.

January 1978 was a cruelly cold month. Columbus was
hit by one crippling snowstorm after another. The temperature stayed below ten degrees day after day, and
newspaper headlines referred to: "Dangerous Storms"
and "Snow Disaster." Finally, on Thursday, January 26,
the worst blizzard in U.S. history—the "Killer
Blizzard"—lashed through the city with eighty-mile-an-
hour winds and a wind-chill factor of sixty below zero.

Claudia had quit go-go dancing at the Latin Quarters
just before Christmas and started waiting on tables in
January at the nude-show restaurant Image Gallery. She
had taken a taxi to work the night of the blizzard, shiver-
ing in her brown cloth coat, but since there was little
business she returned home early—just after midnight.
As she came up the stairs she heard voices, and when she
entered the living room, she saw a stranger sitting in the
easy chair.

"Laudie, this is my new pool pal," Bobby said.
"Can't make it home tonight because of the blizzard, so
he's gonna stay over. He can sleep on the couch."

He was a small, slight man with dark-rimmed
glasses and timid eyes that avoided looking directly at
her. He had a high forehead and a mustache and goatee a

bit fuller than Bobby's. He seemed shy. She got them two beers at Bobby's request, then went back into the kitchen to do the dishes.

She heard scattered fragments about the bad weather, then the stranger's voice crying out, "I never wanted to do it."

She turned the water on to make them think she had started washing and moved close to the door to listen.

"He made me . . . oh, God, I didn't want to . . ." Then came the sound of retching as he threw up.

She stayed in the kitchen listening for a while and then went to bed. Though she lay awake for a long time trying to understand what he'd been talking about, his voice and others in her head were all mixed up now.

Remembering her vision of a woman stabbed in the alley, the trouble it had caused, and how everyone made fun of Crazy Claudia, she decided Bobby would say she had been hearing things if she asked him about it.

So she put it all out of her head, took a Dalmane 30, and let herself float into a deep and dreamless sleep. When she woke up, Bobby's guest was gone, and she complained that she resented having to scrub the carpet in the living room where his new pool-playing buddy had vomited.

Seventeen

1

One gusty afternoon in the spring of 1984, Claudia and I talked for a while, had lunch at a nearby Chinese restaurant, and then went back to her place. I asked her some background questions about the murdered Vicki Hancock, and after we talked about her for a while, and Claudia aired her own fears of being killed in the same way, she said, "Vicki's spirit is here, probably listening to us right now."

I was sitting with my back to the kitchen door, and Claudia—who was facing it—suddenly stared past me, her eyes opening wide in a look of horror, and let out a prolonged piercing scream. For several seconds I couldn't move, a prickling sensation sweeping over my skin, but then I jumped up and turned, half-expecting to see Vicki's burned body drifting towards us.

The kitchen door, through which we had entered, had swung open.

"It's just the goddamned wind," I said, when I was able to breathe again.

Fist to her mouth, she shook her head. "Vicki's spirit was here because we were talking about her. She's gone out."

"Oh, come on, Claudia. When we came in, I was behind you. I just didn't pull the door tight enough for it to catch. You see how strong the wind is outside."

"Vicki just left."

"Well, then, how do you know it wasn't her coming in instead of going out? Maybe she's here right now. Hi, Vicki. How's tricks?"

"You just don't have faith, Dan. You've got to believe."

"I believe what I see and hear with my own eyes and ears." Almost as soon as the words came out of my mouth, I knew I'd made a mistake. It gave her an opening.

"I guess that means you will never believe what happened the night of the McCann murders. Since you weren't there."

"Claudia, you know I believe you. Otherwise I wouldn't be going on with this. What I mean by *my own eyes and ears* can include evidence, testimony of an eyewitness. Now, like the court, I wouldn't accept hearsay evidence. But you were there and saw the murders, and I'd believe what you told me."

"I never said I saw the murders."

"Yes, you did."

She looked perplexed. "I did? When?"

"In your confession to Howard Champ."

She relaxed and smiled. "Oh, that. I made all that up to confuse Howard. I wove lies in with the truth. All that stuff about Bobby and Deno. I knew it would never stand up."

"Why did you tell him you committed the murders?"

"To save myself. I didn't want to die."

"You've got me confused now. Would you explain that?"

She brushed me off with a wave of her hand. "Not yet. When I trust you."

I should have known by now that—even though the spirits had given their okay for her to confide in me—it was going to be this way until the end of our relationship.

"How long is that going to take, Claudia? It's been more than two years. What do I have to do to prove myself?"

"You have to be careful when you interview people. I tell you things, and then find out you went and told them."

"That's the way it works. I have to corroborate the things you tell me."

"That shows you don't trust me. So why should I trust you?"

"It doesn't show I don't trust you. That's how a writer of nonfiction or a reporter has to work. I have to have at least one—and preferably two people who confirm what you say. It's like navigating at sea or surveying on the land—checking out the unknown point by using two other known points of reference and then triangulating."

She looked at me as if I were an idiot. "You're not a surveyor or a navigator. You're writing a book about me, and all you have to do is put down the things I tell you."

"That's not all I have to do, Claudia. I have to put down the truth."

"You're implying that I'm not telling you the truth."

"You often don't *remember* the truth. You've told me that a hundred times since we began. Isn't that so?"

"Yes."

"And I've got to put together the story by talking to everyone I can reach who was involved or who knows anything. I've got your angle on some of these things. When I get their angles, I can—"

"Triangulate?"

"Right."

"But when you talk to them, you don't have to say, 'Claudia told me.' You can just say, 'I heard such-and-such, and I'd like to ask you about so-and-so.' Can't you do that?"

"I guess I could. But what difference does it make?"

"A lot. My mother called me and she was furious that I told you certain things about her. And my father called my mother. Now they're angry with me."

"Well, I had to check them out. And because they both deny the things you said, I won't repeat those things in the book. If I just accepted your accusations, I'd be irresponsible."

She was studying me.

"But you're right about one thing," I said. "I don't have to say: 'Claudia said.' I can just ask them the facts. If my interviewing techniques have caused you any trouble, I'm sorry."

"Okay," she said. "As long as you're careful in the future."

We went over some minor details and then I settled back and looked right into those innocent-looking green eyes.

"I want you to go back mentally to that period, just before the McCann murders."

She groaned. "Do we have to? It upsets me."

"I'm sorry, Claudia. But that's the heart of the story."

She hunched back in the chair and closed her eyes.

I spoke in a soft, hypnotic monotone. "Now to get you back there, I'd like you to think of the weather. It was cold . . . it was snowing . . . for days and days . . . harder and harder . . . Cold . . . deep . . . snow . . ."

She was nodding as I spoke, and then suddenly her eyes popped open. "Oh, my God. I remembered something."

"Go ahead. Tell it."

"I worked that evening of the Killer Blizzard. But there wasn't much business and my boss closed the Image Gallery early that night. When I got home, I walked into the apartment and saw the back of a head of someone sitting in a chair. Bobby told me it was someone he played pool with, someone who couldn't get back home because of the blizzard, so he'd invited him to sleep on our couch."

Her eyes were wide and shining as she seemed to be visualizing that time. "I said hello, and then I went into the kitchen and let the water run to do the dishes. But I kept my ear to the crack in the door, and I heard him and Bobby talking. The man was saying something about two women in Newark—talking and crying at the same time. He was saying it was his brother who forced him to do it. And he felt sick about it. Then he threw up all over the carpet."

"You've told me that already—"

She gripped my wrist. "No! No! Just wait. Later,

when they caught the .22-caliber killers, I recognized him on TV. The man who threw up on my carpet was Gary Lewingdon."

I suddenly recalled her story about seeing the faces surrounding her on the TV sets in the discount appliance store, and now I understood why she had run out screaming.

"Why didn't you tell the police about it?"

"How could I? Until I saw his picture, I never made the connection."

"And why didn't you tell the police when you finally did realize who he was?"

"He'd been arrested already. And I started getting those threatening phone calls, hinting I was going to be killed. I knew it was too late to make any difference. They were caught. The murders were over. So I just kept my mouth shut. I didn't want to die like Vicki."

I struggled to keep my composure. I'd learned never to show excitement in front of Claudia. "Go on," I said.

"With what?"

"And then what happened?"

"That's all there is."

"Oh, come on now! There's got to be more about Gary Lewingdon."

She crossed her arms and shook her head. I knew it would be useless to probe deeper today. But as I left I wanted to cry out to the world that, up to this moment, no one—neither the detectives nor the attorneys nor the newspapers—had ever shown a direct connection between Claudia and the .22-caliber killers.

2

For weeks, I couldn't get her to say anything else about meeting Gary Lewingdon. She kept insisting that was all. But I knew Claudia was still hiding the truth from me. Though my nerves were stretched taut, I warned myself not to lose patience.

One day after I'd been rereading Gary's confession, I brought it up again. "I've been thinking about what you told me about Gary Lewingdon spending the night of the blizzard at your apartment. Did the police ever learn that?"

She looked at me as if I was a fool even to think that. "Of course not! I never mentioned him."

"During Gary's confession to the police, he denied ever having met you. Why would he do that?"

"Bobby probably told him my name was Laudie—what he always called me. And those pictures in the papers didn't look at all like me. So Gary probably thought Claudia Yasko was someone else. He probably didn't even know he'd met me, and slept on my couch the night of the blizzard."

She shook her head. "You know the worst thing," she said, "was after he was gone the next morning, I had to scrub his vomit out of the carpet. You try doing that sometime."

"I've wiped up vomit, Claudia. I was a purser-pharmacist's mate on board ship. I had to do a lot of messy things."

"So you know what I mean."

Then I remembered what she had said once about the smell of vomit making her relive the gang rape, and I felt terrible.

"Yes, Claudia," I said. "I do."

She smiled sweetly, sitting back in her rocking chair, hands folded one over the other—a sexy *Whistler's Mother* in repose—and waited for me to proceed.

"Do you trust me now, Claudia?"

She nodded.

"Enough to tell me what happened on the night of the murders?"

She stopped the rocker forward, brought her face close to mine, and looked into my eyes. "Yes," she whispered.

My chest felt tight.

"But you have to ask me questions," she said. "That's the only way."

"All right. Going back to the night of the murders. You worked that night?"

"What night was it?"

I consulted my chronology chart. "Saturday night was February 11, 1978. The murders happened in the early hours of Sunday morning."

"Yes, I worked Saturday night."

"And then what?"

"When I got done work, early Sunday morning, Pig-man took me and Ginger to breakfast at the Western Pan-cake House. The one on Morse Road."

"Go on."

"Then Ginger was going to drive me home, but she had a flat tire, and Pigman gave us both a lift in his eighteen-wheeler. First he took her home, and then he dropped me off at my apartment. I remember it took me a long time to walk upstairs because on the stairs Bobby had left parts of the car he was repairing. I'd bought it for him, and it was parked out front for months while he worked on it. Anyway, I went upstairs, and let myself in and I remember when I got inside I saw someone sitting in a chair with his back to the door. I just saw the back of his head. And when I got inside that's when I saw it was Gary."

"Lewingdon?" I asked incredulously. "A second time?"

"Yes. He was sitting there drinking beer with Bobby, and I excused myself and went to take a bath. Only I didn't take a bath. I just let the water run so they'd think I was, and I listened through the door I'd left open a crack."

She was rocking now, in slowly increasing rhythm as she spoke. I had questions to ask, but I had learned not to interrupt her recall.

"Gary was saying he just murdered Mickey and Chrissie and Mickey's mother. He went into details. He was crying and said it was his brother Thaddeus's idea, and he had to go along or his brother would kill him. He talked about everything, like he had to get it off his chest."

I must have sat there openmouthed, astounded at her revelation that Gary had come to talk to Bobby after the murders.

"Later, when he was gone," she said, "I was terri-fied to know that he had been in my apartment that morning after committing those terrible murders. I couldn't sleep a wink that afternoon because I was afraid he'd remember what he told Bobby, and he might figure out I overheard, and he'd come back and kill us both."

She was getting more and more upset as she got deeper into her story, and it worried me when I saw how terribly it affected her to bring all this buried material to the surface. I didn't want to play amateur psychiatrist with a mentally unstable woman, yet as a writer doing what she had sought me out to do, I had to help her overcome her resistance to uncovering the past.

I sat quietly, trying to hide my own anxiety. Finally, after two years, I was learning the connecting link between the Lewingdons and Claudia.

"Then what did you do?"

"I looked up my astrological forecast."

"Do you remember what it said?"

"That it was a good day to discover something—a good day for probing."

"Ahaaaa!"

She laughed and echoed, "Ahaaaa!"

"You're not making this up?"

"No . . . I'm remembering . . ."

"Whose astrological books were you using then?"

"Sidney Omar. His forecast for Gemini."

I nodded. "This is great, Claudia. Go on."

She stopped rocking. "That's it. That's how I knew all those details."

Suddenly I was deflated. I looked at her incredulously.

"What?"

"That's how I knew the murder scene. That's what you've been trying to find out all these months, isn't it?"

I spoke slowly to hide my disappointment. "The only problem is that I can't believe Gary would go into such detail—the hazelnuts on the floor, the snow blower in the garage, the blue bowl of cereal in the sink. He would never have described such things to Bobby. You must have learned about them another way."

She pouted. "You don't believe me."

"How can I? When you tell me things that don't make sense, I don't know what to do."

I was ready to argue it out, but as her eyes went wide

and pleading, I knew it was no use to press her. She'd lied under interrogation by experts.

Still, we were getting close to it. The answer was there, if only I could make her trust me.

3

The following week, we went through the same material, this time beginning with events later in the day of the murders—after Gary Lewingdon had described the murders to Bobby.

"I remember Pigman told me the week before," she said, "that we'd be celebrating Valentine's Day early because he had to be on the road, and he'd take me and Ginger to dinner at the Kahiki before we went to work. I got dressed—it takes me forever to get ready—and he picked me up. Ginger met us at the Kahiki."

"Pigman took you out to dinner before work? And then out again to breakfast after work on that day?"

"He was that kind of guy. He liked to do that."

"Go on, what happened at the Kahiki?"

"I was pretty upset after overhearing Gary talk about the three people he and his brother had just murdered. I told Pigman and Ginger that I had to make a phone call, and I went to the lounge and called a neighbor to pick me up at the Kahiki, because I needed to be driven somewhere. Then I told them to go on ahead, and I asked Ginger to sign in for me at the Image Gallery because I knew I'd be a little late. They didn't like the idea of leaving me alone, but I told them there was something important I had to do, that a friend was on his way, and I'd be all right . . ."

"Go on," I whispered, not wanting to break the spell.

"A little while later my friend arrived."

"What's his name?"

She shook her head. "I don't remember. And why do you say *his*? I can't recall if it was a man or a woman. Really I don't. But whoever it was had red hair. Maybe the name will come to me. Anyway, whoever it was left Columbus a long time ago."

"Where were you driven to?"

She looked at me imploringly and put her hand on top of mine. "You're sure I won't be charged with a crime? I don't want to be sent back to prison for this."

"I can't see how you would. We've been through this before. With the murders solved, what prosecutor in the world would want to reopen the case?"

She thought about that a moment and nodded. "All right. I asked the person to drive me to the McCann house."

It was so simple it left me stunned. "Why?"

"I just had to see if what I'd overheard was true. In the past, time and again, I'd been accused of having hallucinations when I overheard something. The time I saw a woman stabbed in my backyard people said it was a delusion—that it never happened. I had to satisfy my curiosity."

"How did you know where the house was?"

"I'd been there before."

"Then Mickey McCann's mother really did invite you to the house for dinner as you told Champ?"

She slapped my hand gently. "You're jumping to conclusions again. No, that's one of the things I made up to confuse Champ. Actually, Mickey's house previously belonged to a woman I know who owned a gay bar in Columbus. I don't want to mention her name. But she had big parties and I was invited a few times. That's how I knew the house so well. I knew every room."

I nodded my apology.

"Where was I before you interrupted me? You mustn't stop me when I'm remembering or I'll lose it all."

"Sorry. You asked this friend to drive you to McCann's house. Did you go inside?"

She swallowed hard and nodded. "I did. I went in and walked—really I ran—through the house and saw the bodies. It was hot inside because Gary or his brother had turned the thermostat up all the way. Do you know why?"

"Tell me."

"To make it more difficult to determine the mother's time of death. Mickey and Chrissie were frozen in the garage, so nobody could tell from their bodies either. I saw

everything I wanted to see, and then I ran out and my
friend drove me to work."

I sat there limp. "So in a way Howard Champ was
right. You *did* go to the murder scene. Why didn't you
just tell him what you told me? Why all that other stuff
about holding the gun, and Bobby pulling the trigger,
and things like that?"

She shrugged. "I knew Champ wouldn't believe me.
I had to tell him something he'd believe, and I had to mix
it up with fantasy so that it wouldn't stand up in court."

"You thought all that out?"

She smiled. "Dan, I'm a very intelligent person."

"Yes, you are, Claudia. I've never doubted that."

She knew I meant it, and I could see that pleased her.

"A few questions about what you've told me."

"I don't like going over it," she said. "It bothers me
to think of those bodies."

"All right. Did your friend with the red hair go in
with you?"

"Oh, no. He or she sat in the car with the motor running."

"In front of the house or across the street?"

"Across the street."

"Was it snowing or had it stopped?"

"Oh, snowing," she said emphatically. "Very hard."

"Did he or she know why you were going into the
house?"

"Not that night. I guess the person found out after
the bodies were discovered and it was reported in the papers."

"What did he or she say to you after that?"

"I never saw my neighbor again. I'm pretty sure he
or she got out of town."

I didn't believe for a minute that she couldn't recall
if her driver had been a man or a woman. Claudia was
holding out on me again, but I let it go for the time being
and shifted the questioning to events of later that morning.

"What did you tell Ginger and Pigman at breakfast?"

"My vision of Mickey McCann being shot to death."

"Wasn't that risky?"

"They knew I was psychic."

"And you used your knowledge that you had gained a few hours earlier to impress them with your powers. You figured that when the murders were discovered and hit the newspapers and TV, they would be astonished at your prediction."

She nodded.

"Did it hit you during that day that you were fulfilling Omar's astrological prediction? That you were discovering things?"

"Definitely."

"You thought of it? At that moment?"

"It was in my mind all along."

"And when you went to the house that night, did you do it *because* that had been your forecast?"

"That had a lot to do with it. It influenced me. Every day I was influenced by what I read."

"Is that what made you go?"

"That was part of it."

"And the other part?"

"I wanted to be sure what I'd heard wasn't a hallucination."

"And is it possible that the third part was your wanting to know what everything looked like so that you could say you used your occult powers and were there spiritually?"

"It was a combination of all three."

She smiled with the innocence of a child pleased with her own performance. "I'm so happy we got that out. I told you my psychic adviser said you'd be able to finish the book. It means more to me now than anything else in the world."

"I don't mean to be a pessimist, Claudia, but you've just given me the tip of the iceberg. We'll have to dig deeper."

"That's what I want, to give you everything you need. It's the one hope that's been keeping me going all these years. Promise me you won't stop until it's done."

I promised.

When I got home, I knew the excitement would prevent me from sleeping. I set to work immediately to put the new pieces of the puzzle into place. Usually, sessions with Claudia left me too tired to write, but now I was delirious to get it down on paper.

It had taken more than two years, but I had it.

All I needed were a couple of missing pieces: to find out if the neighbor who drove her to Ongaro Drive was a man or a woman, and to get her to recall the events *after* she left the McCann house. But compared to what I'd gone through to get today's revelations, those would be easy.

I celebrated that evening with a glass of champagne because the mystery was finally solved!

Eighteen

1

A few days later I found myself pacing back and forth in my room, restraining the overwhelming impulse to smash my fist into the wall. What she had told me was all a lie.

When I reviewed both Lewingdon brothers' trial transcripts and confessions, I realized they didn't match Claudia's version of what had happened. Gary had told the detectives that Thaddeus had driven his own car that night, picked him up, and that they'd gone home together from the McCann house.

How then could Claudia have heard Gary confide in Bobby Sunday morning at her place, right after the murders? I didn't believe Gary would then drive about fifteen miles from Kirkersville, Ohio, all the way back to Columbus during a heavy snowstorm. And if he hadn't come to the apartment directly from the McCann house, how could Claudia have heard about the killings and known enough to call her neighbor to drive her there?

All lies! Or were they? Maybe she'd mixed lies in with the truth to confuse me just as she had done to Howard Champ.

I confronted her with it at our next meeting.

"How could you have known about the murders?"
She appeared confused. "I didn't," she said.

"What do you mean? You had to have known before
you made the trip there with your neighbor."

"Not necessarily," she scolded. "There you go again."
It was like a slap in the face. "How then?"

"You know when I told you I called my neighbor to
drive me there?"

"Yes."

"Well, that wasn't how it happened. What happened
was this person knew about it and took me there."

"*What?*"

"Yes, that's it. He was the one who knew, and I went
along with him."

"Why did you go?"

"Because I didn't know what to expect. And this person had a gun and threatened me with it."

"So you made up that whole lie about Gary Lewingdon coming to your apartment a second time after the
murders and describing it in detail to Bobby?"

"Yes. I'm sorry."

I am not a violent person, but I felt like breaking furniture. "Where do we go from here?"

"What do you mean?"

"How do I continue writing about someone who
keeps lying to me about the important events?"

"I *said* I was sorry. I'm not lying on purpose."

"And you think that takes care of it?"

"What do you want me to do?"

"I want you to tell me the truth about what happened. How you came to know all you did about the murder scene and the murders themselves."

She looked chagrined. "I was there. I was really in
that house."

"When? During the murders?"

"No, afterwards."

"With this neighbor of yours?"

"Yes, that's true. I swear to God that part is true."

"All right then, Claudia, let's review the day of the
murders. I'm having trouble believing you don't remember if the neighbor who drove you was a man or a
woman."

I could see her stiffen. "You don't trust me," she said, looking offended.

"Claudia, you admitted you lied to me about most of that story."

"Well, I *said* I was sorry."

"And I believe that. But dammit, *sorry* isn't enough! Now we have to go over the events of that night again."

"I'm getting upset now."

I turned off the tape recorder. "Then maybe we'd better stop. Maybe we ought to just call it quits."

"I don't want that, Dan. I've told you again and again how much this book means to me."

"What else can I do?"

"It bothers me that you don't believe me," she said.

"Claudia, I've got a problem. I don't want to upset you but I've got to be very careful about what I write."

"Please don't stop, Dan."

"If we're going to continue, I have to know what really happened."

"I just don't remember."

"Do you want to work at it?"

She nodded. "I'll try."

I turned on the tape recorder and hunched forward. "You're in the car being driven to the house."

"What house?"

"McCann's house."

"At 4187 Ongaro Drive . . . ?"

"Right."

"Okay. What's the question?"

"I want you to tell me what you see, hear. . . . Give me a description of what happened."

"I remember it was snowing heavily. I can see the windshield wipers going back and forth making two pie-shaped wedges for us to see out of. We were on the highway. And we passed a sheriff's cruiser. I was frightened . . ."

"Go on."

Her eyes went wide. "I remember! I can see him! Sitting beside me driving the car!"

"Him?"

"I told you about red hair? Now I also see a red beard. Tall, red beard, wearing a khaki military-style jacket. Ohmygod!"

"What?"

"Now I realize why I couldn't remember if he was a man or a woman."

I waited and she gazed at me in awe of her own discovery. "Because he was a *bisexual*. . . . *Bisexual Brady*."

The maddening thing was that it made sense. "You told Champ in your confession that a *Biracial Mickey* was in the house."

"I did that to confuse him. Bobby's other friend, Joker, is mulatto. I guess I combined them."

"Do you have a last name for Brady?"

"Just Bisexual Brady. That's why I felt confident about phoning him. I've always been uncomfortable around straight people."

She was looking right at me accusingly.

"I'm sorry," I said. "Forgive my life-style. I'm as straight as you can get."

"Maybe that's why I've been lying to you. I know you can't really understand my world."

"I've got to make the attempt, Claudia, but I'll need your help."

She smiled her saintliest smile. "I'll try."

"Okay, now," I said. "I know you don't drive. And you have no sense of direction or how to get from one place in the city to another. How would Bisexual Brady have been able to find McCann's house?"

"All the time we were driving there, I hoped he wouldn't know who owned it."

"Did he have the address?"

"I have no idea."

"Had he been to parties at the house before?"

"How could he have?"

"You said the house had formerly been owned by the woman who owned the Casbah. Gay parties. I figured maybe—"

"I meant to tell you, Dan. I don't think that was really the house she owned."

"But you told me—"

"That's when I was lying to you. *Now* I'm telling you the truth."

I slumped back in my chair. "You mean you made that whole thing up too?"

"Just parts of it."

"You know what I realize now, Claudia? You're doing to me exactly what you did to Champ. Giving me bits of the truth, but throwing in enough fantasy to make the whole thing worthless. I resent it. Hell, I really do."

She leaned forward, her eyes wide in innocent surprise. "You're right, Dan. . . . I'm very sorry."

She took my hand, her fingers cool and smooth to the touch. "Be patient with me. Give me time to trust you. When I know you won't hurt me, I'm sure I'll remember what really happened, and I'll tell you."

I looked down at the long fingers, each with rings and tapered blood-red nails. "How much time, Claudia?"

"When your aura changes. Right now the aura around you troubles me, and I can't remember things. I know you expect me to tell you everything, so I make things up to satisfy you. You were right when you said that's what I did with Champ. That's why my confession confused everybody."

I didn't say what suddenly occurred to me: that she saw me in the same role as Champ—as an interrogator. It made me feel lousy.

"What do you want me to do, Claudia?"

"Keep on, as we've been doing. You can't stop now. We're close. I know everything's going to turn out all right."

I sat silently for a long time to let myself simmer down. Then I looked deep into her green eyes. "Okay, let's start over, Claudia. Were you telling me the truth when you said you actually entered the house?"

"What house?"

"The goddamned murder house!"

"On 4187 Ongaro Drive?"

"That's the house. Mickey's house. The murder house."

She gave me an exasperated look. "You *know* I was there. Why are you asking me that? Howard Champ figured out I was there. I *told* you I was in the house. Don't you *believe* me?"

"Yes, Claudia." I pressed my fingers into my throbbing temples. "I do believe you. I really believe you. Believe me, I believe you. What I'd like you to do now is tell me your feelings while you were in the house."

"Why do you want to know?"

I whispered, not trusting myself to raise my voice again, "So . . . I can . . . put it . . . into the book."

"Oh . . ." She smiled as if just remembering what I was doing here and what our conversations for two years were all about. "I was very frightened to be in the garage alone with two dead people. And then when I went up the steps into the kitchen and saw Mrs. McCann I felt very sorry she was dead too."

"You said to Champ you had been invited to the house often before by Mrs. McCann, whom you called *Mamma*. You've since told me you hadn't. Which is true?"

"I never even knew her. I was never even in that house *before* the night of the murders."

"Are you telling me the truth about having been there the night of the murders?"

She held my gaze. "Yes."

"Did your friend—Bisexual Brady—go in with you?"

"No, he stayed out in the car."

"With the motor running?"

"Yes, I remember he had the motor running, because when I came out and got in, I said, 'Let's get away from here.' And he pulled away from the curb saying, 'You look like you've seen a ghost.' And I didn't know what to answer."

"And then what happened? Tell me about the drive home."

"I don't remember."

"Did he ever bring it up, after he saw the news reports of the murders?"

"No."

"Were you afraid he'd go to the police?"

She thought about it. "I guess I did wonder if I could trust him. I tried to get in touch with him, but I heard from some people that he left town right away."

"Let's back up then. I'd like to know what really happened before you went."

"I don't remember."

"How about anything that happened that day?"

She shook her head. "It's a blank."

"Then I'm afraid this is all hopeless."

"The spirits will help us, Dan. I know they will. My dreams are giving me good signs."

"All right, let's talk a little more about your beliefs in the spiritual area. You're a born-again Christian involved with Jesus, right?"

"Yes."

"How did you feel when you were studying witchcraft? That's the opposite of Christianity, right? That's denying Jesus. When did you turn from witchcraft to Jesus?"

"When I saw Him. He came to my cell before I got out of prison. That's when I knew there had to be something to it."

"Do you actually believe you saw the real Jesus there?"

"I *know* I did."

"When you were involved in witchcraft, did you ever see the Devil?"

"Oh, many times. I saw a man with a black hood over his head, beckoning to me. And that really frightened me."

"Was that in dreams or—"

"In dreams, but also when I was awake."

"It must have been a frightening time," I said.

"Not just that time. All through my childhood I felt the presence of spiritual beings in the room with me." She looked around and then whispered confidentially, "There are spirits here *now*, Dan. I can see them. And hear them. Some of them are even helping me find out the answers for you."

When I left her apartment that afternoon, I was frustrated again and uncertain about going on with the interviews, but I was even more concerned about the effect on both of us if I stopped.

She called me at home late that night, awakening me, and told me not to worry about anything because she'd phoned her anonymous spiritual adviser, who assured her that everything was going to work out all right.

"I had the feeling you were upset today," she said, "and I figured the news would help you sleep better."

2

"Claudia, I'm going in circles," I said to her the following Thursday. "I don't know what to believe anymore."

She touched my shoulder and stared deep into my eyes. "I'm sorry, Dan. I trust you more, but not completely yet."

"How much time is it going to take? Are we going to be able to solve the mystery?"

"The spirits tell me you're going to solve all the problems."

She sat back in the rocking chair and smiled a gentle smile. From the way the lamp was positioned today, it cast a halolike glow around her hair. I think that's what set me off—seeing her posing as an angel. I knew the anger was rising in me again, and I couldn't control my words.

"I'll tell you what bothers me, Claudia. All your life, you've put yourself into the hands of sadists, con men, criminals who seek you out to manipulate you, abuse you, destroy you. I'm someone *you* sought out . . . to do something *you* want. You trust them, but not me. Can you tell me why?"

She shrugged. "I just listen to the advice of my spiritual adviser. I call her, and we talk for long periods on the phone. She gives me advice."

"And what is her advice?"

"To be careful about what I tell you."

I got up and paced back and forth. "I don't know what I'm going to do, Claudia. I've been as patient as possible. I've tried to be understanding. But I think I'm going back to writing fiction. I think I'll put these two years down to experience, cut my losses, and take off."

"You don't have to do that, Dan. It's going to come."

"As Rhett said, 'Frankly, my dear, I don't give a damn.'"

Her laugh came out deep and girl-like, as she pointed a finger at me. "Clark Gable in *Gone With the Wind* . . . right?"

It was the childish innocence that got me. "Yes, Claudia."

"I've seen it twice on TV."

I believed her. I visualized her sitting alone in her bed, with the kitchen knife stuck above the hinge of the kitchen door, watching old movies. The anger drained away.

I sighed. "What do you want me to do, Claudia?"

Her eyebrows went up. "I want you to keep working at it, of course. We're committed to it. One thing I've learned about you, Dan, is that you don't give up. You're going to dig it out . . . but it won't be easy. The problem is I don't remember most of what happened. And when I don't remember, I fill in the spaces with what I *think* is true, and then I don't remember what's true and what's not."

"That's what psychologists call *confabulation*."

"Psychologists have a word for everything," she said with a disparaging wave of her hand. "But I can only tell you what I remember—or what I *think* I remember. It'll be up to you to figure out if it's real or not."

"Beautiful," I said.

"You can do it," she said.

"Do you trust me to do it?"

"That," she said, "is another story."

I sat there for a long time considering the challenge.

I got nothing new that week or the next or the next. Every time I tried to bring her memory back to the McCann house on the night of the murders, her thoughts seemed to slip away. Then one hot, muggy evening after we'd spent some time going over background details, I was reminded of a question I had planned to ask Claudia based on some material I had gotten from the files of David Long, her civil lawsuit attorney, a reference to an interview Claudia had given to a TV reporter named Dave Layman.

"There's something I want to check out with you here."

She sat forward in her rocker, expression serious, hands clasped. I showed her the note in Long's handwriting: *"Did she tell Dave Layman that she tried to tip off McCann through his girlfriend Christine Herdman?"*

She looked up at me with an expression of sudden insight. "I did! I did try to warn him."

"How?"

"I phoned Mickey's Eldorado Club."

"And what happened?"

"The line was busy. I kept trying, but the line was busy."

I settled back in the couch and stared at her. She looked like an excited little girl who had just been given a present. "I remember . . . I remember . . ."

Very slowly I asked, "What is it you remember?"

"Calling to warn Chrissie that Mickey was in danger."

Sharp as she was, she obviously didn't see the significance of what she was saying. I held my breath and waited to let it sink in.

"That could only mean one thing, Claudia."

Her eyes opened wide. "What's that?"

"That you knew *ahead of time* that Mickey McCann *was going to be murdered.*"

She sat very still, looking straight into my eyes.

"Which would blow away your story of having learned about it afterwards from overhearing Gary describe the murders to Bobby."

She looked like a doe caught in the bright headlights of an onrushing car, frightened but unable to flee.

"Which would also explain how you were able to predict his murder to Pigman and Ginger at breakfast. Not the morning of his death. But probably days before he was murdered. Because you *knew in advance* Mickey was going to be murdered."

The air quickly went out of her. She nodded, trembling.

"How did you know?" I asked.

"I knew."

"How?"

"From the *second* time I saw Gary Lewingdon . . . No . . ." She held up her hand. "Wait! Not *saw* him. I didn't see him that second time. I *overheard* him talking to Bobby."

"When was that?"

"I don't remember."

"Before or after he spent the night during the blizzard?"

"After."

"Before or after the murders?"

"Before."

"During the week, or on a weekend?"

"It would always have been on weekends," she said, "because Chuck and Gary worked during the week."

Her habit of referring to Thaddeus as "Chuck" threw me off for a time, as I assumed it meant she had known him personally. But she hadn't. Then I thought it meant she had overheard Gary refer to him as Chuck. But all the testimony I had read showed that Gary and Delaine referred to Thaddeus only as "Charles." So her calling him Chuck was just another pose and a lie. Another frustration to deal with in silence.

I took out my 1978 annotated calendar. "The Killer Blizzard happened the last week in January. The triple homicide took place on the second weekend in February. That leaves only one weekend."

She pointed to the date February 4 on which I'd printed the historical note: *Carter and Sadat start peace talks.*

"What's that?" she asked.

"In checking the headlines for the period of the crimes, I also jot down major political events, just for myself, to help me understand what else was happening in the world."

"Well, while Carter and Sadat were talking peace, I was overhearing talk of murder."

I checked to make sure the tape recorder's red light was on and said, "Tell me about it."

3

The Saturday before the McCann murders, Bobby had sent her to Cokley's to buy groceries. Cokley's was more expensive than the supermarkets, but it was within walking distance, so they shopped there often. She had bought the beer, milk, and bread, and as she passed the meat section, she slipped a package of frozen steak into her coat pocket. As she started down the aisle to the checkout counter, her cart knocked over a display of breakfast cereal, and when she stopped to pick up the boxes Mr. Cokley came to help her.

When they were done, he looked at her sadly. "Now don't you want to put back that package you have in your pocket?"

"Oh, I was going to pay for it," she said quickly, pulling it out and tossing it into the shopping cart. "I just did that without thinking."

He shook his head. "Well, a beautiful woman like you shouldn't have to shoplift groceries."

She laughed to hide her embarrassment and paid for everything with her last ten-dollar bill and food stamps. She trudged through the snow, back to the apartment, remembering the time Mr. Cokley had caught Bobby stealing frozen turkey drumsticks and made him pay for them. "I think you owe me an apology," Mr. Cokley had said. But Bobby had stared him down and said, "I don't think I have to apologize for being hungry."

Bobby always knew the right thing to say.

Claudia climbed the stairs at the side of the apartment, because with packages it was always awkward to climb over the tools and parts Bobby had left on the front steps.

When she got to the second-floor landing, she maneuvered around the refrigerator Bobby had told her he was thinking of buying from his new pool-playing buddy. She got the kitchen door open with one hand, trying to squeeze in, but she got stuck. She was about to call out for Bobby to help when she heard voices. First Bobby and then—it took her just a second to recognize it was him—the pool-playing buddy who'd slept over during the blizzard.

He was saying his wife had drawn two maps: one from their house in Newark to Ongaro Drive, and the other from Mickey's Eldorado Club to Ongaro Drive. "My brother and I have been there twice already, casing the place. We know exactly how long it will take to get there from my house, and how long it will take Mickey to get home from his club. We'll be waiting for him."

"Lower your voice, Gary, for God's sake," Bobby

said. "People downstairs might hear you through the ventilator."

"Even though Charles knows the setup, I'd rather do it without him. But I need help. I couldn't take Mickey on alone."

"What makes you think he'll have a lot of money with him next Saturday night?"

"Everybody knows he always carries a big roll. And Dee has inside information, from someone who should know, that it'll be bigger than ever Saturday."

"I wish I could help you," Bobby said. "But my knee is in bad shape, and I wouldn't be much good to you. You'll find someone else."

"No one else I trust, except you or my brother, and I'm worried about Charles. After what happened to the two women in Newark, I'm beginning to think he enjoys shooting people."

"What about you?" Bobby asked.

"I can't eat or sleep for days afterwards. But I'm doing this one to stop Dee's nightmares."

On the porch, Claudia backed away from the door. With the groceries in her arms it was difficult to free herself, pinned as she was between the refrigerator and the door, but she managed to pull loose and set the bags down. She took off her boots and tiptoed down the stairs.

The man Bobby had called Gary was a crazy killer. And if he knew she'd overheard him, he might also murder her.

Once on the street, she pulled her boots on again over her wet stockings and ran to the pay telephone down the block. She phoned Ginger and begged to move in with her. Ginger said she'd have to ask her roommate and she'd let Claudia know later at the Image Gallery.

When Claudia hung up, the realization that she had to go back and get changed for work terrified her.

She returned to the apartment, relieved to find that Gary had left, but Bobby was in a foul mood. The haunted look in his eyes told her he was having to put off his fix longer than he could stand it. The heavy snows and the blizzard were making it tough for drug connections to get through to Columbus, and the prices were going up. Though her penny-pinching boss kept his place open six days a week—snowstorms or not—there wasn't much business, and not many tips. Cabs were so hard to get she had to call them two hours ahead of time, and some days the fare was more than she earned.

"We've got to get money," Bobby said. "I can't stand this much longer. Why don't you get a better-paying job?"

"Why don't *I*?" she screamed. "Why don't *you*? I'm fed up with supporting you and your goddamned habit."

That started the shouting. Claudia let go with everything she had, but she was careful not to let him know what she'd overheard.

Ginger couldn't give her an answer that evening, and Claudia knew she was stuck with Bobby for a while longer. She suddenly wanted to go back to Hawaii, where the weather was warm and where she could feel safe. She considered going to the police and warning them about Gary's plan to kill McCann, but she remembered the two women he and his brother had murdered in Newark.

During a lull in tending the few customers that night, Claudia said, she used the pay phone outside the rest rooms and called the Eldorado Club to warn Mickey. But she got a busy signal. She planned to try again later, but she forgot.

During the week Pigman called and said he'd decided to celebrate Valentine's Day next Saturday night instead of waiting until the following Tuesday.

At the Kahiki, Pigman and Ginger noticed she was mentally far away and asked what was wrong.

She shook her head. "I'm having a vision. . . . Someone is going to die. I know it . . ."

They had heard her talk of her psychic powers before, and though Pigman made fun of spiritualists and mediums, Ginger took her seriously.

"Who's going to die?" she asked.

"His name begins with M," Claudia said. "The spirits tell me he will be shot to death. I can see him lying in his own blood."

"When is all this going to take place?" Pigman asked.

"This weekend."

"Can we go and watch?"

"You're making fun of me," Claudia said.

"Look, I'm just a truck driver," he said, "and I don't know much about this prophesying stuff, but I guess if you can really predict a murder, we'll be reading about it in the newspapers."

"You will," Claudia said. "And then you'll believe I can foretell the future."

Pigman shrugged and lit a cigar. "You know how much I think of you, Claudia. But you've got to admit that with the murder rate in this country, someone, somewhere, whose first or last initial is M, will be shot tonight."

"I believe in your visions, Claudia," Ginger whispered. "Do you see anything else?"

"I'm too upset now," Claudia said. "Maybe at breakfast I'll see what else I can tell you."

When they left the Kahiki at six-thirty, it was already dark and snowing again. Pigman said he had to move his truck, but he would pick them up at two-thirty for breakfast.

"I want to hear more about the murder," he said.

It was a quiet night at the Image Gallery because the snow had gotten worse, and when Pigman came to pick them up he suggested they go in his truck because Ginger had no snow tires. They got to the Western Pancake House at 2:30 A.M., had a big breakfast, and while they were drinking their coffee, he brought up the subject again.

"So, Claudia, any more details of the murder of M?"

Claudia settled back and turned her vision inward as she had learned to do at the Occult School in Honolulu. "The spirits see him," she said hollowly. "Someone is shooting him . . . He's bleeding . . . It's Mickey McCann."

"Jesus," whispered Ginger. Do you see the killers?"

The tightness in her throat told Claudia she had said too much . . . seen too much . . .

"Oh, my God!" she screamed.

"Are you all right?" Pigman asked, suddenly concerned.

She felt cold and drained. Maybe there was still time to warn Mickey, if he hadn't left his club. She thought of going to the pay phone. Then she had a vision of Vicki

Hancock being shot and stuffed into the trunk of her car and set afire because she talked too much.

"No more!" she gasped. "I can't say any more."

"Why can't you say any more?" Ginger asked.

"I meant I can't *see* any more," Claudia said. "I don't feel well. I want to go home."

Pigman drove them to pick up Ginger's car and then he followed, to be sure they'd get there all right. As it turned out, Ginger had a flat tire on the highway, and Pigman had to change it, drive Ginger home, and take Claudia back to her apartment.

He walked her to the door and studied her anxiously. "Look," he said, "if you leave Bobby, I'll take care of you."

"You're married, Lenny. You have a wife and a daughter."

"I'll set you up in an apartment. I'll support you."

She laughed and kissed him on the cheek, then took out her key and let herself in. He was a good man, she thought, as she stepped over Bobby's tools on the stairs. Why, she wondered, couldn't she be happy with a good man?

When she got inside the apartment, she saw that Bobby had fallen asleep reading a book. She turned out the lights and looked out the window. The snow was still falling.

Nineteen

So she had known, a week before it happened, that McCann was going to be murdered. I felt sick at the thought that she might have prevented it. But she was mentally ill, I rationalized, bona fide, certified, paranoid. Not responsible. And she had been terrified that she might be killed if they knew she knew. The following week I went to interview her, determined to follow through with my questioning.

"I want you to remember what happened after you got home the morning of the murders."

"I must have gone to sleep."

"You couldn't have gone to sleep."

"I took my medication—Haldol and Cogentin—I'd have been a zombie."

"Yet we know you went to the McCann house."

She looked at me in amazement. "Yes I did, didn't I?"

"What do you remember?"

"We were driving on the highway and passed a sheriff's cruiser. I was terrified."

"Yes?"

"And when we turned down Ongaro Drive, I remem-

ber him pointing in the headlight beams, at some tire
tracks, and saying, 'Oh, my God, we must have just
missed them,' and then turning off the car lights and the
engine and just letting the car glide to a stop at the curb
across the street from the McCann house.''

"How did you know which one was the McCann
house?''

"I don't know.''

I wanted her to remember. She had to remember.
Then I did something I had never done during all the
time we'd worked together. She'd often put her hands on
mine for a moment to make a point or to soothe me. But I
had never touched her. I did now. I held her hands—cool
hands, with long fingers—and warmed them with my
own.

"Does it bother you that I keep coming back to it?''

"You don't bother me,'' she said. "My memories
do.''

"All right, but I've got to keep coming back, pulling
it out of you. Okay?''

"I want to remember.''

"Then we'll do it this way. What we're about to do is
not hypnosis but suggestion. I want you to remember.''

She giggled in a warm eager way. "*You* want me to
remember, but do *I* want me to remember?'' I laughed
with her and she sighed. "I can feel the muscles in my
body tensing, just thinking I'm going to try to remember.''

"We've got to break through, Claudia. I have to know
if you went into the McCann house on your own or were
forced to go.''

"I was forced to go. Howard Champ believed—''

"Don't get sidetracked, Claudia.''

"—that I was forced to go—''

"I don't want to hear about Champ. We know you
bullshitted Champ. We're not talking about that. If you
don't remember going there, how do you know you were
forced?''

"I do know.''

"How do you know?''

"How can I explain it to you? It's something I just
know. I know I was *unwilling* to go there.''

I saw her trying to slip that by me. "Come on,

Claudia. Being *unwilling* is not the same as being *forced*."

She gave an impatient sigh. "What I did, I did under duress. I was coerced."

"All right. Tell me the duress. Tell me the coercion. That's what we need."

"I don't know how to explain it to you."

"You don't have to explain. Just tell what happened."

"From what point? Where am I?"

"It's the morning after the murders. You've worked at the Image Gallery, and Lenny White—Pigman—has brought you back to the apartment after breakfast with him and Ginger."

She let out a groan as if reviewing it tormented her.

"You go home," I said. "And in your mind you know damned well you heard Gary Lewingdon say he planned to murder Mickey. How did you get to McCann's house? Did Bisexual Brady pick you up? Did you go over to his place?"

She frowned. "I'm trying hard to remember."

"Don't try hard. Just relax. Let it come in. . . . As you listen to my voice . . . open your mind . . . relax . . . see if you see anything. When you come home, is Novatney alone or is somebody with him? . . . Did Lenny walk you to the door or did he stay in the truck? . . ."

Her voice was low as she whispered half to herself, "I don't want to get different nights mixed up. I have a real quick picture of Bobby standing at the top of the steps with a gun. . . . But that was another night when Ginger brought me home late after breakfast, and he accused me of going back to her apartment and going to bed with her. But that never happened."

"Go on."

"Now I remember something. He wasn't asleep when I first got there. He wasn't even home. He came a short while later. *I know that!*"

"Great! Something we hadn't known before."

She took a deep breath.

She thought, eyes closed, and frowned. "Nobody was there, but I figured Bobby must have fallen asleep earlier because in the kitchen there was the smell of burnt pizza and I saw he had thrown one into the gar-

bage. And I could tell somebody had been there earlier.
More than one person."

"How could you tell?"

"I smelled traces of marijuana in the living room.
n the ashtray I saw different brands of cigarettes. If
.   d been one person, there wouldn't be different
brands. I always checked the ashtrays when I came
home."

"That's excellent deduction, Claudia."

"I'm a good detective. I was watching Bobby. He
didn't realize how much I was watching him."

"So he wasn't home. Then what happened?"

"I took my medication . . . and . . . wait, I remember
now . . . I found a note on the dining room table. It said
Laudie, be right back. I'm trying to remember what room
I was in when he came back . . . mmmm . . ."

She pursed her lips as she thought aloud. "I
figured he was armed when he left because in the bedroom the dresser drawer was open and his gun was
gone. And I could tell he had just cleaned and loaded it
because there was a dirty pipe cleaner with grease on
it. He'd spilled some Borax inside the dresser drawer
and on the floor, and he didn't bother to clean it up,
so that gave me the idea he was in a hurry when he
left . . ."

"Excellent, Claudia. It's all coming back to you.
Keep it up."

Her voice was very low again. "And when he came
back, up the steps, I could hear conversation. He was
talking to at least one other person. Mmmm . . . I still
don't remember what room I was in."

"It doesn't matter. Just keep going."

"Wait . . . I was in the bedroom we shared. I remember I thought of taking my purse and the things I'd
brought home with me and hiding in the closet so I could
listen to what they were talking about. . . . But then I
thought, oh no, if you get caught in the closet you might
even get shot."

She looked directly into my eyes and shook her head.
"I didn't do that." Then she looked away thoughtfully. "I
did hide in the closet once when somebody came into the
apartment looking for something. I think it was something that Bobby or Deno had. Nothing ever came up

missing though, so I don't know what that was about. And then another time—"

"Let's not digress. Stay with this. Bobby comes in. You hear voices coming from the staircase."

"Deep voices . . . masculine voices . . ."

"Could you recognize them?"

"I could hear some laughter. Someone was joking about something."

"Does Bobby come in alone or with someone?"

Her mouth suddenly gaped. "I know what they were laughing about. They were making fun of *me*!"

"Really?"

"Yes. He didn't know I was listening. Or I guess he wouldn't have said it so loud."

"What was he saying?"

"Something about me being in a fog all the time. And then Joker was saying, be sure she doesn't run out of medication."

"Joker was with him?"

"I don't remember."

"But this is the first time you've mentioned Joker talking to him on the stairs."

"It's a very long staircase."

She was silent for a long time, then I took her hands again and said, "Close your eyes and visualize them."

"I couldn't see them from the bedroom. I could just hear them talking. . . . They were always making fun of me."

"Because of the medication you were on?"

"My whole personality. Just me. In general."

Another long silence, but I waited it out, letting the tension build in her to fill the emptiness. Then she looked at me curiously. "What's the question?"

"Bobby. When he comes in, what does he say to you?"

She didn't answer.

"Were you in bed? Were you dressed or undressed?"

"I came home in my working outfit—black pants . . ." She nodded. "I hadn't been there long enough to change."

"So what did Bobby say to you? Did he say, 'Tonight's the night'? He didn't know you'd overheard Gary Lewingdon. You never discussed that with him."

She shook her head. "Uh-uh!"

"So how in the world did somebody get you to go with Bisexual Brady that night?"

"Bobby could get me to do *anything*!"

"Yes, but I'm asking *how*?"

"Through conversation. Just by ordering me to go."

"All right. Who told you to go? Who told you what?"

She hunched her shoulders as if preparing herself to break down a door. "When I was in the bedroom, he called my name as soon as he got into the living room. He said, 'Laudie, are you home?' When I said yes, he said, 'Come here, we want to talk to you.' He told me I should go over to the McCann house because Mickey had more than one hiding place and he didn't think it was possible for the Lewingdons to find every hiding place and get all the money."

I didn't believe her. I let go of her hands, got up, and paced, making no attempt to hide my annoyance.

She glanced at me, upset at the effect of her words. "Dan, did you know Mickey had much more cash than the press reported?"

"I know."

"How do you know?" she asked.

"I know."

"Because Mary Slatzer counted the money that night, and she told you?"

"Yes."

I was angry because I sensed that she had shifted from telling me what she remembered to telling me what she thought I wanted to hear. She was weaving fantasy in with the truth again. As much as I hated to, I had to press her. I pointed a scolding finger. "Now you're saying that at this point Bobby tells you to go over to the McCann house. Wouldn't you ask why? And why would he mention the Lewingdons if he didn't know you'd overheard them? He didn't know that you knew there was a murder."

"Sometimes I just did what Bobby told me to without question. He got very upset if I ever questioned him. He had a lot of control over me—"

"My question—"

"—not complete control. I still had my freedom. But he had a lot of control over me."

"My question is: Why would he send you? He knew you were on medication. He felt you were not dependable or stable—"

"I've always said that didn't make any sense."

"So how did he get you to go?"

"No one else was willing to go. Brady didn't want to go there alone."

"How do you know?"

"In fact, I remember now that Bobby wanted me to be armed before I left the house. He wanted each one of us to have a gun, but I refused to carry a firearm. I had no intentions of using it, so why carry it? You know Bobby slept with a gun. He slept on the side of the bed closest to the door, and me on the other side, so that if anyone came in and he had to shoot them, I wouldn't be in the way."

"Who was he afraid of?"

"He had so many enemies. He owed people for drugs. Even in the summertime when it was hot, he'd wear layers of clothing so that he could have a shoulder holster for his gun. He was afraid of being murdered. Even indoors, he wanted a gun close at hand or on his person. Real paranoid."

"Were you afraid you might be murdered?"

"Yes, I was."

"Even at that time?"

"Yes!"

"You told me you had a gun—the derringer."

"With a mother-of-pearl handle. Bobby bought it for me at Christmas."

"Did you carry it in your purse?"

"Bobby wanted me to keep it between the two bottoms of my purse so that I wouldn't get in trouble for carrying a concealed weapon. He said he could fix it so I could have access to it real fast."

"You've mentioned that false-bottomed purse, but I can't visualize what it looked like."

"It was navy blue, genuine leather, with a leather handle. I couldn't carry it on my shoulder, which I didn't like; I like shoulder bags. It had a satin-lined bottom. I can't remember what color it was, but if you dumped everything out of the purse you'd see the lining. It had a gold little diamond-shaped pattern. And there was about two inches under that."

"Did you carry that purse when you went to the McCann house?"

"I don't know for sure. I don't want to lie to you."

"After more than two years of working together, I appreciate knowing you're going to tell me the truth once in a while."

She laughed. "No . . . I tell you the truth all the time."

"But you don't tell me *all the truth*."

"That's because I didn't want any trouble."

I sat down again and stared deep into her eyes. "Can't you see my problem, Claudia? I've got to separate truth, fantasy, guesses, and lies. That's a big knot to unravel. I appreciate your helping me. Do I still have to ask you every time—'*is that true?*'"

"You don't have to ask that anymore."

"And one other thing. If you say, 'I don't remember,' when you do, that's also a lie."

"I don't do that anymore."

"And you realize also that blanking out is a way of obstructing our search for the truth."

"That's involuntary . . . that's unconscious. I'm not consciously saying, 'Shut your mind down. Don't talk to Dan anymore.' I'm not doing it on purpose."

"I believe you, Claudia, but it's still *you* doing it. That's something we have to deal with."

She smiled and waited.

"Soooo . . ." I said, taking her hands again. "Let's get back to that morning . . ."

"I'm getting very upset."

"Do you want to stop?"

"No, because next week it might be even more difficult. I want to get this over with. I want to give you as much material as I can, so that you can sit down at your typewriter at five in the morning—the way you said you do—and write."

"Good. Claudia, if we could put together this little section of time, I feel I could probably let you alone for a few weeks. Because then I'd go and work. But I can't even get started until I visualize it all. It's as if we have a chain over here, and another one over there, and we have to link them together. And you've just started doing that."

"I did?"

"Yes. When you said that after Lenny brought you home, Bobby wasn't there, you added a new link to the chain. That's good. Then you said you heard voices on the stairs. You positive of that?"

"I'm positive."

"That's beautiful . . . that's going along."

"All male voices."

"Good. Was it daylight yet? Can you see if it was daylight?"

"It was dark."

"Okay. Who's coming up the stairs? How many people?"

"I'm thinking three. I can see their winter coats but I can't see their faces."

"Describe the coats."

"I can see feet. I can see boots. I can see heavy coats. I can see Bobby's face, of course, but I can't see the other faces."

I couldn't restrain a chuckle. "I don't say it's intentional, Claudia. But that's real censorship. Your unconscious is censoring. And I'm trying to bring it out. Now, you're doing fine. Don't get upset. You've taken me a couple of steps forward."

"I'm upset because I can't remember."

"I know but it's coming out. Don't fight it. Tension will block it."

"I'm really tense."

"I can feel it in your hands. My God, they're cold. Now visualize . . . visualize those three people. Was Bisexual Brady one of them?"

"Hmmmm. Bobby and Deno were both head and shoulders taller than Joker. So if I can just see from here down," she said, pointing to her neck, "I'd be able to see Joker's face."

"Did you? Do you?"

"No."

"Okay, you're doing very well, Claudia. If we can just keep it going this way. What does Bobby say to you when he asks you to come into the living room?"

"He says he needs my help."

"Fine."

"He's real tired. He wanted me to sit down, but he couldn't sit down because he was pacing back and forth in the living room. He'd stop at each ashtray in the room and look at me . . ."

"Good . . . good . . . keep telling details like that . . . it'll come."

She stared into space for a long time, and I tried to prompt her. "Did he bring up the name Gary Lewingdon?"

"No."

"Did Bobby mention McCann?"

"I don't remember. I've got a headache. I'm going to get some aspirin."

When she returned, I asked her again if she preferred to stop, but she insisted she wanted to keep going to get through it. She knew as well as I did that to stop the tormenting memories—or ghosts, as she put it—she had to face this ordeal.

"It's very strange," I said. "I'm wondering what there was about those few hours that upset you so much. Even more than what happened later. I wonder what it could be."

"I just don't know. I try to think about it when I'm alone—each time after you leave. I try to figure it out."

"Well, little by little you're remembering."

"Joker planned the whole thing," she said. "But he isn't the one who got me to go. He had no influence over me, but he knew the tremendous influence Bobby had over me, so he told him to make me go."

"Are you saying Joker was there with Bobby that morning?"

"Yes, he and Bisexual Brady." She said it in a matter-of-fact tone, as if she were surprised at my question.

"Are you remembering that, or just guessing?"

"I remember."

"But five minutes ago you said you couldn't see the faces and you didn't know who came up the stairs with Bobby. Now you say you do."

"I know."

"Claudia, you're driving me crazy."

"Don't get so upset. When I went to get the aspirin I was thinking about it and it came to me. Now don't interrupt me or I'll forget."

"Okay, please go on."

"I feel so relaxed now. I even feel relieved."

We both laughed at that.

"What's the question?" she asked.

"I just want you to tell me anything that comes into your mind. Don't hold back. Don't think about it or examine it. Just let it come out. And free association will lead us. Bobby is pacing up and back. . . . He must be saying something. . . . What are you thinking now?"

"That I knew they wanted to trick me into doing something. I walked out of the living room into the dining room. I don't know where I was going, but Bobby followed me. He shoved a chair against me hard. . . . Then I went back into the living room . . ."

"What were your feelings?"

"Real upset and fearful."

"Now if he pushed a chair at you, it doesn't seem as if they're trying to trick you. They're angry and trying to force you—"

"No. You don't understand. They *were* trying to trick me. And they were running out of time and losing patience with me and getting short-tempered."

"Okay . . . okay . . . what was the trick they were trying to do?"

"That's what I don't *know*."

I had her free-associate again. I sensed she was on the verge of breaking through to the memory of that morning. She was silent for a long time, and I realized she wasn't telling me what was in her mind.

"What are you thinking about now?"

"It's not connected."

"It doesn't matter. Say whatever you're thinking."

"I was remembering the Kleenex in the bathroom with blood on it because Bobby had shot up, and he dripped some blood on the bathroom floor. But that doesn't have anything to do with what we're talking about."

"That's all right. It's still free association."

"But it doesn't have any connection."

"Yes it does."

"What's that got to do with where we were going?"

"It doesn't matter. That might be connected to something else. Just keep it going. That's a very good detail."

"But blood doesn't upset me. Some people are disturbed by it, but not me."

"There still might be a connection. Not a logical connection, but it could be linked to something in your mind. I'm glad you thought of that."

"I don't even know why I thought of it."

"Because in some ways, blood is connected to blood."

Her eyes opened wide in recognition. "Oh, Dan . . . oh, Dan . . . oh . . ."

"You see how free association works? Anything else that pops into your head, just say it."

After a long pause she said, ". . . about doing my laundry . . . I was wondering what it was like when I was doing my laundry in the laundromat. I don't know why I'm thinking about that."

"That's okay. It's an association."

"Association with what? What's laundry got to do with anything?"

"Well—"

"Oh, I know why I was thinking about doing the laundry! Because Bobby had his long-sleeved shirt soaking in cold water in the bathroom. When he shot up he rolled up his sleeve, but he got blood on his sleeve and he was using cold water to get it out . . . ohhh . . . laundry . . . blood . . . Oh, Dan."

"See how beautiful the associations are?"

She laughed and nodded.

"Okay, laundry. What does that lead you to think of?"

"Later I wanted to wash the clothes I was wearing when I came back from McCann's . . ."

"That makes sense. Keep associating."

"I remember, also later, Bobby cleaning my gloves with lighter fluid . . . cleaning . . . cleaning . . . I can see Brady cleaning snow off the windshield so he could see to drive, and then the windshield wipers cleaning off the snow . . . I don't remember if it was a car or a truck . . . windshield . . . bad weather . . . tire tracks on the street or the driveway . . . somewhere . . ."

After a long silence, I asked, "What does that make you think of?"

"Lewingdon's car driving away . . ."

I tried to keep my voice even, not to betray my excitement as she free-associated details. When the pauses got intolerably long, I prompted her.

"What does that make you think of?"

"Brady was driving, looking through the windshield at the road, and then he turned slowly and looked straight at me with a surprised expression on his face. I don't know if I asked him a question or made a statement, but I recall him turning slowly to look at me. Now I remember he was wearing a military jacket . . . olive or drab green . . . I think last time I described him to you I said he was wearing something else. But now I remember it was military. What I told you about his red facial hair . . . that's the same as I said before . . . and now I'm thinking of the bodies in the house, and that makes me very sad . . ."

Her associations stopped, and after a while I told her to think about herself back in her apartment living room with the three men whom she said were trying to trick her.

"What does that make you think of?"

"Being in a conference room with doctors and feeling they're ganging up on me . . . trying to trick me into taking medicine and being hypnotized . . . taking shock treatment . . . all the treatment plans I didn't really want to participate in . . ."

"Being tricked by doctors and being tricked by criminals—an interesting parallel. But we still don't have the trick. How did they trick you into going? Where did they say you were going?"

"I don't remember. What are we going to do?"

"Keep trying. I told you when we started, Claudia, I don't give up."

"I can't come up with anything logical."

"Forget logic."

"I can't even come up with something dumb."

"Don't force it. Just free-associate as we've been doing. Where in the world could they have told you you were going? Not too many places you could go at five or six in the morning during a blizzard."

"There were times at that hour when Bobby would run out of cigarettes, and he'd drive me to an all-night place and make me get out of the car and buy them for him. But this wasn't about cigarettes . . . I don't think . . ."

She paused, and there was a distant look in her eyes. "I remember somebody telling me I had to go visit some people . . . and then I remember being in the car with the snow coming down real heavy . . . and telling Brady, 'You told me we were going to visit some people, but you didn't tell me the people were dead.' I'm positive . . . I really am positive that happened."

"Keep it going."

"That's when he turned his head and looked at me that strange way. They didn't think I knew anything about it. They didn't know about me standing on the back porch and listening or about me running the water in the bathtub and listening at the door. They thought I was always in a fog and didn't know if I was coming or going . . . walking north and facing south . . . I remember him turning his head and shoulders towards me, real slowly . . . his wide eyes . . . his gaping mouth. He asked me how I knew everybody was dead . . . I doubt I told him the truth."

"What did you tell him?"

"I don't know . . . but I can hear myself crying . . . I can picture myself upset . . . my eyelashes wet from tears . . . mascara burning my eyes . . . and I can hear myself telling him to just leave me alone."

"I'm wondering what caused you to say to him, all the people you were going to visit were dead."

"It was something he said to me . . . I can see the right side of his face . . . his profile . . ."

Another long, interminable silence that made me want to tear my hair. "Where did you think you were going?" I asked over and over softly, trying to pry it from her memory.

"*I know,*" she said, suddenly alert. "*I know. They told me somebody was real sick and needed a faith healer. They asked me to go . . . pray for somebody that was real sick.* Oh, my God. That's spooky. Somebody sick and dying . . . I used to do that—go and pray over sick people."

It made sense. It rang true.

She was silent again for a while, eyes glazed as if her mind was searching the past. Suddenly she jumped up. *"I remember!"* she screamed joyfully. *"I remember everything!"*

It was her turn to pace up and back.

"There was a couch in the dining room," she said, "and another couch—more of a Hollywood bed—in the living room. And above the doorway between them was a piece of artwork—a plaque of . . . of . . . Jesus praying in the Garden of Gethsemane. . . . Oh, my God!" She lifted her arms over her head in triumph. "I remember everything now! I remember! I remember! I remember!"

It sent a chill through me. I remained silent, afraid to break the spell. Visualizing the image of the religious plaque had somehow brought it all back to her. She began speaking very fast, in contrast to her usual measured speech.

"I think they didn't *know* what they were going to tell me when they came to the house! And Deno said— No! . . . No! . . . Deno wasn't there. That was another night—he used to sleep on that couch—Deno refused to sleep there because of the plaque of Christ above his head. He said, 'How do you expect me to sleep with him staring at me?' Bobby took it down, and later I stood on a chair and put the thing back up.

"But *that* night, when Bobby was pacing back and forth, looking around the room, he stared up at that plaque of Jesus praying in the Garden of Gethsemane, and he said he wanted me to go pray for somebody who was sick. I realize now he just thought of what to say to me right at that moment when he saw the plaque. He was tricking me. That's it, Dan! That's it! I remember!"

She laughed with more happiness than I had ever seen her express before. She grabbed my hands and squeezed them. "I never thought I would ever remember. I can see and hear it all as if I were right there. . . . Bobby was always making fun of Christ. He'd say he was gay . . . or having an affair with the Apostle Paul . . . things he knew would offend me. I remember them making fun of Jesus that night, and I was very upset."

"It makes sense, Claudia. Because I think that's one

thing they could get you to go out for, even in a snow-storm."

"Oh, yes. That's something Bobby would know I'd do. Even if I'd taken my medication . . . even if there was a blizzard . . . if I believed someone was lying somewhere in a bed sick or dying . . . and they weren't saved . . . or a born-again Christian, I would go."

"And you thought you were going to someone's home?"

"Yes."

"And you believed it?"

"I sure did. God, it was all the farthest thing from my mind! Just now, when I really started to picture Bobby glancing around the room, in my mind, I looked at what his eyes were seeing, and I knew it was the plaque. I had a religious tapestry too, of the Last Supper, hanging in the dining room. Deno once complained that I had the place decorated by the Church."

Her laugh was rich and happy. I found it a good sign that through all this, she could still laugh at herself. She was shaking her head and screeching. "Now I remember exactly what I said in the car with Brady. I said, *'You told me these people were sick, not dead!'* That's it! That's it! That's it! I never dreamed . . . I'm starved. Can we go out and eat now?"

"There's one more piece we have to fit in about the trip to the McCann house. One more question we need answered."

"Not about inside the house," she groaned. "Not to-day."

"No. About the trip *to* the house."

She pouted, and sat on the edge of the chair, hands clasped as if waiting for the teacher's last question before lunch recess. "Then can we go eat Chinese food?"

"Sure," I said, "as soon as we finish this part of the story. But first, at what point did you know it was a trick? What made you realize you weren't going to pray over the dying, but were really going to McCann's house?"

"When we were almost there."

"What made you know it—?"

Even as I spoke she was whispering, contradicting herself. "No . . . no . . . no . . . not even then . . . not even then . . . not even then . . . It was when I got inside the house and saw the first body . . . Mrs. McCann by the fireplace . . ." She put her hand to her mouth. "No . . . no . . . no . . . that's not true. It had to be while I was still in the car. He told me when we were almost up to the house . . . he told me when we were a few streets away . . . he told me. Remember when I told you he saw some fresh tire tracks in the snow—in the street or the driveway—and he said, 'They must have just left'? It was then that I knew what he was talking about. I knew what he meant. And when I said that about there being sick people for me to pray over, he said, 'You're the only sick person here.'"

"Did you really believe it when Bobby said he wanted you to pray for a sick person?"

"I was suspicious. But I had to go anyway or I wouldn't have been able to sleep with a clear conscience."

"Is what you're telling me this time really true?"

"Oh, yes," she said vehemently. "It's really true."

"Well . . ." I said, sitting back. "How do you feel now that you have this part out in the open?"

"As if a tremendous weight was lifted from my shoulders. I think you've done it. I don't think they'll torment me anymore."

"We're done for today, but you still have to take me verbally through the McCann house—step by step—the night you were there."

"Okay," she said. "Next time. But now let's go eat."

Twenty

At our next interview, the following week, Claudia recalled that walking to the car that night in the snow, with Brady leading her, she had a premonition that the people she was going to pray over would die before she got there. She hoped they would be alive. Bobby usually laughed at her claim that she had the power to talk with the spirits, and that those from the other world could intercede for the sick and dying. She could hardly believe he was encouraging her now to use her power to help others.

She remembered vividly how Brady unlocked the door of his snow-covered Volkswagen and let her in the passenger side. As he got in on the driver's side, she saw him take a gun out of his belt and slip it into his olive-drab military jacket.

"What do you need that for?" she asked.

"Never without it," he said, looking straight ahead.

The starter whined. She thought maybe they wouldn't get going, but then it coughed and he revved the engine a few times. He never once looked at her.

She'd always had mixed feelings about Brady. She disliked his cold aloofness, but because he was bisexual she felt a kinship towards him. Other people couldn't understand bisexuality—neither the straights nor the gays—that you could love everybody.

As they turned off I–70, they passed a state trooper's cruiser, and again she had the feeling of something ominous before her.

"I hope we're in time," she said.

Brady gave her a strange glance.

As they drove, she couldn't tell where they were because the street signs were covered with snow. Then he turned into a tree-lined street of expensive-looking houses. The whiteness covering everything made her think of a beautiful Christmas card.

As they rounded the corner, his headlights illuminated two sets of fresh tire tracks. "Holy shit!" he whispered. "We must've just missed them." He turned off his lights and cut the ignition, coasting to a stop at the curb.

She could see that all the houses were dark, except one across the street up ahead with its garage door open. She heard the sounds of gunshots, and though their windshield was rapidly being covered with snow, she saw a man run out of the garage, and another one in a ski mask following and shooting at him. Then Brady grabbed her head, pushed her face down into the seat, and hunched over beside her. She heard more gunshots, but as she squirmed to look, Brady held her down.

"They just shot McCann," he whispered. "Keep down and quiet or we're both dead."

They lay hunched over in the front seat for what seemed like hours, though it was just ten or fifteen minutes later that she peeked through a clear spot in the rear window only partially covered with snow. She saw two men in parkas and ski masks walking down the middle of the street in the opposite direction from where Brady had parked. When the men reached the end of the block, she lost sight of them, and then she heard a car starting up and driving off.

Brady opened the car door and pulled her out.

"Come on," he said. "We've got to move fast."

She saw that the garage door that had been open when they were shooting was now closed, and she hung back. Brady pulled out his gun and pointed it at her. "Don't make me use this, Claudia. We've got to go in there. Remember what Bobby said. There are people who need your prayers."

She believed he would use the gun. A drug addict would do anything. She wondered what they would find inside that house. In front of the garage she saw bloodstains, and the marks of where the killers had dragged McCann's body back into the garage from the front of the house—all of it being covered up by the heavy falling snow.

Bisexual Brady tried the front doorknob and then peeked through the small window beside the door. When she wanted to look, he pushed her aside.

"Let's check the other doors," he said.

"Why?" she demanded. "What do you see?"

"Nothing. I forgot Bobby said to use the side door by the garage."

She didn't believe him. She knew she was still being tricked somehow. But why? What did Bobby want her there for? Brady tried the side door and found it open. She could see that the doorjamb was splintered where someone had broken in. Brady gestured with the gun for her to go inside.

"Why me?" she asked.

"Why not?"

The door swung open at her push, leading to a summer porch with African-style wicker furniture and spears and masks on the walls. Past that into the kitchen. She almost stepped on something, and when she looked closer she could see hazelnuts on the floor and bullet casings. She started to back out, but Brady was behind her, pushing her towards the dining room. On the floor in the passageway between the rooms, lying partly on the hearth, she saw an elderly woman in a blood-spattered dressing gown with blood on her face and her shoulder. The staring eyes told Claudia she was dead.

"Oh, dear God," Claudia whispered. She looked at Brady reproachfully. "Bobby said there were sick and dying people who needed me. I never thought he wanted me to pray over someone who was already dead."

"Move!" he said, pushing her forward.

"I want to leave!" she screamed.

He put his hand over her mouth. "Shut up. We're not leaving till we're done."

"What are we doing here? Why did we come to a house where people were murdered?"

"This is Mickey McCann's house."

"I know that. But why are we here?"

He looked at her, and spoke slowly, as if explaining something to a child. "Because Gary and his brother came here to murder Mickey. They aren't very bright, and they don't do drugs, so it's a sure bet they missed some of the shit. There's got to be dope around here."

"How do you know?"

"The dancer was a dealer, and she'd be carrying her stash in a place they would never think of looking."

"My medication is making me sleepy."

"Stay awake, Claudia. We've got a lot of ground to cover."

"I have to pee."

"Well, you can't use the bathroom here. You'll have to hold it. And don't take off your gloves. You search that room with the round bed and the living room. I'll take the other bedrooms and the basement."

The frilly room with the round bed, she guessed, had been the mother's. The mattress had been turned over and drawers had been emptied out onto the spread. On the dresser Claudia saw a white jewelry box. It was empty, but she pulled up the blue velvet lining and found some Delaudids. She knew that was what Brady really wanted, and she gave them to him.

Terrified but curious, she got involved in the search. In the living room, she noticed a small end table. The drawers were empty, but underneath one of the drawers was a space that held a flat box. When she opened it she found crisp bills stacked neatly—twenties, fifties, and hundreds. Her heart pounding, she shoved the money into her coat pocket.

She heard Brady go down to the basement, heard him opening and closing doors. From the head of the stairway she could see him taking down sections of the false ceiling. She wondered if he was finding anything there, and if he would share what he found.

Moving from the living room back to the kitchen, she opened the door leading to the garage. She saw Christine Herdman's body sprawled out on the floor. There were bullet holes in her face, and the blood was still wet . . . and she screamed.

Brady came running with his gun drawn. "You god-damned bitch! What the hell's wrong with you?"

"It frightened me," she sobbed. "Poor Chrissie."

Why had there been a busy signal when she'd tried to call the Eldorado Club? Why hadn't she tried again?

Brady pushed her into the garage and she saw the big red Cadillac with the white top.

"Mickey's got to be around here somewhere," Brady said. "That must have been him running outside when they were shooting at him."

But she couldn't take her eyes off Chrissie's body. Her books were standing beside her, and her purse had been emptied, the contents dumped on the ground: combs, brushes, tissues, and a red address book.

"Here he is," Brady said, looking down between the front of the Cadillac and the wall. She went to look and saw Mickey McCann sprawled on his back, feet facing the garage door through which he'd been dragged. His toupee had come loose and was covering his forehead almost down to his staring eyes. She wondered if someone had lifted it to see if he had money or dope hidden under it.

Brady searched McCann's pockets, his jacket, inside his shirt and socks, but he found nothing. He looked at Claudia. "Search her."

"What are you talking about?"

"She must be carrying."

"I'm not touching a dead body."

Brady pointed his gun. "Goddammit, Claudia, do what I say or there'll be a fourth body here with the rest. One more dead chick won't make much difference."

She realized he meant it. She understood the desperation of drug addiction, and she knew he wouldn't hesitate to put a bullet into her face, too. She bent over and started patting down Chrissie's slacks. The faint odor of the dancer's perfume made her want to throw up.

"Search her," Brady shouted again.

"I am! I am!"

"Take her slacks down."

Claudia saw that the zipper was already open, that

someone had torn it down to the crotch. Brady became impatient and yanked them down to her thighs. Beneath her slacks, Chrissie was wearing white, beaded go-go panties. Brady pulled them down, revealing cold white skin and dark pubic hair.

"Now search her!"

Claudia suddenly understood what he was asking her to do, and she pulled back, terrified and disgusted. "I can't put my hand in there!"

"You're a woman, you goddamned bitch. You've done it lots of times with your lesbian lovers. Do it, or I'll kill you." He put the gun to her head. "We've got to get out of here, but I'm not leaving without knowing if she's carrying dope."

Tears streaming down her cheeks, Claudia bent over and put her gloved fingers into the dead woman's vagina. She felt sick to her stomach, afraid she was going to throw up over the body. She wondered if a person could be identified by her vomit. What was she doing here? Why had she ever gotten involved with Bobby and his drug-crazed friends?

"Anything?"

She shook her head, not trusting herself to speak.

"Take your glove off," he commanded. "You can feel around better in there."

He pulled off her glove and pushed her hand towards the crotch. With her long fingers, she felt inside where it was still wet, and touched something and pulled out a small plastic bag with the end tied into a knot. There was white powder—a lot of it. She handed it to Brady, and he shoved it quickly into his jacket pocket.

"Bingo!" he said. "Let's go."

Claudia pulled Chrissie's go-go panties up again so that she wouldn't be found half-naked. She cried hysterically, unable to move, when Brady pulled her to her feet and said it was time to get out of there.

"I have to go to the bathroom," she said.

"You can't. We're leaving right this minute."

She started towards the door from which they'd entered, but he pulled her out the open glass patio door and slid it shut behind them. Outside, the icy wind numbed her face. She stumbled around in a daze, running from him, with her arms flapping as if she were trying to fly away, but he caught her, slapped her, and led her back to the car.

"Hysterical bitch!" he snorted, pushing her into the seat. "Stay put, or I'll really blow you away." He scraped the snow off the front and back windows, started the car, and took off.

"Now listen," he said. "You're gonna tell Bobby and Joker that we never went into that house."

"Why?" she sobbed.

"So I don't have to split the dope with them."

"What'll we tell them? How do we explain being gone so long?"

"Look, it's snowing bad. Say we got stuck in a snow-drift and had to wait for someone to help us get out. To-morrow, I'll come over and back you up. We'll say we didn't make it. You're guilty of a crime now, Claudia, just as much as I am. And if they know, they can use it against us. Bobby might let something slip when he's drunk or high, and tell Gary. And he and Charlie would kill us to protect themselves. You saw what they're capable of."

She nodded, her teeth chattering. She was furious with Bobby for the way he had used her. She had no intention of sharing the money with him. She would buy a plane ticket to Hawaii. She would get away from all this snow . . . and death . . . and be where it was warm and beautiful all the time.

When they pulled up in front of her apartment, it was almost daybreak. Brady said, "Remember, you must never tell anyone you were in the McCann house."

She nodded and wiped her tears. "I swear."

When she got to the top of the landing, the light from inside the apartment, through her purple curtains, out-lined Bobby's shadow. He was waiting for her. She let herself in.

"Well?" he asked. "What happened?"

"Nothing."

"What do you mean, nothing?"

"We got stuck in the snow. We never got to wherever it was we were going."

She spoke quickly, repeating what Brady had told her. She saw the rage in Bobby's face, but there was noth-ing he could do about it. As long as Brady kept his mouth shut—and she was sure he didn't want to split the heroin and the Delaudids with anyone—there was no way Bobby or anyone else could know where they'd been.

Bobby kept following her around, asking questions about what had happened. She knew he was upset because he'd been hoping she'd bring him some dope. Finally, he stopped talking to her and slumped into a chair mumbling to himself.

In the bathroom she put the money into her false-bottomed purse. She took a bath and went to bed, afraid to sleep . . . afraid of the dreams that might come. . . . Then sleep came, and in the nightmare it was Bobby and Deno who were in the house with her . . . killing everyone. . . .

She woke up a few hours later crying . . . drenched in sweat. Bobby was looking at her strangely.

"Bitch! You've been talking in your sleep!" he shouted. "You overheard Gary, didn't you? You must have been eavesdropping." He shook her by the shoulders. "If you ever tell anyone—if you ever speak of it— you'll be dead." He put his finger to her temple as if cocking a gun. "They're killers, and they wouldn't hesitate to blow your brains out. So you must never tell anyone what you know."

By the time she stumbled into the kitchen, the pain in her throat was intense. She knew she would soon lose her voice again. Why did she always lose her voice? She turned on the kitchen radio, wondering if she would hear anything about the killings. There was nothing about McCann or his mother or Chrissie.

She stayed home all day Sunday and by nighttime her voice was very hoarse. Bobby said it was a relief not to hear her bitching.

She cried herself to sleep, and the nightmare came again . . . with the restless spirits of Mickey trying to grab her and pull her down on top of him . . . and Chrissie and old Mrs. McCann reaching for her . . . begging her not to kill them . . . pleading with her to pray for them.

Then she took more pills to help her sleep . . . and nights drifted into days. . . . It wasn't until Tuesday afternoon—Valentine's Day—that she heard it on the bathroom radio.

She was brushing her teeth when the newscaster

mentioned the murders of Mickey McCann, his mother, and Christine Herdman at 4187 Ongaro Drive.

Claudia listened to the news and watched her face in the bathroom mirror. Her mouth, filled with toothpaste, had dropped open, and she watched herself listening to the description of how the bodies had been discovered.

She closed her eyes and swallowed the toothpaste and tried to call Bobby. . . .

But by then her voice was gone, and she couldn't remember what she had wanted to tell him.

As we sat facing each other in the darkening room, I was moved by the awesome tragedy in which mentally ill Claudia—through no fault of her own—had played a role. It was terrible to realize that if only she had remembered and told someone the truth sooner, only Karen Dodrill and Joyce Vermillion would have died, the other eight .22-caliber victims might not have been murdered.

Claudia looked at me with misty eyes. "I just realized I never did what I went there to do in the first place. I was so confused, so terrified, that I forgot. Maybe that's why their spirits have been restless, tormenting me, these past six years, because I buried their memories inside my head without saying a prayer over them. I've got to do it now. Will you help me?"

I knew what she meant. Weeping fully now, Claudia got out of her chair. I rose and stood beside her. She held out her hand, and I took it, bowed my head, and joined her as she finally kept her promise and prayed for the immortal souls of Chrissie . . . and Mamma . . . and Mickey McCann. . . .

Epilogue

If this were a novel, the story would end there. But since this is a true story about real people, the reader may care to know what happened to them.

I know what happened to some—not all—of the people in this book. Others were not accessible either because they were in prison, or had disappeared, or would not talk to me. Here, as of this writing, is what I've learned about the changes in some of their lives:

Gary James Lewingdon: still at Lima State Hospital for the Criminally Insane, his face now hidden by a full, bushy beard, was retried in February 1983 for the tenth murder. The state of Ohio was eager to convict Gary of the Joseph Annick slaying (to which he had confessed the first night of his arrest) so that if the other eight convictions were ever reversed on the grounds that his second confession had not been voluntary, he would still not be released from prison.

A Hamilton County jury in Cincinnati quickly found him guilty, and another life sentence was added to the others.

Public Defender James Kura filed appeals to overturn the convictions on the grounds that statements

Gary Lewingdon had made to Womeldorf and McMenemy had not been of his own free will, that his right to remain silent had been violated, and that "the use of the emotionally upset wife had the effect of overbearing his will and rendering his confession anything but the product of an essentially free and unconstrained choice."

Kura had agreed to ask his client if he would speak to me, and took a list of questions to Lima State Hospital for him to answer. Kura later told me he had showed him my questions but at the same time advised him not to answer any of them, nor to see me, because his appeal was still pending.

Thaddeus Charles Lewingdon: still incarcerated in Lucasville for nine life sentences, is (according to several sources) one of the most feared inmates of the prison. He took over all trial material and transcripts from his attorney, Gary Tyack, in order to conduct his own appeal to the U.S. Supreme Court, and filed a writ of habeas corpus on December 24, 1984.

On January 6, 1985, the Associated Press reported that Thaddeus thought he had discovered a legal loophole that could free him from prison. In an article entitled "Is Ohio a State?" included in a prison ministry newsletter at Lucasville, Thaddeus argues that since Congress did not formally accept Ohio into the Union until 1953 (although that acceptance had been made retroactive to 1803) all state laws approved in the interval are not valid. He also interprets the Ohio Constitution as providing that amended laws are considered repealed and that the Ohio General Assembly cannot define crimes and penalties.

Thus, Lewingdon contends, all Ohio criminal laws should be considered repealed, and inmates should be released.

Pointing out that might not necessarily be a good thing, Lewingdon said, "There are people in here who shouldn't be out in the street. I don't want them out any more than you do. I have a wife and children out there." Lewingdon said he would drop the litigation if he and several other inmates he considers "decent" are freed.

According to the AP report, the executive director of

the American Civil Liberties Union of Ohio said the courts have rejected similar arguments in the past.

Prosecutors George C. Smith and James O'Grady: have both become Columbus Municipal Court judges.

Claudia: Shortly before we had begun working on this book, Claudia had met a tall, handsome young criminal defense attorney who told me he had first seen her in court during her arraignment for murder. He recalled how she had looked around the courtroom with a lost expression but with an innocent smile. He had thought her very beautiful, he said, and very brave.

On August 7, 1984, Claudia and he were married in the same Franklin County Courthouse. She tells me she knows they will love each other always and will live happily ever after. . . .

I wish them happiness.

Daniel Keyes

Ohio, 1985

Acknowledgments

This book was developed after hundreds of hours of interviews over two years with Claudia Elaine Yasko and law enforcement officers, attorneys, judges, and "street people" of Columbus, Ohio. As I interviewed relatives, friends, and enemies, it soon became clear to me that many people feared to admit having known her. Although most people spoke to me openly and freely, some agreed to talk to me only if their names were withheld. Others refused.

Those people who wished to remain anonymous, those who could not be found or reached for comment, and those who, in my judgment, should not be identified, are represented by fictional names. In scenes involving them, as well as several scenes from Claudia's background in which I was not present, dialogue is re-created from summaries by third parties—here I have taken dramatic license.

For example: although selected material from news conferences and court testimony of the late Robert Ray Novatney is quoted verbatim, his dialogue in the scenes in which he appears is re-created from my interviews with his mother, brother, sister-in-law, attorneys, acquaintances, and—of course—Claudia.

I did not speak to Gary, Thaddeus, or Delaine Lewingdon. Material about them was developed from interviews with the law enforcement officers involved, with anonymous attorneys, and from confessions, trial transcripts, and news stories. My thanks to those who provided this material.

Though trial documents are public records, I should like to acknowledge my debt to the meticulous court reporters who enabled me to report verbatim dialogue in all court scenes and confessions. Though selectivity is always essential when using trial transcripts in a work such as this, omissions are indicated clearly by ellipses.

I should like to thank the following individuals for their invaluable assistance:

Attorneys: James Kura, Gary Schweickart, Lew Dye, David Long, Stephen Enz, Don Ruben, Lew Friscoe, Gary Tyack, Thomas Vyvian, and Prosecuting Attorney Michael Miller. *Judges:* Paul Martin, George C. Smith, James O'Grady.

Franklin County Sheriff's Department Deputies: Former Deputy Director Howard Champ, Detective Tony Rich, Sergeant Steve Martin, Detective George Nance, Deputy Director Inga Shulman of the Women's Correctional Institute, Deputy Donna Zag, former Auxiliary Deputy Robert Slatzer.

Columbus Police Department Officers: Detective Sergeant Bill Steckman, Officer William Brinkman, Detective Jerry McMenemy, Detective Charles "Sam" Womeldorf, and public information officer Mary Helen Van Dyke.

Claudia's friends: Tom House, Vicki Weals, Jim Stahl, Phil Gary Scianamblo, Michael Finnell, Tom Schramm, Diane Harrington. *Claudia's family:* Claudia's sister Nancy and her parents, George Yasko (deceased) and Martha Yasko.

Other participants in the events: Deno Politis, Mary Slatzer, Mary Lou Novatney, Andy Novatney, Licking County Sheriff's Detective Paul Short, senior editor of *Playboy*, William J. Helmer, *Playboy*'s private investigators Russ Million and Lake Headley.

For making my burden of work easier, thanks to: the Franklin County Sheriff's Department; the Franklin County Public Defender; the Franklin County Prosecutor; the Columbus Division of Police, and Chief of Police Dwight Joseph; *Playboy;* Ohio University's Alden Library; the Public Library of Columbus; Micro Center of Columbus; and Ohio University (for a one-year fellowship to pursue my writing).

Thanks to Alison Acker for her invaluable help in handling detail and dealing with problems promptly, efficiently, and thoughtfully.

My special thanks and gratitude to my perceptive and dedicated editor, Nessa Rapoport, whose editorial creativity helped me find the form and voice for this book.

Thanks to my daughters, Hillary and Leslie, for caring and understanding.

Above all, for her insightful editorial suggestions, for her tireless efforts in listening to the tapes and logging them into a retrieval system so that I could cross-check details, and for her loyalty, patience, and constant encouragement, thanks to my wife, Aurea.

ABOUT THE AUTHOR

aniel Keyes is the author of the award-winning novel,
wers for Algernon, and the award-winning nonfiction
portrait of a multiple personality, *The Minds of Billy Mil-
an*.

raise for Joseph Wambaugh

mbaugh's characters have altered America's
e."   —*Time*

is a master artist of the street scene."
                             —*Publishers Weekly*

is a writer of genuine power."
                             —*New York Times Book Review*

etter than any other contemporary writer,
able to convey just what it is that makes cops
the rest of us and, more important, why."
                             —*Library Journal*

NOBODY WRITES ABOUT COPS BETTER THAN WAMBAUGH

DON'T MISS ANY OF THESE BANTAM BESTSELLERS

☐ **#26217 DELTA STAR**   **$4.50**
☐ **#26302 GLITTER DOME**   **$4.50**
☐ **#27148 LINES AND SHADOWS $4.95**
☐ **#26021 SECRETS OF HARRY**
              BRIGHT   **$4.50**

and his latest bestseller:

☐ **#26932 ECHOES IN THE**
              DARKNESS   **$4.95**

Look for the above books at your local bookstore or use the handy coupon below: